Automated Athens

Automated Athens

Ancient Greek Ideals in the Early Age of Automation

MICHELE KENNERLY

The University of Chicago Press
Chicago and London

The University of Chicago Press, Chicago 60637
The University of Chicago Press, Ltd., London

Published 2026
Printed in the United States of America

35 34 33 32 31 30 29 28 27 26 1 2 3 4 5

ISBN-13: 978-0-226-85216-4 (cloth)
ISBN-13: 978-0-226-85217-1 (paper)
ISBN-13: 978-0-226-85219-5 (ebook)
DOI: https://doi.org/10.7208/chicago/9780226852195.001.0001

Library of Congress Cataloging-in-Publication Data

Names: Kennerly, Michele author
Title: Automated Athens : ancient Greek ideals in the early age of automation / Michele Kennerly.
Description: Chicago : The University of Chicago Press, 2026. | Includes bibliographical references and index.
Identifiers: LCCN 2026026171 | ISBN 9780226852164 cloth | ISBN 9780226852171 paperback | ISBN 9780226852195 ebook
Subjects: LCSH: Automation—Western countries—History—20th century | Automation—Philosophy | Automation—Social aspects | Automation—Historiography | Labor supply—Effect of automation on | Automation—Greece—Athens | Civilization, Western—Greek influences | Athens (Greece)—Civilization
Classification: LCC T59.5 .K45 2026
LC record available at https://lccn.loc.gov/2026026171

♾ This paper meets the requirements of ANSI/NISO Z39.48-1992 (Permanence of Paper).

Authorized Representative for EU General Product Safety Regulation (GPSR) queries: **Easy Access System Europe**—Mustamäe tee 50, 10621 Tallinn, Estonia, gpsr.requests@easproject.com
Any other queries: https://press.uchicago.edu/press/contact.html

This one's for you, Dad

Contents

Introduction

Athens Appeals

The fact probably is that each age gets what it likes out of antiquity.
GILBERT HIGHET, *The Classical Tradition*

Ancient Athens receives frequent credit as the starting place of democracy, and as a direct, demanding, even pure form of it.[1] "People power," the literal meaning of δημοκρατία, meant that political decisions were not made by a small class of the superrich or by one all-powerful person who could not be challenged. Thinking, speaking, listening, and deliberating with the polity foremost in mind became essential governmental arts. The prizing of community and communication meant that public matters could be set to meter by playwrights and heard by thousands, or argued for hours by hundreds serving in offices drawn by lot. At the individual level, one could come to know, develop, and exhibit oneself as long as one did not threaten democratic norms. The preceding is, of course, an idealized, incomplete view of a place that is storied largely because the stories it told about itself have so often proven compelling to subsequent advocates of democracy.

Any democracy, in whatever time and place, needs an asterisk to shine upon those living in the polity who are primarily subjected to, rather than the subjects of, that people power. This fact rightly tempers zeal to find purity at its purported origin—or in any subsequent democracy. Any appeal to ancient Athens as a model democracy is complicated, but the complexity does not lie solely with ancient Athens: As classicist Niall Livingstone has observed, "Ancient democracies would not count as democratic by modern standards—and vice versa."[2] Anyone writing about democracies decides whether to position such caveats as quick asides or central plot points in the story they tell.

For its part, Athenian democracy in its Periclean phase, its most famously self-celebrating years, excluded from the power-holding demos anyone not born in Athens to two Athenians and recognized as a man. Exclusions—of the not-Athenian, of women, of enslaved people—not only informed the language of citizen excellence but also enabled those who were considered citizens to avoid thinking about and attending to repetitive tasks like managing a household. Further, when engaged with their democratic work, the laboring poor were not hammering helmets or shoes.[3]

This book concentrates on a particular—and, on its face, unintuitive—strain of appeals made to ancient Athens as political and cultural site par excellence: those during the early age of computerized automation, a time of purportedly momentous technological change and social and public adjustment to that change. What recurringly has tied together ancient Athens and automation has been an expectation that automation would "free" people—the language of liberation is common—from uninteresting physical or cognitive labor so they could attend to creative and communal pursuits, developing themselves and their communities. The idea is that automated systems and machines would perform the sort of tasks performed in ancient Athens by enslaved people, or metic craftsmen, or free yet subordinated women. As such, automation would bring an improvement over ancient Athens, since the category of "the people" would be far more inclusive, and (or, more precisely, *because*) the slaves and underlings would be machines or automated systems rather than people.

That kind of expectation might seem of recent commencement, but it was prominent in the mid-twentieth century and even started to appear in the machine age with the rise of industrial capitalism and democracy across the Global North in the nineteenth century. True automation—that is, a self-regulating system using an electronic computer—did not exist before the twentieth century, but the discursive tracks it traveled upon arrival were laid a century earlier. Linking the liberatory promise of machines to ancient Athens seems to have started in the United States in the second quarter of the nineteenth century as a rejoinder to dire concerns about the welfare of the laboring classes and humankind as a whole expressed in premiere Scottish periodicals, Scotland having industrialized with ferocious rapidity.

No doubt the most enduring piece came in 1829. In an immediately influential essay, "Signs of the Times," Scottish cultural critic Thomas Carlyle calls his stretch of time "the Mechanical Age," observing all around him "cunning abbreviating process[es]" that drove "the living artisan from his workshop, to make room for a speedier, inanimate one. The shuttle drops from the fingers of the weaver, and falls into iron fingers that ply it faster."[4] His concern, though, extends from workshops into all domains of life. "Men are grown mechanical in head and in heart, as well as in hand," he diagnoses. In his estimation, living well as a human requires dynamic elements and mechanic ones; the problem comes when the latter overpower the former. Paradigmatic of the dynamic are wonder, love, religion, and poetry: of the mechanic, the management and counting of external things, be it a routine or an institution. In Carlyle's estimation, a purely mechanical mindset in a person or the mood of an age constitutes a grave dehumanizing danger.

In 1831, a young US American lawyer named Timothy Walker anonymously penned an essay titled "Defence of Mechanical Philosophy," directly in response to Carlyle's "Signs of the Times."[5] Walker's piece bears an ambitious, impatient competitiveness. Carlyle's animus against the mechanistic perplexes him: "Machines are to perform all the drudgery of man, while he is to look on in self-complacent ease. But where is the harm and danger of this?"[6] Frequent rhetorical questions convey Walker's breezy assurance not only that he has the correct opinion but also that his readers hold it, too, or are persuadable. "We maintain," he continues, "that the more work we can compel inert matter to do for us, the better it will be for our minds, because the more time shall we have to attend to them."[7] Our embodiment presents the core nuisance: "So long as our souls are doomed to inhabit bodies, these bodies, however gross and unworthy they may be deemed, must be taken care of." Bodies make their constant demands, and we attend to them, necessarily. Keeping people fed, clothed, and sheltered is busy work, especially when considered at the scale of a society. "If," however, "machines could be so improved and multiplied, that all our corporeal necessities could be entirely gratified, without the intervention of human labor, there would be nothing to hinder all mankind from becoming philosophers, poets, and votaries of art."[8] Anticipating scoffs, Walker adds that even the steady pursuit of such a condition, unattainable as it may be, would yield rich cultural returns.

Keeping his focus on Carlyle's disparagement of the emergent epoch, Walker asserts, "The mechanical enterprise, with which our age is so alive, far from being unfavorable to our spiritual growth, is the one thing needful to furnish the freedom and leisure necessary for intellectual exercises."[9] Within the speedy history of humans and labor-abbreviating machines that follows, meant to support Walker's attitude toward progress (continual, though not constant), comes ancient Greece. He treats ancient Greece as a marvelous paradox, since it established itself as a culture for the ages without the benefit of labor-easing machines. He asks another question he knows people will answer in a way that suits his argument:

> How came Greece to achieve her high intellectual supremacy, when all her work was performed by hand? The answer, so far as it respects this discussion, is ready. The Greeks themselves did not toil. Every reader of their history

> knows, that labor, physical labor, was stigmatized as a disgrace. Their wants were supplied by levying tribute upon all other nations, and keeping slaves to perform their drudgery at home. Hence their leisure. Force did for them, what machinery does for us.[10]

Using the generic moniker "the Greeks," Walker presents an exclusive, elite-centric experience and attitude of no work as the norm for all Greek people. He does not mention the working poor, who comprised the great majority of the demos and participated directly in its political activities. The imperialistic and enslaving ways of the Greeks supported what he calls their "high intellectual supremacy." Though distant in time, ancient Greece is purportedly proximate to the culture he claims greater mechanization could deliver. In a dualism addressed to those intent on resisting machines, Walker argues that we *could* "spurn all mechanical improvements" and earn our leisure through aggression, or we could face the likely prospect "that that nation will make the greatest intellectual progress, in which the greatest number of labor-saving machines has been devised."[11] If Walker's argument entails the emancipation of the millions of enslaved people in the United States, he does not say so. His concern seems limited to those for whom the burdens of life are already comparatively light but could be lighter still, freeing them for "thought, reflection, study, and contemplation."[12]

As Carlyle's essay and Walker's apologia indicate, developments in mechanization prompted debate about their effects, especially whether they would minimize or maximize the human experience. In point of fact, it was not unimagined by ancient writers that freedom would function differently, even in purportedly freedom-loving Athens, if there were *automatoi*—self-moving objects—that could replace assistants and enslaved people.[13] With the coining of "cybernetics" in the late 1940s and the popularizing of "automation" in the early 1950s, such outlooks were reenergized, since the processes to which those words referred seemed to deliver, at last, what people in previous centuries had thought was possible or even imminent.

This book scrutinizes attitudes toward ancient Athens as a model for the United States during the early age of computer-based automation, 1948 through 1968, in the writings of mathematicians, philosophers, industrialists, economists, sociologists, and socialists. In a time of disruptive technology, those writers used ancient Athens to coin new terms, identify problems, articulate ideals, and generally think, communicate, and plan with others.

Entangled with ancient Athens are discourses of freedom and enslavement, leisure and work, democratic participation and disenfranchisement. References to ancient Athens show attempts—sometimes riffing on one another, sometimes not—to make the democratic potential of an emerging technology legible and tangible.

It is not spoiling things to point out that automation has *not* been a technology of personal liberation or enhanced democratization.[14] The strain of discourse I trace was sometimes very high profile, but it proved unable to put up much of a fight against powerful entrenched interests. Ineffectual public discourse of the past may not be of historical consequence, but it is of historical interest: It is a record of contestation over what matters. Such discourse is never inert. Though it was either rejected or ignored in its time, it may hold elements worth reanimating now or in the future.

In the favorable instances, which are more plentiful, ancient Athens functions as what I call a *eutopos* (from *eu*, "good," and *topos*, "place"), which I explain by showing how this concept works within the traditions of three place-based formulations: topos, utopia, and technological utopia.

Topos

Because critical vocabulary for organizing iterative claims, frames, stories, metaphors, or images is not lacking, a critic should be choosy. Historians of technology, for their part, often identify "patterns."[15] "Theme" is also a serviceable analytic. Langdon Winner has clearly used it—and tried, too, "notion," "idea," and "central obsession"—to point to recurring anxiety that the speed and unpredictability of technology's interactions with human life has outpaced planning and policymaking.[16] Literary critics are predictably metacritical about their categorizing vocabulary. Fredric Jameson, for instance, expresses dissatisfaction with common terms for identifying sustained yet distributed forms: "It may help to discredit the facile word *theme* which seems at one and the same time methodologically unavoidable and overly humanistic or anthropomorphic."[17] He didn't think "motif" was much better but figured it allowed critics to suggest "pattern" without obliging them to offer interpretations about the purpose or meaning behind it.

A useful yet—outside of the study of rhetoric—underused concept for understanding and organizing recurrence over time is topos.[18] *Topos* (plural *topoi*) is an ancient Greek word for "place" or "space." In addition to functioning as a general terrain term, *topos* held a specialized meaning in ancient Greek rhetoric (the systematic art of public speaking) and dialectic (philosophical argumentation). Due to their sheer helpfulness, topoi used to be most famous as what the ancient Greek philosopher Aristotle designated as rhetoric's *koinoi topoi*—that is, "common topics" or "common places," meaning general ways, such as using comparison or providing the meaning of a word, of generating something to say that ostensibly could be applied to any matter whatsoever.[19] Anyone who learned the so-called topical system of rhetorical invention could venture to those "places" to get thinking and talking going. The topical system emerged from observations of subject-independent moves that arguers commonly made, and the system's being taught assured that the moves would continue to be made. As a result, the use of common topoi could be anticipated by opponents and audience members who also had received topical training and could be identified later on by those who read a published speech, for example. Aristotle also specified kinds of topoi called *idia*, meaning particular places to which a speaker could go when doing the specific work, for instance, of praising someone. In contemporary rhetorical theory, which has a strain extending ancient rhetorical terms, a topos is a recurring feature within a domain of discourse or a set of images.[20]

Topos offers a lot to the study of talk over time—and especially so when the same *place* is brought up, again and again.[21] Ancient Athens, my topical focus, is a topos in several senses. For starters, it was an actual place. It would more commonly have been referred to in the ancient Greek world as an *astu* (city) or *polis* (city-state), but, generically, it was a place. Additionally, the common topic of the meaning of a word is remarkably commonplace when "democracy" is under discussion; its ancient Greek etymology is often supplied, usually narrowing into attention to (and often praise of) ancient Athens.[22] Furthermore, ancient Athens recurs in talk about automation—making it a specific topos—because it yields useful lines of claim-making about the optimal conditions of the good life, often imagined to depend on democracy, which (recall the caveats, and I will, too) those ancient Athenians who were included in the demos are said to have practiced exuberantly because others did the work and labor.[23] Even if one is flummoxed by the social or political implications of an automated technology, one can eke out a few hundred words by bringing up ancient Athens, and so the place remains a commonly visited region in discussions about technology. Additionally, it might seem brainy through classical allusion alone; obviously, one reason ancient Athens is invoked so often in discourses of all sorts is because of the status it continues to enjoy as a "classical" place—that is, one both long ago and first class.[24] It is the case for several of the people who feature in this book that ancient Athens was an easy go-to for analogies and examples because they had received an education in classics, which would have valorized so-called classical Athens (and Rome).

My concept of *eutopos* adds the ancient Greek adjectival *eu*, meaning "good," to *topos*. In actual ancient and contemporary Greek grammar, adding *eu* to *topos* in hope of yielding a noun can only be done as *eutopia*, a form I use occasionally but hold separate from my ungrammatical but theoretically useful modification of *topos*. Most basically, I take *eutopos* to mean any positively valenced, repeating realm of argument; more specifically, a eutopos can be any instance of a class of arguments that attempts to orient people in disorienting times by indexing a familiar place that enjoys a presumption of goodness. It may help differentiate eutopos from eutopia (a good place) to say that when ancient Athens is treated as a eutopia, the positioning and the argumentative structure that supports it constitute a eutopos. Deemed a good place (by and for some, at least), ancient democratic Athens is a place of argument-making and an argument of place-making within discourse about automation.[25]

Utopia

The second place-based formulation to which my conception of eutopos connects is utopia, usually interpreted to mean "no place" literally but "ideal place" functionally within some plan, program, or story. The word *utopia* appears to be ancient, visibly founded on *topos* as it is, but *outopia*—what the word, as "nowhere," would be in proper ancient Greek—does not appear in ancient works. Still, as a concept, utopia is commonly retrojected to that time and place. Since this book looks in that direction, too, I will briefly sketch how utopia has been hellenized.

The "golden age" invoked by the archaic Greek poet Hesiod in his *Works and Days* has been hailed regularly as a vision of utopia.[26] Also treated for utopian themes is *Birds*, the 414 BCE comedy of Athenian playwright Aristophanes that sees two Athenian men abandon their lawsuit-happy polis and plan out a new one among the avian set.[27] Most commonly of all, Plato's *Republic* receives credit as the first work to set forth a full utopian program. In 1922, for instance, cultural and media theorist Lewis Mumford opened his *Story of Utopias* with a chapter on Plato. Mumford points out that the physical site of Plato's "ideal community" is not some imagined place but Athens itself, evidenced by Plato's "referring repeatedly to the soil in which Athens was planted, and to the economic life which grew out of that soil."[28] As for the radically antidemocratic ideas Plato's Socrates talks through in the dialogue, Mumford asks readers to "remember that Plato wrote in the midst of defeat; a great part of his region, Attica, has been devastated and burned; and he must have felt that makeshift and reform were quite futile when a Peloponnesian war could make the bottom drop out of his world."[29] With this mix of contextual analysis and psychoanalysis, two modes appropriate to Mumford's post–Great War, post–Freudian moment, Mumford labored to repatriate a work that has been taken far from the time and place in which it was written.

Sixteen years later, on the day Germany invaded Austria, the Austrian philosopher Karl Popper decided to write what he would ultimately call *The Open Society and Its Enemies*. The first volume, *The Spell of Plato*, makes a lengthy case against what Popper calls "Utopian engineering," a mode of polity planning exemplified by Plato's *Republic*. Everyone who is or who hopes to be involved with the running of a polity plans with certain objectives in mind, of course, but "the Utopian attempt to realize an ideal state, using a blueprint of society as a whole, is one which demands a strong centralized rule of a few, and which therefore is likely to lead to a dictatorship."[30] Published in 1945, *The Spell of Plato* treats the *Republic* as a totalitarian project, a closed, antidemocratic society the essential likes of which were being manifested in the twentieth century to horrific effect. Similarly to Mumford, Popper sympathetically details Plato's situation and intentions, but sympathy for Plato does not mitigate the danger of what is sketched out in the *Republic*: the break with the norms of democratic Athens.[31]

As for the *Republic* itself, Plato nowhere uses the word *outopia* (or *eutopia*), but the character Glaucon once refers to the place being conjured by Socrates as his "kallipolis," a beautiful city-state—so different, we are meant to note, from Athens as it had been legally, politically, and socially constituted during the time of the historical Socrates.[32] Characters decide to make a polis from its very starting point; reckon they are establishing a "paradigm . . . of a good polis"; claim that were there but one person suited to carrying out their polis-plan, that person would effect what now seems "unbelievable"; and praise Socrates for describing convincingly just how such a polis would come to be "if it were ever possible."[33] Such moments underscore the unattainable nature of this beautiful place *not* absolutely but given the then-current givens.

Yet the word "utopia" does enjoy a firm connection to the *Republic*, despite not being there in literal name. In the fifteenth century, the dialogue was an artifact of and contributor to the more general frenzy for ancient Greek works.[34] "Utopia" seems to have been coined by the Catholic adviser-to-the-king Thomas More, who could read ancient Greek, when he used it in the title for his 1516 work, titled and composed in Latin, *De optimo reipublicae statu deque nova insula Utopia* (On the best state of the republic and on the new island Utopia). For his title, More is thought to have dropped the *o* in *outopia* (*ou* + *topos*, "no place"). In a poem in the second edition, however, it is suggested that what he actually started with was *eutopia* (*eu* + *topos* = "good place"), and what he dropped was the *e*: "Wherfore not Utopie, but rather rightely my name is Eutopie, a place of felicitie."[35] The tricky matter of what vowel he dropped provides us with productive ambiguity about what sort of place a utopia actually is.

As Sarah Hogan has explored, More's *Utopia* is a "parodic reworking" of, most prominently, Plato's *Republic* and the English estates satire, the latter a genre emerging alongside capitalism as wealthy landowners began to fence off their land.[36] The combination of philosophical capaciousness with a narrow, nation-based focus made for an easily adaptable form: More's *Utopia* begat a proliferation of utopian visions. Some, like a (serious) plan for Ireland, even went by the name "eutopia."[37] The use of "utopia" and "eutopia" in the sixteenth century shows that new words resembling old Greek toponyms were powering visions of the spatial and cultural effects of incipient structures of politics and power. Only "utopia," though, noticeably pressed on into later centuries. It is one of those fun flukes of intellectual history that the word keeps getting applied to Plato's *Republic*.[38]

Since its appearance in early modern England, "utopia" has come generally to mean an ideal place that *could* come to exist if certain preconditions were encouraged and plans adopted. The machine-powered industrial age saw an explosion of utopian imaginings, variously manifested but with technology often at its core.[39]

Technological Utopia

The third place-based formulation whose tradition is important to my conception of ancient Athens as a eutopos in discourse about automation is a special variant of "utopia" traced in attitude if not in usage to the nineteenth century: the technological utopia, or technoutopia. The name is attributed (and often by critics) rather than claimed. Technoutopianism describes the notion that technological "advances" will deliver us unto a place so vastly better than what we have that the usual, bungling, not-optimized ways of managing ourselves, both socially and individually (e.g., government, prison, war, marriage, work, and even food as we know it), will no longer be necessary. It will transpire that all manner of stubborn social ills merely awaited a technological solution. Howard P. Segal, an explicator of technoutopianism as it manifested in the United States between 1883 and 1933, points to confidence that technologies-to-come would eliminate humanity's "major chronic problems," such as poverty and sickness, as well as ones deemed characteristic of modernity, such as "nervousness, rudeness, aggression, crowding, and social disorder, in particular."[40] At every level, technology will structure and sustain society—and an improved one, at that. The technocrats were the first unified, official technoutopian group; the schism within their ranks in 1933 explains why Segal stopped his study with that year.[41]

In 1966, nuclear scientist Alvin Weinberg surveyed the sociopolitical scene and the persistent problems at which activists and policymakers—whom he calls, using the parlance of the time, "social engineers"—were directing their determination and persuasion. He did not see how they would budge matters much, let alone ensure long-lasting progress. In "Can Technology Replace Social Engineering?," he entertained the possibility that social problems could be translated into technological problems, that "Quick Technological Fixes" could either eradicate or ease without deliberation, persuasion, or violence.[42] His first example proceeds on the claim that "the Marxian view seems archaic in this age of mass production and automation . . . for the brilliant advances in the technology of energy, of mass production, and of automation have created the affluent society." Weinberg concedes that his times are not *quite* what Marx had hoped for: "Technology has expanded our productive capacity so greatly that even though our distribution is still inefficient and unfair by Marxian precepts, there is more than enough to go around." But this abundance points Weinberg to the conclusion that "technology has produced a 'fix'—greatly expanded production of goods—which enables our capitalist society to achieve many of the aims of the Marxist social engineer without going through the social revolution Marx viewed as inevitable. Technology has converted the seemingly intractable social problem of widespread poverty into a relatively tractable one." Widespread poverty is not long for a techno-fixable world. Weinberg casts technological engineering as the benevolent mitigator of human misery—and of what he takes to be the slow and often fruitless effort to shift it through communication, struggle, compromise, and revolution. What Weinberg envisions has been called a "practical utopia," since it sits seemingly within a much more reasonable reach than an expansive technoutopia.[43] That seemingness is its power.

The technoutopian lexicon continues to meet with refinement. In 2013, tech critic Evgeny Morozov observed that tech companies increasingly take a solutionist stance, offering "sexy, monumental, and narrow-minded solutions—the stuff that wows audiences at TED Conferences—to problems that are extremely complex, fluid, and contentious."[44] He calls it "technological solutionism." Data journalist, programmer, and professor Meredith Broussard refers to "the belief that tech is always the solution" as "technochauvinism." A technochauvinist perpetually transmits or believes the hype that "tech is something new and potentially revolutionary." An attendant view tends to be "that if the world just used more computers, and used them properly, social problems would disappear and we'd create a digitally enabled utopia."[45] And, of course, it would take a form envisioned and designed by the wealthy-white-men-led companies of Silicon Valley, a place dubbed "brotopia" by tech journalist Emily Chang, who thereby appended another toponym to the plot of tech's domains.[46] Tech billionaires drive what science writer Adam Becker terms "the *ideology of technological salvation*," whereby we don't have to maintain, care for, or limit what humans currently have because technology we don't yet have (and likely never will have) will save us from scarcity and danger.[47] It encourages maximalism in nearly all things (e.g., energy use, artificial intelligence, having babies, space exploration) but regulation. What maximalism could yield registers as utopian for a certain sort of person (usually a billionaire), but, for the rest of us, "if you want a picture of that future, imagine a billionaire's digital boot stamping on a human face—forever."[48]

The Athens Eutopos

Apart from the odd adaptation of a George Orwell quote, those more recent concepts and studies, present- and future-oriented as they are, seldom look back to the 1940s, '50s, and '60s, where there are significant antecedent attitudes toward technology.[49] Appeals to ancient Athens in discourse about automation in the mid-twentieth century are related to technoutopianism but importantly different for two main reasons. The first reason is that ancient Athens sits in that underscrutinized space between utopia and eutopia. On the one hand, since ancient Athens was an actually existing place, it can never be a no-place or a purely imaginary blueprint; on the other hand, since any access we have to it is mediated by ancient materials and forms (e.g., texts, inscriptions, sculptures) interpreted by generations of thinkers, poets, architects, and the like, many of whom have been trained or habituated to valorize them, ancient Athens tends to get a lot more attention for aspects deemed good—and deemed good largely because its own artifacts set the criteria for goodness in the first place.

The most well-known instance of admiring Athenian self-reflection comes in a speech honoring Athenian war dead given by the Athenian general Pericles in *The History of the Peloponnesian War* by the Athenian historian Thucydides. He speaks the city back to itself, emphasizing the qualities—like an unlikely mix of daring and deliberativeness—that made Athens "the school of Greece."[50] Though Plato's Socrates would later joke that citywide eulogies have a low level of difficulty, that particular speech persuaded more than ancient Athenians that their polis was one for the ages.[51] The facts are, as Johanna Hanink and Demetra Kasimis put them, that "the Athenians were not inherently made of miraculous or even ingenious stuff. They were, however, exceptionally committed to debating with each other, documenting themselves, and to projecting civic identity in media that have managed to survive to the present day. They were also unusually skilled at convincing others that their city and civic community were extraordinarily special, and that its memory was truly worth preserving, studying, and celebrating."[52] In his sizable study of the ancient Greek city-state as such, classicist John Ma suggests that examining its reception history shows that "the *polis*'s own discourse, if read with the grain, produces an idealist, utopian history."[53] That is especially true in the case of Athens, so persuasive was the polis-promotion of its speakers and writers.

The second major dissimilarity between the Athens eutopos and technoutopianism is that in the period during which "cyber" became a prefix, some believed that ancient democratic Athens offered a cultural-governmental blueprint automated technologies would help us have, and in an improved form. As such, the Athens eutopos operates differently from at least the most radical technoutopian discourse in that the former usually gives dynamic, inclusive democracy—people talking to and listening to one another, and their communication having real, institutional power to shape events—central importance, whereas the latter commonly leaves behind old things deemed to have been necessary only because our ways of life could not supply what each of us *really* required and desired. In the far reaches of technoutopian talk, the view is that people who favor democracy as it has manifested thus far, even in ancient Athens, have sold their technological imaginations far too short.

The ancient Athens eutopos in discourse about automation comes with a certain social vision. It looks forward—by looking backward—to increased free time, education in talking to strangers, a florescence of culture, and intensified citizen commitment.[54] When the harms of ancient Athenian enslavement *do* come up, it is often to emphasize that we can do ancient Athens better than ancient Athens did because we will not need to subordinate or enslave *people* to do it; the object of the slave concept shifts from human to machine. Athenian exceptionalism, imperialism, xenophobia, and misogyny are less commonly mentioned. The same goes for the ongoing and unresolved history of slavery in the United States, as well as for US American exceptionalism, imperialism, xenophobia, misogyny, and their intersections, and how they ensure that the costs and benefits of automation will not be equally distributed. They are not popular topics for everybody who appeals to Athens and to whom Athens appeals, but they are not entirely absent, either.[55] The propagators of the Athens eutopos in early automation discourse are highly educated, economically comfortable, often left-leaning white people. Though black US Americans do use the classical tradition, react to and organize in the face of automation, and engage in utopian imaginings, the three infrequently coincide.[56]

The seemingly incongruous pairing of ancient Athens and automation became prominent in the 1950s as the term "automation" exploded into public discourse. The pairing indexes emotions about the future of work and of democracy not only informative of years gone by but also instructive for our own time, since ancient Athens and automation continue to be paired, as I exhibit toward the end of the book. Telling a history of the recurring cultural claim that democratic ancient Athens has something to offer as a modern democracy automates is of importance in our current phase in the age of automation, when we are struggling to figure out what is new, what is old, what outcomes we ought to expect or to demand, what plans we should make, and when. A prominent keyword before "automation" was "cybernetics," so we start there.

1
Why Plato Is Missing (Norbert Wiener)

> Few philosophers of politics nowadays care to confine their investigations to the world of Ideas of Plato.
>
> NORBERT WIENER, *Cybernetics*

Before "automation," there was "cybernetics." Popularly attributed to US American mathematician Norbert Wiener (1894–1964), the term is credited with defining an era.[1] Now, outside of histories of science and technology, we encounter it primarily as "cyber-," and even that prefix does not abound as it once did.[2] Simply put, cybernetics is the study and theory of relationships within interactive systems, which come in mechanical, biological, hybrid, and even cultural forms. The word's wide applicability is clear, but its politics are not. How did Wiener come up with it? What effect did he reckon cybernetic logic and design would have on the world?

Wiener's account of how he decided on "cybernetics" changed over time, particularly after the word made him famous. His politics can be seen in his writing, and his citations reflect them as well. As I show, "cybernetics" comes from an ancient Greek word Wiener likely encountered while translating Plato's *Republic* as a teenager, but he never links "cybernetics" to Plato, despite scholarly pressure for him to do so. Wiener deeply values the classical education he received, but he does not think that ancient Athens or Plato's *Republic* have much to offer a modern, multiracial democracy that places a high value on both engineering and social mobility. Citing Plato would confuse matters.

The Launch of *Cybernetics*

In *Cybernetics; or, Control and Communication in the Animal and the Machine* (1948), the work that introduces the term, Wiener explains the immediate context of its provenance. While in France for a conference in 1947, he met with Enrique Freymann, the Mexican director of a small, niche French publishing house, Hermann et Cie, that was founded in the previous century by Freymann's father-in-law, a professor of mathematics.[3] Freymann invited Wiener to contribute a short book on "communication, the automatic factory, and the nervous system" to his series.[4] Neither of them expected it to turn a profit, let alone christen a cultural age.

For this book and its subject, Wiener needed to come up with a name capacious enough to capture his and his collaborators' wide-ranging work but narrow enough that it had no entangling etymons. Prior to 1947, Wiener had been part of several interdisciplinary research groups that had struggled to coin a term for their shared enthusiasm, across their knowledge domains, in matters pertaining to communication and control within dynamic systems.[5] Ultimately, it was the need of a book title that pressed a new form of an old word into service.

Because he composed the manuscript for *Cybernetics* in a flurry during a research stay at the Instituto Nacional de Cardiología in Mexico City, then the institution of the Mexican physician and physiologist Arturo Rosenblueth, his friend and former MIT colleague, Wiener uses the "we" of collaborative science to introduce "cybernetics."[6] He describes how he and Rosenblueth, to whom he dedicates the book, had long been stymied by the lack of a superintending concept that would unify their various projects, but then arrived, at last, at a name:

> After much consideration, we have come to the conclusion that all the existing terminology has too heavy a bias to one side or another to serve the future development of the field as well as it should; and as happens so often to scientists, we have been forced to coin at least one artificial neo-Greek expression to fill the gap. We have decided to call the entire field of control and communication theory, whether in the machine or in the animal, by the name Cybernetics, which we form from the Greek χυβερνήτης [*sic*] or *steersman*. In choosing this term, we wish to recognize that the first significant paper on feedback mechanisms is an article on governors, which was published by Clerk Maxwell in 1868, and that *governor* is derived from a Latin corruption of χυβερνήτης [*sic*]. We also wish to refer to the fact that the steering engines of a ship are indeed one of the earliest and best-developed forms of feedback mechanism.[7]

Extant words exerted themselves too much. A neologism it had to be. Perhaps poking fun, Wiener points to "artificial neo-Greek" as an inexhaustible resource for scientists stuck for nomenclature. In what seems like a wink at etymology, he acknowledges ship steering as one of the first and sturdiest cybernetic systems. The mention of Maxwell adds yet another element related to ships, where governors, invented by James Watt in the late eighteenth century, got their start in steam engines; the reference also acts as an informal scholarly citation. That is all that Wiener volunteers in *Cybernetics* about the origins of the word.

The chapter titles of *Cybernetics* index the wide applicability of the formation it names, ranging from time and statistics to psychopathology and the nervous system. Overall, *Cybernetics* is a technical book, replete with equations. But it also displays considerable political awareness. For instance, Wiener closes the introduction by attending to what he calls a "social potentiality of unheard-of importance for good and for evil" that he deems on par with atomic energy: the automatic factory.[8] What it holds for humanity is the promise of "a new and most effective collection of mechanical slaves to perform its labor."[9] Calling automated systems (or, more typically, machines) "slaves" predates this instance.[10] For example, "The Book of Machines," a pamphlet that appears in Samuel Butler's 1872 satiric novel, *Erewhon*, uses the language of master, servant, and slave to imagine how human-machine relations might change over time.[11] The pamphlet had split the Erewhonians into machinists and anti-machinists, resulting in a protracted civil war, the victory of the anti-machinists, and the destruction of machines. Wiener mentions the book frequently.[12]

These days, Butler's *Erewhon* is not often identified as a literary source of the machine-slave comparison. That honor usually goes to the Czech playwright Karel Čapek, who introduced the word *roboti* in his 1920 play, *RUR* (*Rossumovi Univerzáini Roboti*, Rossum's Universal Robots), formed from the Czech word *robota*, meaning forced or drudge work, and used it to describe human-like beings created to work for humans.[13] Here is how the general manager of RUR, Harry Domin, imagines the future: "All work will be done by living machines. Everybody will be free from worry and liberated from the degradation of labor. Everybody will live only to perfect himself."[14] Before long, the robots revolt and kill all humans but one. The names of the characters evince etymological play; Domin is short for *dominus*, Latin for "master" (all the named robots have singular Latin monikers). Wiener devotes only one sentence to *RUR* in his published work, but he delivered a prologue before a performance of the play in 1950.[15]

In *Cybernetics*, Wiener goes on to observe that "such mechanical labor has most of the economic properties of slave labor, although, unlike slave labor, it does not involve the direct demoralizing effects of human cruelty."[16] We find him emphasizing an economic and moral incongruity in likening machines to enslaved people; he does not qualify the former, but the latter he seems to judge as an improvement over the enslavement of humans. Yet, in a piece published in *Science* more than a decade later, in 1960, Wiener provides a retrospective look at the consequences he predicted in *Cybernetics*, and from another angle. In a section titled "Man and Slave" he writes:

> The problem, and it is a moral problem, with which we are here faced is very close to one of the great problems of slavery. Let us grant that slavery is bad because it is cruel. It is also, however, self-contradictory, and for a reason which is quite different. We wish a slave to be intelligent, to be able to assist us in the carrying out of our tasks. However, we also wish him to be subservient. Complete subservience and complete intelligence do not go together. How often in ancient times the clever Greek philosopher slave of a less intelligent Roman slaveholder must have dominated the actions of his master rather than obeyed his wishes! Similarly, if the machines become more and more efficient and operate at a higher and higher psychological level, the catastrophe foreseen by Butler of the dominance of the machine comes nearer and nearer.[17]

Using Butler's novel to catalyze the comparison, Wiener draws parallels between a machine more advanced than any of his time and a shrewd Greek "philosopher slave," and between a human and a less astute Roman enslaver soon outwitted and disobeyed. Through this ancient Roman example, Wiener implies that both brute force and sociocultural power are vulnerable to intelligence, by means of which the conquered can undermine the conquerors. A few issues later, *Science* would publish a rebuttal to Wiener's piece that calls the machine-to-slave analogy "misleading" and "fallacious"—a debate that continues to this day.[18]

In *Cybernetics*, Wiener refuses to come down on either side of the question of whether machine slaves would be a boon for humans: "It may very well be a good thing for humanity to have the machine remove it from the need of menial and disagreeable tasks, or it may not. I do not know."[19] Constantly alert to unintended consequences and human fallibility, he recognizes that cybernetically automated machines would be operating in a capitalist system. Whereas the first industrial revolution devalued the human arm, this second one will devalue most human brains, such that what he calls "the average human being of mediocre attainments or less has nothing to sell that is worth anyone's money to buy."[20] This is precisely why Wiener insists that cybernetic tech decisions cannot be made according to market logics—a typical US American tendency. In fact, he asserts that "the answer, of course, is to have a society based on human values other than buying or selling" that does not balk at the prospect of "a good deal of planning and a good deal of struggle."[21] He himself felt duty bound to seek out as many labor union leaders as he could to prepare them for what was coming, and he did.[22]

Wiener is remarkably honest about the situation in which he and his collaborators find themselves, calling their "moral position . . . not very comfortable." They have set forth "a new science" that "embraces technical developments with great possibilities for good and for evil," and they "can only hand it over into the world that exists about us, and this is the world of Belsen and Hiroshima."[23] He describes what is unfurling as unstoppable and enjoins those doing cybernetic projects "to see that a large public understands the tread and the bearing of the present work, and to confine our personal efforts to those fields, such as physiology and psychology, most remote from war and exploitation."[24] The only naivete to be found in the entire book may be this belief that research into matters of communication and control can be protected from potential mobilization for war and exploitation. That said, Wiener highly valued scientists' moral agency; resistance would be futile only if too few of them took theirs seriously. To encourage resistance, Wiener had allowed *The Atlantic* the year previously to publish, as an open letter, a private response Wiener addressed to a scientist with military connections who had been seeking access to Wiener's wartime research.[25] Wiener knew how valuable and far-reaching the study of interactive systems could be. It didn't take long for everyone else to catch on.

French Critics School Wiener

The unlikely popularity of *Cybernetics* begat the rapid uptake of "cybernetics" as well as an invitation for Wiener to write a less technical, more essayistic cybernetics book. It also gave him another chance to reflect on his choice of the term. However, in the first edition of *The* Human *Use of Human Beings*, published in English in 1950, he shares even less than he did in *Cybernetics*: "Its name signified the art of pilot or steersman. Let it be noted that the word 'governor' in a machine is simply the latinized Greek word for steersman."[26] Wiener also engages critical reactions to *Cybernetics*, including an excerpt from a review by a Dominican friar named Père Dominique Dubarle that ran in the leading French newspaper *Le Monde* on December 28, 1948.[27] Though *Cybernetics* was not translated into French until 2014, the book—which had been published, after all, by a Parisian press—was read immediately in English. The intensity of the French reaction to the cybernetics craze is well known (and the bibliography vast).[28] For my part, I'm interested in the fact that French critics educate Wiener in the history of the word he claims for his new science, demonstrating how easy it was to discover he was not the first to give ancient Greek vocabulary for ship steering a metaphorical application to some other system. The early users most frequently credited by the French are Plato and André-Marie Ampère.[29]

For example, 1953 saw the publication of *La pensée artificielle: Introduction à la cybernétique* by science correspondent Pierre de Latil.[30] Among the three epigraphs in its front matter is a quote from Plato's *Gorgias*: "La cybernétique sauve des plus grands dangers non seulement les âmes mais aussi les corps et les biens." [Piloting/cybernetics saves from great dangers not only souls but also bodies and goods.][31] This line is actually a clause from the middle of a sentence in *Gorgias*, one of several Platonic dialogues about rhetoric, the systematic art of the speaker. Regarded among the most shameless of Socrates's interlocutors, Callicles insisted that rhetoric helps one evade danger and stressed its salvific function; here, Socrates attempts to refute that point with reference to navigational piloting, which, unlike rhetoric, is a true *technē* (the word means something like "learnable system") and one truly based on the preservation of life. Yanked out of context, this line from *Gorgias* establishes an early start for cybernetic terminology. Latil plays up that provenance by finding or rendering a translation that uses the French *la cybernétique* for the Greek τὴν κυβερνητικὴν rather than *le pilotage* or *la navigation*. The result is the chronologically true and untrue implication that "cybernetics" has a long history.[32]

Latil opens the first chapter of *La pensée artificielle* as if he has been listening to a conversation and must get a word in: "Cybernétique? . . . Le mot vient brusquement à la mode." [Cybernetics? . . . The word suddenly comes into vogue].[33] Most of the chapter is about Wiener. Latil reviews the narrative Wiener provides about how he came up with "cybernetics" and asks, "Mais <cybernétique> est-il vraiment un néologisme? . . . Pour la langue anglaise, peut-être. Pour la langue française, non." [But is "cybernetics" really a neologism? For the English language, perhaps. For the French language, no].[34] In French, the word had appeared in the writings of André-Marie Ampère more than a hundred years before *Cybernetics* emerged.

Through the eponymous "amp," short for *ampere*, the base unit measure of electric current, Ampère flows through circuits of wire. Less commemorated than his contributions to electrodynamics is his two-part work classifying all of human knowledge, *Essai sur la philosophie des sciences: Ou, Exposition analytique d'une classification naturelle de toutes les connaissances humaines* (1834–43). In the second volume, Ampère addresses the political theory of good government and finds himself needing a concept that does not exist in French. He seeks a term that will cover how those who govern will develop and use their knowledge of their polity—"its character, its customs, its opinions, its history, its religion, its means of existence and of prosperity, its organization and its laws"—to "guide it in each particular case."[35] Ampère explains that he will name what he refers to here "cybernétique, du mot κυβερνητική, qui, pris d'abord, dans une acception restreinte, pour l'art de gouverner un vaisseau, reçut de l'usage, chez les Grecs même, la signification, tout autrement étendue, de l'art de gouverner en général." [Cybernetics, from the word *kubernētikē*, which, taken first, in a limited sense, as the art of governing a vessel, received from usage, among the Greeks even, the quite different meaning of the art of governing in general.][36] Ampère does not specify an ancient Greek text featuring that extended usage, and he limits his focus to political governance, strictly speaking.[37]

The year after the publication of Latil's book came mathematician Georges-Théodule Guilbaud's *La cybernétique*, a nimble explainer-type text that, like Latil's, draws only from *Cybernetics*.[38] Guilbaud opens with a chapter titled "Notes for a Dictionary Entry," where he imagines he has been asked to define the word "cybernetics" for a major dictionary and so must trace its "origin, history and evolution."[39] The very first citation establishes the ancient Greek derivation: "The word occurs fairly often in Plato, both in this literal sense and in the metaphorical sense of the art of guiding men in society, i.e. the art of government."[40] Guilbaud does not provide references, but, again, we can hazard a guess: As Latil pointed out, Plato's Socrates uses *kubernē*-based words in debates throughout *Gorgias*, but their use in the *Republic* pertains much more directly to government. Guilbaud concedes that Wiener mentions the term's derivation from the ancient Greek *kubernētikē*, but he gets in this little dig: "He seemed to be unaware of the *kybernētikē* of Plato and imagined that the term was a new one."[41] Wiener's recognition of the word's ancient Greekness but not its use by Plato suggests that Wiener does not know Plato well enough to be aware that he uses many *kubernē*-based terms. After all, if one anglicizes a word one knows from reading Plato (in ancient Greek, no less), surely one would highlight its Platonic provenance to lend authority to the term and to the term's user. Or Guilbaud may wish to suggest that Wiener owes recognition to Plato because, just as Plato used *kubernētikē* to talk about something other than ships (i.e., democracy), so does Wiener use "cybernetics" to talk about a whole range of subjects (i.e., democracy, animal physiology, human labor). Perhaps, in Guilbaud's view, the metaphorical capaciousness Wiener relies upon when he chooses "cybernetics" starts with Plato, and Plato deserves credit.

To capitalize upon the fervor around *Cybernetics*, Wiener wrote *The* Human *Use of Human Beings* quickly, and the manuscript underwent a radical revision (cuts, mostly) before being republished in 1954 (the same year Guilbaud's book was published, in fact). In the second edition, when discussing how "cybernetics" came to be, Wiener moves from the first-person plural of his account in *Cybernetics* to the first-person singular and at last acknowledges Ampère's place in the word's intellectual history:

> Until recently, there was no existing word for this complex of ideas, and in order to embrace the whole field by a single term, I felt constrained to invent one. Hence "Cybernetics," which I derived from the Greek word *kubernētēs*, or "steersman," the same Greek word from which we eventually derive our word "governor." Incidentally, I found later that the word had already been used by Ampère with reference to political science, and had been introduced in another context by a Polish scientist, both uses dating from the earlier part of the nineteenth century.[42]

Plato remains largely absent. But not entirely. In a later chapter, to prepare readers for—and to justify—an extended metaphor, Wiener writes that "phantasy has always been at the service of philosophy, and Plato was not ashamed to clothe his epistemology in the metaphor of the cave."[43] The cave is, of course, the most famous of all of Plato's metaphors, and it features in the *Republic*.[44] Still, one need not have read the *Republic* to know that.

For French critics like Latil and Guilbaud, the citation of Plato in any discussion of "cybernetics" is a matter of conducting honest intellectual and conceptual history. The question of why this was not the case for Wiener becomes difficult to ignore in the face of this philological insistence. It becomes yet more difficult to ignore once we know about Wiener's early years.

Wiener's Greek

Wiener writes about the background of the name "cybernetics" in one other place. While working on major revisions to *The* Human *Use of Human Beings*, Wiener, encouraged by his celebrity, decided to write an autobiography, the two volumes of which contain additional insights into how he came up with the term. For instance, we learn in the second volume that *kubernētēs* was not the first ancient Greek word he considered:

> I first looked for a Greek word signaling "messenger," but the only one I knew was *angelos*. This has in English the specific meaning "angel," a messenger of God. The word was thus pre-empted and would not give me the right context. Then I looked for an appropriate word from the field of control. The only word I could think of was the Greek word for steersman, *kubernētēs*. I decided that, as the word I was looking for was to be used in English, I ought to take advantage of the English pronunciation of the Greek and hit on the name *cybernetics*.[45]

What does Wiener mean when he says he "looked" for ancient Greek words that would work? Where was he looking? When he says he "knew" or "could think of" these two words, he is telling us he is relying on his own previous knowledge. *Angelos* is common enough, but how did *kubernētēs* occur to him? He does not explain directly in any of his published work or unpublished papers, but the first volume of his autobiography holds intriguing clues, since there he looks back on his classical training, even recording the difficulty of retaining his reading knowledge of ancient Greek.

The son of a Harvard professor of Slavic languages who aggressively managed his education, Wiener started learning ancient Greek as a child and continued his study of the language while a teenaged undergraduate at Tufts.[46] His father grew fond of his son's Greek-language professor, whom he invited over to the Wiener home, where Norbert would "play on the floor and listen with fascination to the wide-ranging conversation between the two men. If anything could have made a classicist out of me, it was these experiences."[47] Wiener also loved reading Spinoza and Leibniz, and his father made the decision that he should pursue the study of philosophy at Cornell. There, during a postgraduate fellowship year when he was sixteen, Wiener took a course in which, he reports, he "read Plato's *Republic* in Greek."[48] In his revision notes for *Ex-Prodigy*, the first volume of his autobiography, Wiener recalls that he struggled through it, but "did not fall down so badly in the Plato course, for this was but the continuation of my father's teaching under another preceptor."[49] For a reason he did not record (perhaps for narrative fidelity only), Wiener decided that detail was worth relating.[50]

Wiener was at Cornell for only a year before his brother fell ill and his father summoned him back to Harvard, where he continued pursuing his PhD in philosophy. Nearly seventeen, Wiener took a class during his first year with George Santayana, who infused the course with "the feeling of continuity with an old culture and the feeling that philosophy was an intrinsic part of life, or art, and of the spirit."[51] In *Ex-Prodigy*, Wiener reports laboring to relearn ancient Greek and Latin, names Homer and Horace as his forever favorites, and recalls another struggle with Plato's *Republic*, this time during an oral examination in Greek philosophy administered by a Professor Woods.[52] His doodle-embroidered, equation-dotted notebooks from this time, the second term of the 1911/12 academic year, show his engagement with ancient Greek philosophical concepts and contests such as "Ηδόνη vs. φρόνησις," which he encountered while reading Plato's *Philebus*.[53] Looking back decades later, Wiener's overall self-appraisal is that he "may not be much of a classicist in the technical, competitive sense, but the roots of a classical education are firm in me."[54] I think the word "cybernetics" grew from those roots.

Translating Plato's *Republic* would have put Wiener in the company of plentiful *kubernē*-based words. In books 1, 3, and 6, Plato's Socrates includes navigating and piloting a ship among a set of *technai* (learnable systems) he uses to make comparisons to the main topics of the dialogue, which, from book 2 on, sketches out "a paradigm of a good polis."[55] In book 6, to impress upon his interlocutors the problem of democracy as he sees it, Socrates deploys a fleet of naval similes to model the challenges of guiding people and the structures designed to carry them safely. More precisely, this *eikōn* (likeness) is suggestive of what happens to philosophers when they try to assert what Plato believes to be their rightful leadership position in a democratic polis. They are like a ship's pilot or navigator—a *kubernētēs*—whose efforts to use his knowledge to help deliver those aboard to safety constantly get blocked by rowdy crew members who try to persuade the ship's owner to let them to do the navigating and steering, even though some have no idea what they are doing. In this "ship of state" analogy, the ship corresponds to the polis (the state), the shipowner to the demos (the people), and the sailors to the rhetors (public speakers) who are attempting to convince the power-holding people to give them the helm. The analogy is meant to clarify the arrangements of Athenian democracy so that the crew's (ostensible) ridiculousness and dangerousness will be identifiable and undeniable to all: Just as one would want a trained steersman to guide one's ship, so should one want a philosopher to guide one's polis. Anyone who reads the *Republic* in ancient Greek will notice the recurrence of *kubernē*-based words in this section of the work. Plato's Socrates himself calls the analogy *glischrōs*, sticky.[56]

The combination of Wiener's sentimental regard for his classical education and his technical proficiency in ancient Greek lead me to suppose that he had at least those two reasons to dwell on the provenance of an ancient Greek word he himself selected to name his research, if he had wanted to do so.

Why Wiener Steers Clear of Plato

Wiener's documented knowledge of Plato's *Republic* in ancient Greek raises the question of why he does not mention Plato in connection with *kubernētēs*. For the French explicators of "cybernetics," Plato is the obvious place from which to start an account of the word. Why not for Wiener?

One potential answer is that Wiener cares to establish only the technical features of the history of "cybernetics," from ancient navigation through Watt's and Maxwell's governors for steam engines. The metaphorical work Plato does with *kubernē*-based terms is irrelevant to Wiener's literal leaning. But, when one considers a manuscript Wiener did not see through to publication, a more intriguing possibility presents itself.

Wiener completed *Invention: The Care and Feeding of Ideas*, in 1954, the same year the revised, much-shortened edition of *The* Human *Use of Human*

Beings appeared, and while he was writing the second volume of his autobiography.[57] The manuscript, finally published in 1993 due to the efforts of Steve Joshua Heims, contains a chapter on "social climate and invention," where Wiener goes into "historical matters not so much for their own sakes, and *particularly not so much for the hope of being able to say anything complimentary about them*, as because I wish to lay the ground for a discussion of social relations in the present day as affect invention."[58] Ancient Athens did not impress Wiener as a site conducive to inventive engineering—or, more importantly, to pervasive human flourishing.

First, he turns a phrase from the *Republic* to establish his invention-based critique: "Paraphrasing the modifying Plato's statement that in the ideal state, kings must become philosophers and philosophers, kings," we might say that, "for a great period of invention, the artisans must become philosophers or the philosophers, artisans."[59] Wiener writes that "little or nothing in the training or orientation" of fifth- and fourth-century-BCE democratic city-state residents encouraged the development of a philosopher-artisan or artisan-philosopher. No surviving writings from ancient Athens center on or celebrate people in whom theoretical, technical, and experimental modes meet in the fabrication of objects or material systems.

He goes on to disapprove of the subordinated status of artisans and craftspeople and of the altogether vaulted plane of the philosopher, "a gentleman, participating in affairs of state and in affairs of war, interested in reflection, but with soft hands."[60] Democratic ancient Athens did not last long, and while it did, he writes, "the gentlemen had the leisure to be philosophers, and the rough work of life was left to slaves and to disenfranchised metics."[61] This contrast between "soft hands" and "rough work" uses sensual words to judge the inclusions and exclusions of democratic Athens as seen by Plato and Aristotle—two aristocrats who were not fans of democracy. Aristotle's view of free people who work with their hands or who manage those who do is that "the best city-state [*hē de beltistē polis*]" will not put them on the roster of citizens; political *aretē*—by which Aristotle means something like virtue or virtuosity in matters of the polis—is not an object simply possessed but honed, which takes what is in short supply for laborers and their managers: time.[62]

Only one ancient Greek figure interests Wiener as a potential relation of the contemporary engineer: Daedalus. Earlier, in *Cybernetics*, Wiener had stationed the techniques of Daedalus, along with those of Hero of Alexandria, at the start of the automaton tradition, stating that "the ability of the artificer to produce a working simulacrum of a living organism has always intrigued people."[63] This fascination with automata continues into—and, of course, beyond—Wiener's time, yet he resists a popular urge to reduce cybernetics to human-like robotics. In *Invention*, Wiener opines that "Daedalus is more a contemporary of Watt in his thoughts than he was of Plato."[64] It was James Watt who invented the governor for steam-ship steering, selecting the word due to its Latin etymology, which is related to *kubernētikē*. Wiener's appreciation for Daedalus does not end with his technical acumen but extends to his communication with the power brokers and decision makers of his day. Daedalus did not restrict his attention to his workshop, and his creations were too impressive for those outside of his guild (so to speak) to ignore.

This manuscript demonstrates that Wiener knew Plato's *Republic* and Plato's Athens well, and that he knew, too, the exclusions and philosophical snobbery that abounded in what ancient Athenians called "democracy." Plato's *Republic* presents not only a polis whose workings are not engineer-centric, but also one whose structure is antidemocratic. Wiener did not think that *actual* ancient Athens (as presented by Plato and Aristotle) was a time and a place from which twentieth-century US American engineers should look for models, either; it lacked what he considered the requisite technical and social climate for an object of serious emulative study or even the stuff of useful analogies. The only democracy Wiener thought worthy of learning from was that of the United States, and its lessons were largely warnings.

Wiener as Theorist of Democracy

Debate about to what tradition Wiener belongs as a theorist of human communication and community shows his status to be unsettled. In the view of N. Katherine Hayles, Wiener talks a good game but holds the positions of a "liberal humanist subject." For instance, she claims, he noted the potential threats of automatic factories but "offered no remedy other than the platitude that men must not let machines take over."[65] That's not entirely true. Wiener pushed beyond platitudes: He reached out to labor leaders to warn them about what was coming and refused to work on any military contracts (or release his past military work so that others could build on it), publicly urging other scientists to join him. Critical information scholar Ronald Day argues that Wiener approached communication as transmission, as information flow from sender to receiver. This conduit paradigm, Day asserts, should be set aside "so as to better account for language and society, as well as to open up the 'information future' in ways that are more open than, and more critical of, dominant political and social institutions that have existed throughout our Cold War society."[66] Though Wiener contributed to early information theory and research, to suggest that his approach to communication is narrow, closed, or uncritical is to ignore not only particular passages in his books but also their entire drift. One of the premier historians of media and communication, John Durham Peters, and his son, Benjamin Peters, an expert on the Soviet internet (or lack thereof), contend that Wiener's thinking and writing bear smudged imprints of pragmatist influence.[67] The evidence is stronger there.

On the whole, Wiener's democratic theorizing has been underappreciated. In his two books on cybernetics, Wiener writes plenty about democracy. And he is not complimentary about its past, or its present. In fact, he neither holds back criticism of it—always a bold choice but especially so during the early years of the Cold War—nor shies away from calling out the antidemocratic tendencies of entrenched powers (e.g., big business) that threaten individual and collective human flourishing.

Wiener intended the title of *The* Human *Use of Human Beings* to be an anthem. Originally, he wanted to call the book *Pandora* or *Cassandra*, summoning a mythic woman with a strange relationship either with hope or with doom. Objecting on the grounds of salability, however, his editor repurposed a line from the manuscript's introduction instead.[68] Here, from the first edition, is the paragraph that enlarges upon the book's central theme and impetus: "Our view of society differs from the ideal of society which is held by many Fascists, Strong Men in Business, and Government. Similar men of ambition for power are not entirely unknown in scientific and educational institutions. Such people prefer an organization in which all orders come from above, and none return. The human beings under them have been reduced to the level of effectors for a supposedly higher nervous organism."[69] Wiener uses the language of cybernetics to critique power relations that are characterized by unidirectionality of communication and the absolute subordination of those designated as the underlings to those designated as their superiors. We might hear an anti-*Republic* resonance in Wiener's disapproval of such an arrangement. In the mid-twentieth century, Plato's *Republic* was a "conscript in the ideology wars" between democracy and cultural forms and institutions deemed undemocratic.[70] I have been unable to find a direct reference to Karl Popper in Wiener's writings, but the heart of Popper's critique of the *Republic* was that a social structure engineered to secure power for a few tended ultimately to concentrate power in a single "great man."[71] Such a structure seems ideal to Wiener's list of capitalized men and men-ruled entities, but Wiener was more than capable of arriving at that conclusion through his own education and observation. Wiener continues:

> I wish to devote this book to a protest against this inhuman use of human beings; for in my mind, any use of a human being in which less is demanded

> of him and less is attributed to him than his full status is a degradation and a waste. It is a degradation to a human being to chain him to an oar and use him as a source of power; but it is an almost equal degradation to assign him to a purely repetitive task in a factory, which demands less than a millionth of his brain capacity. It is simpler to organize a factory or galley which uses individual human beings for a trivial fraction of their worth than it is to provide a world in which they can grow to their full stature. Those who suffer from a power complex find the mechanization of man a simple way to realize their ambitions.[72]

Here, he rages against those who would press people into configurations that are meant to make them small, manageable, and predictable. To reduce the variety, complexity, and magnitude of a person's life is to do a great wrong. From the perspective of the etymology of cybernetics, it is striking that Wiener uses a nautical example that calls back to a time before steam power. Moreover, the factory, that fixture of the Industrial Revolution, is a place whose operations cybernetics is poised to disrupt. Foremost, Wiener stands for humans being used in ways commensurate with their humanness. Throughout *The* Human *Use of Human Beings*, he arrives at the meaning of this use indirectly, by enumerating current constraints on humans living to their full measure. Remarkably, this introduction does not appear in the book's second edition, leaving readers who may be curious about its title somewhat adrift.

Wiener knows his own country well and presumes that cybernetics will unspool there the most quickly. He cannot separate the many dangers he foresees from his view of the national character. Throughout the book, he asserts that US Americans, in general, worship progress, the end result usually being that they make bad things more efficient; are complicit with a government that has dealt and continues to deal unfairly with Indigenous people, especially when it comes to interpretations of treaties; do not seem to care about their unsustainable devastation of nature; display a swaggering prioritization of "know-how" (what we technically know how to do) over "know-what" (the principles and ends to which our "know-how" should be directed); and do not handle gloom and doom well and so have no stomach for the tragic view of life. He believes that US American business commodifies everything, is ruthlessly profit driven, and is oriented to short-term gain, all of which stand to work against any new technology or other resource being managed responsibly and democratically. He also thinks that US American antagonism with the USSR is ridiculous. All of this adds up to the country mishandling the opportunities that cybernetics presents.

Again and again, the substance of Wiener's projections about how cybernetics will affect the United States show him to be an early alarm-ringer about how cybertech could further entrench extant systems of asserted superiority. For example, Wiener points to dangers related to actual histories and potential futures of domination that have limited and will limit human possibility. In a chapter titled, "Rigidity and Learning: Two Patterns of Communicative Behavior," he ventures into human communication. He offers Inuit "social community" as an example of a communication structure with little subordination, and Indian social community, with its caste structure, as one "in which the means of communication between two individuals are closely restricted and modified by their ancestry and position."[73] Where does the United States fall on that spectrum? He opines that "most of us in the United States prefer to live in a moderately loose social community, in which the blocks to communication among individuals and classes are not too great. I will not say that this ideal of communication is attained in the United States. Until white supremacy ceases to belong to the creed of a large part of the country it will be an ideal from which we fall short."[74] Despite many of the national notions of the era, people in the United States did *not* enjoy open and unrestricted communication. In calling out pervasive anti-blackness as a pattern of hierarchy, separation, and exclusion, Wiener casts doubt on whether unbound, unblocked social community is something white US Americans even want.

Insofar as democracies depend on citizens communicating and treating one another as equals, what the United States has going is, at best, an inchoate democracy. Still, Wiener assesses that "even this modified formless democracy is too anarchic for many of those who make efficiency their first ideal," a poignant observation to make in 1950, when the United States was heralding itself as the bastion of democracy and its freedoms.[75] Wiener details how "worshippers of efficiency" would much prefer that each of us were born into—and die having moved in—a "social orbit" we cannot alter, serving a function we cannot change.[76] They would never explicitly say so, of course, but in many ways that "show[s] that the democracy to which they pay their respects is not really the order in which they would prefer to live. The regularly ordered state of pre-assigned functions toward which they gravitate is suggestive of the Leibnizian automata and does not suggest the irreversible movement into a contingent future which is the true condition of human life."[77] This is the inhuman use of human beings for which Wiener is on guard. Though he associates it here with the automata of Leibniz, what Wiener describes is not far off from the strictly ordered conditions of human life within the ideal polis as articulated by Socrates in Plato's *Republic*. At bottom, one's designs for social life depend on one's definitions and understandings of the human.

The category of the human has long been (and continues to be) contested and controversial. In the introduction to the first edition of *The* Human *Use of Human Beings*, Wiener addresses the trickiness of defining humans: "The problem of the definition of man is an odd one. To say that man is a featherless biped is merely to put him in the same class as a plucked chicken, a kangaroo, or a jerboa. This is a rather heterogeneous group, and it can be extended to our heart's content without throwing any further light on the true nature of man."[78] Wiener does not note that "featherless biped" is the infamous genus for the human offered by Socrates in Plato's *Statesman*.[79] For Wiener, "what does differentiate man from other animals in a way that leaves us not the slightest degree of doubt, is that he is a talking animal. . . . There are animals besides man which are social, and live in a continuous relation to their fellow creatures, but there is none in whom this desire for communication, or rather this necessity for communication, is the guiding motive of their whole life."[80] Using "communication," which his research helped make a keyword of the twentieth century, Wiener joins ancient Greek thinkers like Isocrates and Aristotle in this emphasis on distinguishing human life through speaking and listening.[81]

In passages following his reference to Leibnizian automata, Wiener professes his belief that "variety and possibility are inherent in the human sensorium—and are indeed the key to man's most noble flights—because variety and possibility belong to the very structure of the human organism."[82] From the level of the individual to that of the species, in order to flourish we need contingency. We need to know that things can be otherwise, that we are not absolutely stuck with things as they are. Conditions that are so regulated as to be determined are optimal for machines, which function best when "probability is negligible."[83] Such conditions harm humans. For Wiener, then, contingency and the need for communication—that is, the ability to talk to and listen to others and know that such processes influence the functioning of the whole system of which we are a part—mark human beings. This attitude, above all, may explain why he does not link "cybernetics" to Plato's *Republic*. Plato may have used the word, but he does not own it.

Norbert Wiener was a mathematician and an engineer trained in philosophy and steeped in the arguments of classicists and their texts. He is not easily slotted. His archives contain one amusing piece of evidence suggesting that his colleagues viewed him as having qualities redolent of an ancient Greek intellectual—or maybe they detected that he viewed himself that way, and they played along. An undated piece credited to Giorgio ("George") de Santillana, a professor of the history and philosophy of science in the Department of Humanities at the Massachusetts Institute of Technology from 1941 to 1967, purports to be a "Life of Norbertos" authored by "the to-be-lost Diogenes Post-Laertius, as uncovered by certain friends of his," and providing select life details about Wiener, a "mathematician and sophist."[84] Diogenes Laertius was a third-century CE Greek biographical historian most famous for his ten-volume *Lives and Opinions of Eminent Philosophers*. De Santillana does not follow his model's biographical template exactly (e.g., we do not get any of Wiener's sayings, but we are told he was a vegetarian). On the topic of where Wiener settled, the mock (and mocking?) piece records that Wiener escaped the tyrant (i.e., Harvard) and took up in "Antipolis," near Boston, where he was "honored by its citizens, who decreed for him a Coronal ('Cyclotron') and the title of Cybernete or governor. He wrote a book on Cybernetics or the art of ruling; in it he teaches how to deceive the people by telling them what they want to hear and he calls this 'feedback.'"[85] De Santillana returns "cybernetics" to its language and culture of origin, amplifying the metaphorical link to governorship and ruling that Plato, too, had emphasized when he used κυβερνητ-based words. The line about *Cybernetics* also smacks of Plato, since his Socrates accuses rhetors and sophists of deceit by telling people what they want to hear and calling that process "rhetoric"—in *Gorgias*, most famously. It is a reach to suppose that Wiener's distance-keeping from Plato was a running joke among his colleagues, but it is notable that de Santillana uses a Platonic approach to have fun with Wiener. As a whole, the piece uses a quirky, archaic style to playfully place Wiener among eminent philosophers.

The influence of his early classical training shows throughout Wiener's work, but his faithfulness to it has limits. He thought that certain cybernetic applications could, under the right conditions, most of them counter to US America's strongest tendencies, amplify human flourishing, but he never looked back to ancient Athens for a productive paradigm for how that might be so. And he certainly never sought inspiration from Plato's *Republic*, even though he would have encountered κυβερνητ-based words while translating it as a teenager. Connecting "cybernetics" to that dialogue in particular risked misrepresenting the message Wiener wished to deliver. Communication within a cybernetic system—be it mechanical, biological, or social—takes forms that are dynamic and distributed, not static or always hierarchical; moreover, he identified rigid social structures and exclusionary social practices as constraining rather than constituting such systems. When Wiener chose to supply a brief etymological gloss of "cybernetics" rather than undertake its intellectual history, he was not doing so out of ignorance or arrogance. Whereas advocates of cybernetics after him took full-on inspiration from ancient Greece, especially Athens, Wiener took only one word.

Automation for the People?

The churnings of mid-century—technological, economic, cultural—cast Wiener's word across the 1950s and '60s. As historian of technology Ronald Kline has documented, cybernetics and other cyber-compounds, such as "cybernation" (coined by Donald N. Michael in 1962) and "cyberculture" (coined by Alice Mary Hilton in 1963), had a major cultural moment but were eclipsed by talk of "information," the swift-propagating keyword of Wiener's student Claude Shannon.[86] A third keyword of the period is, of course, "automation." Wiener himself hated it: "Convenient as this word is for its brevity, it is barbarously constructed," he and MIT colleague Donald Campbell bemoaned in a 1954 draft of a coauthored piece titled "Automatization," their preferred form.[87]

That same year, Wiener either dictated or typed pages later archived as "Untitled re: Automatic Factories." In them, he takes up a topic on which he does not spend much time in his published books: leisure. In a chapter of *The* Human *Use of Human Beings* titled, "The First and Second Industrial Revolutions," he returns to a posture of doubt he had assumed in the introduction to *Cybernetics* about whether automated machines would be good or bad for humanity.[88] In *The* Human *Use of Human Beings*, he reckons that if automated machines put an end to repetitive factory labor, then, "in the long run, the deadly uninteresting nature of the repetitive task may make this a good thing and the source of leisure necessary for a man's full cultural development. It may also produce cultural results as trivial and wasteful as the greater part of those so far obtained from the radio and the movies."[89] He does not enumerate activities he finds less trivial and wasteful, but he does take the opportunity the second edition affords him to revise the views he had expressed in the first, four years earlier:

> Since the publication of the first edition of the book, I have participated in two big meetings with representatives of business management, and I have been delighted to see that awareness on the part of a great many of those present of the social dangers of our new technology and the social obligations of those responsible for management to see that the new modalities are used for the benefit of man, for increasing his leisure and enriching his spiritual life, rather than merely for profits and the worship of the machines as a new brazen calf. There are many dangers still ahead, but the roots of good will are there, and I do not feel as thoroughly pessimistic as I did at the time of the publication of the first edition of the book.[90]

In "Untitled re: Automatic Factories," he extends his worry about the short-term livelihood of factory workers to whether workers in future automated factories will enjoy the good life. The pages conclude with an exhortation: "We must have more arts and crafts and less television, more reading and less looking, more baseball fields and less [*sic*] bleachers. Whether we shall get what we must have, or whether the rpoletariat [*sic*] of the factories will turn as an earlier proletariat did in Rome into a proletariat of bread and spectacles, is something only the future can tell us. May it give us the right answer."[91]

Wiener urges creative, active, participatory uses of one's time rather than mere spectatorship. This recommendation speaks to a concern that Wiener was not alone in expressing: that automated factories would lead to increases in leisure time, which US Americans would not know how to use generatively. Wiener hopes that workers will not behave like proletarian ancient Romans, whom the satirist Juvenal judged to have traded their political agency for large-scale performances they sat and watched and for food they did not bake or buy themselves, both intended to keep them quiet and obedient to whoever entertained and fed them.[92] Wiener does not seem to have liked imperial Rome any more than he liked imperial Athens, though, of course, hating on imperial Rome, with its panem et circenses, was (and is) far more common.

The proliferation of "automation" (rather than Wiener's preferred "automatization"), in newspapers and magazines, full of affective charge of one kind or another but never clearly defined, induced the US Congress to hold hearings in October 1955 on the subject.[93] A common refrain during the proceedings was that "automation" had not yet appeared in standard dictionaries, thereby contributing to the word's power to index all manner of technologies and attitudes toward them. Another topic of much discussion was leisure, which representatives from both management and labor highlighted as a great promise of automation.

From the management side, John Diebold, the founder of an automation consulting company, led off the hearings. He was the ideal choice, since he had popularized the word "automation" in his 1952 book, *Automation: The Advent of the Automatic Factory*.[94] *Automation* contained a brief section titled "The Problem of Leisure" in which Diebold had asked whether "we as a people [can] learn to utilize leisure," a challenge "automation accentuates but has not produced, for the problem has been with us, to an ever-increasing extent, since man first found means for providing the barest material essentials of life."[95] In his testimony during the hearings, he addressed the matter of training for this expected increase in leisure: "I think considerable attention must be given to our education system to see that we use this leisure creatively, that it is used in a manner that benefits all of our society."[96] He also entered into the record the opinion of psychologists that people would not know how to use a boost in leisure time.[97] It may be tempting to think that Diebold's worries smack only of paternalism and capitalist productivity obsession, but they were not unique to mental health specialists friendly with big names in private enterprise—nor were they new.[98]

Labor representatives also spoke to necessary adjustments in knowledge priorities. The most prominent speaker from labor was Walter P. Reuther, then-president of the Congress of Industrial Organizations, to whom Wiener had written about the cybernetic future of labor in 1949, in Reuther's capacity as president of the Union of Automobile Workers, a role in which Reuther served until his death in 1970. Reuther opined that "what we need to do is match our scientific, technical, and production know-how with comparable human and social and moral know-how. The production process is not the end. It is the means to an end. The end is the enrichment of human life. The end is to meet man's basic needs, within the framework of an expanding intellectual, political, and spiritual freedom."[99] Earlier in his testimony, he had linked the reduction in the work week, made possible by automation, with a potential surge in leisure activities including education, horticulture, and travel. On the whole, the discourse dedicated to leisure during the hearings indicates agreement between management and labor that the country and the culture had a lot of adapting to do. Where might everyone look for different patterns of life?

2

Athens Emerges in the Age of Automation (Hannah Arendt)

> The word "automation," which came into use in 1952, became popular with the press, and stories about electronic monsters and giant super-brains, of robots that were a combination of Tik-Tok from the Land of Oz and Martians began to appear in Sunday supplements. Curiously enough, nobody seriously worried about people.
>
> ALICE MARY HILTON, "Cyberculture—The Age of Abundance and Leisure"

Academics, too, got a word in about leisure in the automation age. The challenge and opportunity posed by leisure for US Americans, who were neither habituated to nor educated for it is the focus of "Recreation in the Age of Automation," the fall 1957 issue of *The Annals of the American Academy of Political and Social Science*.[1] The issue's programmatic purpose is to begin to understand "the leisure mode of tomorrow's living," with "leisure" as perhaps the very fundament of those "enjoyments once reserved for a privileged elite [that] are becoming widely distributed."[2] The more historically and philosophically grounded essays point out that the Greek noun *scholē*, usually translated as "leisure," gives us our word for "school," with one contributor joking that "if we take the word of the Greeks for it, all school education is a leisure activity—however much three thousand years of groans and sighs from youthful learners suggest the contrary."[3]

Political scientist James Charlesworth, in his essay "A Bold Program for Recreation," mentions democratic ancient Athens directly. His main point is that attitudes, programs, and policies that advance recreation education lagged behind the frenetic activity of business leaders that automates repetitive taskwork and thereby (potentially) frees up a laborer's day. Here's why: "The leaders who preside over our industrial civilization are individualists and make no pretense of being architects of societies. They are neither trained nor motivated in the general public interest. Accordingly, civic minded people, like educators and recreationists, must follow after the industrialists, assess the social and cultural effects of what they are doing, and periodically enunciate social programs to supplement or correct those effects."[4] In addition to social programs is the need for a sort of cultural deprogramming. He marks the attitude of living to work as redolent of an immature economic system, but he knows how deeply it is embedded.

Charlesworth's solution to Christian (particularly Protestant) attitudes toward work is to bypass Christianity and go yet further back, to an older inheritance: "We must consider all of the little and big iron men as our slaves and ourselves to be entitled to the demigodlike personal development of the Athenian citizens of the Periclean age."[5] Here, automation takes the form of humanoid robots, which Charlesworth calls "slaves" to set up an analogy between human beneficiaries of such "slaves" in the twentieth century and a small, select group in the fifth century BCE. A causal relationship holds the analogy together: Because of slaves, human or not, citizens of particular eras may achieve a degree of self-enhancement that exceeds the usual limits. Charlesworth urges a consideration of such an arrangement as an entitlement. Though he emphasizes "personal development" and not, say, public-mindedness as the focus of Periclean-period democracy—the viewpoint expressed in Thucydides's version of Pericles's funeral oration, that public business is every citizen's business, springs to mind—he also gives three cheers for democracy. He fears, however, that "intense specialization" and the resultant shrinking of broad expertise means that people will treat democracy the way they do sports: watch professionals do it rather than participate themselves and risk being anything less than "superlative."[6] Again, the frame of spectatorship is used to mark disengagement. Yet others at the end of the 1950s anticipate a reluctance—even a culturally habituated incapacity—to use the inevitable, automation-gifted free time to participate actively in the messy project of living well together.

Hannah Arendt and *The Human Condition*

The subsequent year, 1958, saw the publication of what would prove to be the most durable mid-century study of humanity in conditions of automation-granted leisure, *The Human Condition*, by German thinker—and US American citizen since 1951—Hannah Arendt (1906–1975). In a short prologue, Arendt establishes the impetus for the book by pointing to the two most jolting technological possibilities of the 1950s: that humans nearly have the power to rocket off the planet we have shaped and that has shaped us (Sputnik had launched the year prior, after Arendt had submitted her manuscript), and that humans nearly have the power to free ourselves from labor. Automation, touted as a great liberator, was more interesting to her than space exploration, since it seemed to be far "closer at hand."[7]

In the book's prologue, Arendt immediately enmeshes automation, labor, and ancient Athens. Automation, she supposes, "in a few decades probably will empty the factories and liberate mankind from its oldest and most natural burden, the burden of laboring and the bondage of necessity. . . . Freedom from labor itself is not new; it once belonged among the most firmly established privileges of the few."[8] We come to understand that she is alluding here to ancient Athenian citizens, specifically the elite, to whom she returns throughout her study; via the enslavement of others, they freed themselves from many demands of everyday, embodied life. She goes on to call our society one "of laborers which is about to be liberated from the fetters of labor, and this society does no longer know of those higher and more meaningful activities for the sake of which this freedom would deserve to be won."[9] Here, she refers to what a very few ancient Greek thinkers have ranked as the most precious potential of their slave-ensured leisure: opportunity for contemplation. Second place went to spirited participation in public life. Arendt believes that the aptitude for both activities in modern US American society is seriously lacking. "What we are confronted with," she writes, "is the prospect of a society of laborers without labor, that is, without the only activity left to them. Surely, nothing could be worse."[10] She suggests that we think about the problem.

Her proposal is not a dodge. Arendt marks "to think what we are doing" as our most solemn responsibility in an age characterized by thoughtlessness.[11] She warns that if thought were to become disconnected from "know-how," then "we would indeed become the helpless slaves, not so much of our machines as of our know-how, thoughtless creatures at the mercy of every gadget which is technically possible, no matter how murderous it is."[12] Before we can think what we are doing, we must come to terms with what it is we do; analyzing what humans do qua humans is Arendt's pursuit in *The Human Condition*. That she frames the stakes in terms of enslavement to our own thoughtlessness makes not technology per se but its unthinking implementation the risky venture. We see here, too, an early sign that she will challenge the deterministic contention that automation will enslave humans to machines.

Three terms structure Arendt's analysis of the activities that constitute the human condition. Together they comprise what she calls *vita activa* (the active life): labor, activities that sustain human life, personally and generationally; work, activities that produce things and objects that stabilize human life through a built world; and action, activities that establish and nourish human *inter*action and thereby constitute the space of public life.[13] Notably, while Arendt draws frequently from her own interpretations of ancient Greek works, she uses the Latin concept of *vita activa* to frame this discussion. As a superintending category, *vita activa* affords Arendt a way to organize her difficult-to-disambiguate central terms—labor, work, and action—and to preserve ancient Greek attitudes toward a life lived in the polis as radically distinct from subsequent political postures. In Arendt's use of the term, *vita activa* is set apart not only from *vita contemplativa* (Latin for "contemplative life") and *bios theōrētikos* (ancient Greek for "theoretical life") but also from *bios politikos* (ancient Greek for "political life"), since that last manner of living—according to the elite ancient Greeks upon whose thinking Arendt relies—vigorously excludes both labor (and laborers) and work (and workers). *The Human Condition* is often called Arendt's "most Greek" project, but the fact that the anticipated disruptions of automation prompt her to dust off ancient Greek standpoints toward labor, work, and action has been underemphasized.[14] It is a detail worth emphasizing, however, because it puts Arendt into conversation with less-well-known figures of the 1950s and '60s who also looked to ancient Athens for commitments that could be renewed in the age of automation.

Automation and the Trifold Active Life

At the core of *The Human Condition* are Arendt's analyses of the past and present states of labor, work, and action. Automation obviously implicates labor and work, but, because of its much-promoted potential to free up time, it also reaches into action—or, at least, it would, if that area of activity had not, in her estimation, shriveled.

Arendt begins her investigation of our trifold active life with labor, classifying mid-century modernity as a laboring society. By starting with labor, Arendt stresses its primacy as an intractable fact of being alive, which no classifiers of human activity had magnified until recently. In particular, she notes the "contempt for labor in ancient theory, and its glorification in modern theory"—namely, in Marx.[15] Ancient theorists, foremost among them Plato and Aristotle, were contemptuous of labor because it results from the never-ending, inescapable cycle of embodied necessity: Our bodies make unceasing demands. The only way to minimize those demands for oneself is to force someone else to attend to as many of them as possible. Arendt is alert to what that imposition meant for both the enslaved and the enslaver in ancient Greece: "The price for the elimination of life's burden from the shoulders of all citizens was enormous and by no means consisted only in the violent injustice of forcing one part of humanity into the darkness of pain and necessity." It also consisted in what it cost enslavers: a significant reduction of the intense, felt "vitality" of life, a feature of the "pain and effort" of labor.[16] Obviously, the cost was staggeringly asymmetrical; a muted life is far less costly than a brutal one.

Arendt argues that Marx named labor *the* characteristic, defining human activity. In her view, Marx considered humans the *animal laborans*, the laboring creature. Arendt's use of the present active participle *laborans* was a way to name a creature in the mode of Linnaeus (for whom we were *Homo sapiens sapiens*) while illuminating how it grammatically performs the continuously ongoing nature of the labor cycle. Arendt posits in *animal laborans* the force of what she views as Marx's rejection of the early modern Latinate designation of humans as the *animal rationale* (rational animal) and of a counter to Aristotle's definition of the human as the *zōon politikon* (political animal) and *zōon logon echon* (logos-having animal).

Marx never calls the human being the *animal laborans*. Notably, in his *Grundrisse*—the drafting notebooks he kept during the winter of 1857–88—he mulled the rise of so-called civil society, powered by what Jürgen Habermas would later call the "bourgeois public sphere." Marx noted the bourgeoisie's use of sociality to attend to and protect their private interests as consistent with Aristotle's definition of the human as ζῷον πολιτικόν.[17] Labor is unapologetically central to Marx's sense of human activity and to his attendant political philosophy; he understands it to be what occurs when a person "sets in motion the natural forces which belong to his own body, his arms, legs, head and hands, in order to appropriate the materials of nature in a form adapted to his own needs."[18] The capacity to activate one's body in this way he calls "labor-power."[19] Every person, whatever their class position, possesses labor-power, which is, along with the products it yields, commodified under capitalism, but a small subset of people also possess means of production, including tools and machines. Marx uses the language of "metabolism" to capture the biological aspect of labor as a response to "the everlasting-nature-imposed condition of human existence" that is therefore "common to all forms of society in which human beings live."[20] He also uses metabolic terms to describe the capitalist labor process, in a gesture of conceptual mirroring that draws attention to that process as "an appropriation of what exists in nature for the requirements of man."[21] This is the human condition in industrial capitalism.

Arendt understands why Marx gave labor this power. In reflections from earlier in the 1950s, she was not condescending when she noted: "It was Marx's great achievement to have made labor the center of his theory, because labor was exactly from what all political philosophy, once it no longer dared to justify slavery, has averted its gaze. But for all that, we are still left without an answer to the political question posed by the necessity of labor in human life and by the paramount role it plays in the modern world."[22] Marx's choice to center labor seems to pull him far from the ancient Greek views on the subject, as well as from subsequent theorists too cowardly to take it on, but Arendt detects in Marx some so-called utopian features that she believes hint at ancient democratic Athens. I return to that tension shortly.

Beyond Marx's observations, calculations, and predictions, Arendt detects in the 1950s a tight association between labor and life that knows no class boundaries. "Even presidents, kings, and prime ministers think of their offices in terms of a job necessary for the life of society," she assesses, "and among the intellectuals, only solitary individuals are left who consider what they are doing in terms of work and not in terms of making a living."[23] Through this framing of "necessary for life" and "making a living," Arendt highlights how all jobs are couched in terms of the unrelenting demands of living, whatever the job title and whatever the job entails, but for a few scattered exceptions. Though kings and prime ministers obviously do not hail from the US American context, one wonders to what degree Arendt's critiques of the dominance of labor resulted from living where she did, when she did. The United States, of course, had been leading the way in labor's ascendency for some time. Taking notes for and writing *Capital* nearly a hundred years earlier, Marx observed that lingering feudal attitudes in Britain meant that certain types of labor were considered disrespectable by elites (he includes a scathing aside about the British elite finding the business of enslavement perfectly respectable), whereas "nowhere are people so indifferent to the type of work they do as in the United States, nowhere are people so aware that their labour always produces the same product, money, and nowhere to do they pass through the most divergent type of work with the same nonchalance."[24] When cultural awareness concentrates on what all jobs, at base, have as their common outcome, and that base is said to be money, then the content of labor becomes immaterial. We all produce, we all consume. Arendt concedes that this state of things makes for an odd sort of egalitarianism.[25] The weird equality amounts to lots of labor, from everyone, and no capacity for leisure.

Turning to "Work," the shortest of the three core chapters, Arendt centers on the construction of *homo faber*, human as maker, the suggestion being maker of useful or beautiful objects. Though she cannot identify its precise starting point as a moniker, she believes *homo faber* to be of "modern, post-medieval origin."[26] Arendt points out that the political theorists of ancient Athens had no serious regard for artisans, manual laborers, and craftsmen, known as *banausoi* in ancient Greek. Aristotle, for example, states that the best polis will not enroll them as citizens, since they tend to have been born elsewhere and do "necessary services for the community"—in other words, their work made a polis habitable and kept them occupied. He proceeds to explain that the constitution of a polis determines the political status of banausoi, and that a democracy with a robust population likely would not include banausic workers or their children as citizens.[27]

But work has its place. Through strength and craft, humans fabricate things and objects, thereby giving semipermanent shape to what is otherwise a fluctuating, inhospitable world. In Arendt's operationalizing of terms, labor's efforts do not produce anything beyond themselves, or, if they do, they produce products that are quickly used up; by contrast, work's efforts yield artifacts that are not only useful but also durable, lending a sense of sturdiness (and, with some artifacts, lasting beauty) to the ephemeral, liquid nature of the world. Arendt points out that work turns into labor when the work must be repeated quickly and cyclically for sustenance—or, much more commonly, to get what gets us sustenance: money.[28] This tendency of work to become labor is an outcome of machines.

Arendt embeds within her treatment of work a brief history of modern technology, starting with the steam engine, and retraces those steps because the discourse about automation insists that automation breaks with what came before. She quotes from Diebold, who popularized the term "automation" and testified first in the 1955 congressional hearings on the subject, to capture the prevailing perspective that automation is *not* the newest version of the oldest instrument, the human hand.[29] The common reaction is that it is altogether different, and as such it disrupts the human condition. Such a claim intrigues Arendt, since it cuts against her view that "whatever enters the human world of its own accord or is drawn into it by human effort becomes part of the human condition."[30] Believing that process to occur as a matter of course, she finds notable "the apparently endless discussion of whether man should be 'adjusted' to the machine or the machines should be adjusted to the 'nature' of man" that has attended the rise of automated machinery.[31] Such discourse speaks to anxiety that machines lie outside of human control and can at best be made to cooperate through forced subordination. Additionally, she acknowledges "the frequent complaints we hear about the perversion of ends and means in modern society, about men becoming the servants of the machines they themselves invented."[32] To her, the more pressing question "is not so much whether we are the masters or the slaves of our machines, but whether machines still serve the world and its things, or if, on the contrary, they and the automatic motion of their processes have begun to rule and even destroy world and things."[33] She fears that what will accompany the rise of automation—with its quick, continuous, independent operations—is the intensification of animal laborans and the eclipse of homo faber. The result would be a world without the durable objects of craft and artistry, a world designed for accelerated cycles of products of mass consumption that either deteriorate after little use or are quickly discarded.[34] Arendt does not reflect on the use of (or on *her* use of) "servant" and "master" and "slave" in discourse about the relationship between automatic machine systems and people, but such terms will make someone who knows ancient Greek texts and terms think of ancient Greek texts and terms.

Arendt studs the final core chapter, "Action," with quotes from Homer (*Iliad*); Sophocles (*Oedipus*); Thucydides, *History of the Peloponnesian War*; Plato (*Gorgias, Statesman, Republic, Laws, Symposium, Phaedrus*); and Aristotle (*Politics, Nicomachean Ethics, Metaphysics, Poetics, Physics, On the Soul, Athenian Constitution*), the premier poets, historian, and philosophers of ancient Greece, that support her view of action as something that humans have not really done right since. Like Wiener, Arendt evinces no fondness for Plato, but even his work contains evidence of the centrality of action to ancient Athenian democratic life (even if he thought it was entirely wrong-headed).[35] The *polis* (usually translated as "city-state"), the key organizing unit of the post-Homeric Greek world, was a sturdy place in which "everybody" could display their uniqueness through word and deed and have some hope that memory of their contributions would endure.[36] Arendt's model for democracy is certainly ancient Athens. Any doubt is allayed by her enthusiastic engagement with Thucydides's reconstruction of Pericles's oration for those Athenians who died in the first year of the war with Sparta, especially his mentions of Athenians leaving traces of themselves everywhere and not needing a Homer to sing their praises in order to be remembered.[37] Odd—to me, at least—is Arendt's lack of engagement with the parts of the speech about deliberation, which is, of course, a collective, future-determining public activity.

The polis, the host of public life, promotes seeing and being seen. It is a place where one cannot hide, since it compels visibility as well as "acting and speaking," through which "men show who they are, reveal actively their unique personal identities and thus make their appearance in the human world."[38] This acting and speaking comprises "the web of acts and words of other men," both past and present, that allows for connection and competition.[39] The polis is "the space of appearance in the widest sense of the word," not only because it is where we appear to others and they appear to us, but also because through speaking and acting with others we certify how things appear to us as shared reality.[40] Arendt does not think that the space of appearance is always open to everyone, and she names representatives from the ages of action, work, and labor to whom it was and is closed: "the slave, the foreigner, and the barbarian in antiquity, like the laborer or craftsmen prior to the modern age, the jobholder or businessman in our world."[41] Not being able or not wanting to speak and act in the open with others endangers the collaborative project of making meaning, which relies on the verification of shared impressions. That she puts the enslaved person of the ancient world and the jobholder of today in the same excluded category is not glib provocation.

By Arendt's calculus, set to the measure of democratic ancient Athens, the promise of reduced labor due to automation suggests a potential intensification of commitment to the realm of action, since it is the realm powered by attenuated or eliminated labor (and work). Yet that outcome seems unlikely to her, due to several factors.

For starters, she believes that the rise both of "the social" as *the* concept characterizing human relations and of the world economy as a scale for ordering and assessing the management of our economic interests has made the traditional differences between the realms of "public" and "private" difficult to maintain.[42] What one has in the age of the social is a social role, and what one manifests is behaviors. Hanna Pitkin, the most well-known analyst of Arendt's negative regard for the social, shows how Arendt uses that category to index "a collectivity of people who—for whatever reason—conduct themselves in such a way that they cannot control or even intentionally influence the large-scale consequences of their actions."[43] These people do not recognize their collective agency or know how to work together to exercise it. Everything is stimulus, response.

There is, too, the matter of the vagaries of terms from the *oikos*, the household, which ancient Greek people considered to be a private space. The world economy takes a word, "economy," born of ancient Greek household management (*oikonomia*), a private affair, and enlarges it to a proportion not even a country can control. Arendt also points to the role of mass consumer society, an ugly combination of the economy and the social, in growing labor and shrinking action. With low-quality consumables being produced in quantity and promoted through corporate advertising, consumers cycle through products so quickly as to be constantly consuming. The other main contributor to the truncated realm of action is the valorization of "the individual," its most toxic form being "the strong man" who pledges to get everything done on his own.[44] What Arendt takes to be lost is a space for equality (we are all the same) and distinction (we are not all the same), by which she means the sense of common reality and of one's own distinctiveness that arises from interacting with other people.[45] Distinction also results from the "agonal spirit" for which ancient Greek culture is well known: Through competition, virtuosity emerges.[46] When each of us focuses on making a living and is more responsive to the calls of the social than to the public, we do not engage with one another on the matters that determine whether we will live well together.

What the United States finds itself with at the end of the 1950s, she thinks, is an epidemic of relentless consumption, loneliness, and unhappiness.[47] In such conditions, more days with less work would not induce action in a person. Arendt's other concern is the relationship between isolation and totalitarianism: When citizens do not come together often to talk, listen, and take action, they become fearful of one another, which makes them withdraw from each other further. Into the notional space where citizens act and communicate together steps that "strong man" who impatiently and violently takes care of everything himself.[48] The two decades prior to Arendt writing *The Human Condition* (and her earlier book, *The Origins of Totalitarianism*, from 1951) testify to the horrors of that outcome.

For Arendt, power is organized togetherness, and organized togetherness is power. Words spoken to and heard from other citizens, and deeds committed with other citizens, have the potential to effect unprecedented events. This potential, for Arendt, is the ultimate value of action and of a jealously guarded space of publicness.

Returning to Marx

For Arendt, "the developments of the last decade, especially the possibility opened up through the further development of automation, give us reason to wonder whether the utopia of yesterday will not turn into the reality of tomorrow, so that eventually only the effort of consumption will be left of 'the toil and trouble' inherent in the biological cycle to whose motor human life is bound."[49] In other words, automation may return labor to what she claims was its original marginal(ized) position, opening up space for action once more. The precise referent of "the utopia of yesterday" comes into clearer view in a footnote, where she opines that "the classless and stateless society of Marx is not utopian"; rather, "these ideas in Marx himself were obviously conceived in accordance with Athenian democracy except that in communist society the privileges of the free citizens were to be extended to all."[50] A few pages later, she adds that Marx's "guiding model" for this society "was doubtless the Athens of Pericles which, in the future, with the help of the vastly increased productivity of human labor, would need no slaves to sustain itself but would become a reality for all."[51] Arendt uses "obviously" and "doubtless" as if the claim of Marx being inspired by Periclean Athens requires no substantiation; moreover, she seems to infer that Marx thinks that technology could be a key part of the liberation of laborers.[52]

Insight into her thinking about Marx's purportedly unmistakable model can be found via the acknowledgments at the end of *The Human Condition*, where Arendt mentions having given a series of lectures at Princeton titled "Karl Marx and the Tradition of Political Thought" in the fall of 1953.[53] Though the lectures did not appear in print during her lifetime, parts of them have been published since. For instance, "Karl Marx and the Tradition of Western Political Thought" contains threads of thought she likely shared in that series.[54]

She begins by saying both conservative critics of Marx and zealous Marxists are wrong when they classify Marx as breaking with the tradition of Western political thought. She argues that "Marx's roots go far deeper in the tradition than even he himself knew. I think it can be shown that the line from Aristotle to Marx shows both fewer and far less decisive breaks than the line from Marx to Stalin."[55] Again, we see Arendt asserting a lineage, only here she proclaims to know better than Marx himself who his formative influences were. A student of classics—he earned his doctorate at the University of Jena in 1841 with a dissertation titled "Differenz der demokritischen und epikureischen Naturphilosophie" (Difference between Democritean and Epicurean natural philosophy)—Marx knew ancient texts well.[56] In addition to what he could access at the British Library, where he conducted his research, he had in his personal library an abecedary of modern editions of ancient Greek and Roman texts, from Aristotle to Horace to Xenophon.[57] The general cultural hold enjoyed by classical material in both Germany and England at that time meant that Marx could create noticeable continuities or breaks in his observations about how humans create value by pairing such ancient material with his observations about capitalism, which was a distinctly modern phenomenon. Marx was certainly aware of his own affection for Aristotle. But it is the century before Aristotle (and Plato) to which Arendt thinks Marx unwittingly connects.

In *The Human Condition*, Arendt notes that those dismissive of Marx's view of a future classless society call it "utopian," a descriptor she also used in her earlier lectures on Marx. She rejects critical dismissal of his prospective view of society on two grounds: First, one ought to endeavor to understand seriously the future Marx imagined that his theories, if enacted, would yield, rather than write those theories off as unrealistic; and, second, "utopia" does not apply to the classless society he imagines, because "if utopia means that this society has no *topos*, no geographical and historical place on earth, it is certainly not utopian: Its geographical *topos* is Athens and its place in history is the fifth century before Christ."[58] Getting literal, Arendt rejects characterizations of Marx's vision as "utopian," because utopia literally means "no place," and fifth-century BCE Athens did factually exist. The stateless future Marx imagines, she continues, "corresponds to life in the ancient Greek city-state, which, although it was based on rulership over slaves as its pre-political condition, had excluded rulership from the intercourse of its free citizens. In Herodotus' great definition (to which Marx's statement conforms almost textually), that man is free who wants 'neither to rule nor be ruled.' "[59] Arendt's parenthetical here refers to what she calls a "pillar" of Marx's "whole theory and philosophy": that "*nobody can be free who enslaves others*."[60] Further, she credits him with recognizing, in his "own words," that "the realm of freedom begins where laboring ends."[61] She must be truncating this line from the third volume of *Capital*: "The realm of freedom really begins only where labour determined by necessity and external expediency ends" (as rendered in the edition I have).[62] Joining Aristotle most prominently but other ancient Greek thinkers as well, Arendt make the antithesis between freedom and necessity central to her thinking; therefore, this line jumps out at her—and strikes her as indicative of Marx's unrecognized affinity for the early decades of ancient democratic Athens.

When Marx says he wants to "abolish labor altogether," he means not only what she has been calling "labor" but also what she has been calling "work": "Hardly anything could be more revealing of Marx's original impulses than the fact that he banishes from his future society not only the labor that was executed by slaves in antiquity, but also the activities of the *banausoi*, the craftsmen and artists: 'In a communist society there are no painters, only men who, among other things, paint.' "[63] Marx does not banish painters, as Plato's *Republic* banished poets, but simply does not confine them to a group; labor and laborers would no longer be divided this way. Arendt envisions what the day of a citizen of fifth-century-BCE Athens would have been like: as entirely structured around opportunities to gather with others for the sort of exhibition, friction, and collaboration through which a public self is formed, displayed, and, perhaps, preserved in history.[64] In sum, Arendt believes that what Marx saw coming after capitalism "coincided rather curiously with the ideal of life associated with the Greek city-states."[65] By absorbing Marx into the realm of action as lived and valorized in fifth-century-BCE Athens—an exercise she justifies by claiming she is "clearly following the central indications of Marx's work itself"—Arendt shows that even labor's greatest champion does not think labor worth keeping.[66]

Why Ancient Athens?

Throughout *The Human Condition*, Arendt uses ancient Athens to think through how automation might condition humans as she finds us in the mid-twentieth century: all labor, little work, even less action.[67] Enthusiasm among scholars for Arendt's use of ancient Athens started early, as I exhibit in the next chapter. But others have questioned why Arendt uses antiquity to understand mid-twentieth-century modernity at all, and whether she objects strenuously enough to the ugly exclusions and conditions of ancient Athenian democracy.

Political theorist Margaret Canovan, who, in the mid-1970s, wrote the first full-length book on Arendt, starts where most people do when keying in on her use of certain ancient Mediterranean ideas: with her education. As is well known, Arendt studied under Martin Heidegger, an enthusiast of ancient Greek philosophy himself, within an educational system still steeped in the philhellenism of the nineteenth century.[68] Intellectual biographies on their own fail to account, however, for the *particular* uses to which a thinker puts what they have learned during their training. To Canovan, Arendt's "knowledge of history, and of the model of life and scale of priorities preserved in the ancient languages, enables her to draw upon a wider range of human experience than we are now commonly aware of."[69] For readers, such expanded awareness can prompt moments of recognition—say, when a thread of tradition or an angle of congruity is identified—but it can also cause confusion. Arendt is not one to connect all the dots.

As we have seen, Arendt's core conceptual work is informed by her knowledge of ancient texts, mainly in the chapter on action. There, Arendt excavates from Homer and Thucydides a vocabulary of virtuosity that links becoming who one is and showing who one is to talking, listening, and acting in the company of peers striving to do the same. The private space of the home (*oikos*) is the space of laborious survival; the public space of the polis is the space of action-packed glory. Canovan anticipates that it is precisely Arendt's view of action that will leave some readers "rather bewildered. In particular, they are likely to want more concrete details about action. What exactly counts as action? What sorts of deeds and words is she talking about? What did the men of the Greek *polis* do, and what relation has that to us? It must be confessed that it is hard to give very precise answers to these questions."[70] Canovan highlights the complication that, in general, Arendt tends to connect action with greatness—and a certain triumphalist, imperialist greatness, at that—rather than with goodness, and she agrees with those who find Arendt's choice to place Periclean Athens at the center of her praise "élitist," in the sense that what she praises was available to only a portion of its denizens.[71]

In the next decade, political theorist Blair Campbell identified Arendt as the promulgator of the view that citizens of the ancient Athenian polis were hyperparticipatory, a perspective that "has functioned as a standard for criticizing developments in contemporary Western (especially American) politics" within political theory.[72] In the belief that Arendt's misrepresentation of ancient Athens has misled three decades of theorists, Campbell goes hardest at the Arendtian attitude that democratic Athens was "an extended debating society, comprising a body of citizens in a political arena or 'public space' ever engaged at developing some essential part of themselves by their political discussion and choices."[73] He cites ancient evidence that democracy was praised and instituted only insofar as it was believed to be the best way to preserve the laws of a polis—that is, democracy made for comparative constitutional stability, which was deemed desirable. The democratic polis was certainly not a place that welcomed radical self-fashioning or radical group action. If ancient Athens offered citizens capacious opportunity for self-discovery (of a kind), coordinated action (of a kind), and reverberant renown (of a kind), that was incidental to its true purpose.[74] And democratic citizens certainly were not political activists, since activism was considered meddlesome or, alternately, absurd, to judge by the choice of Aristophanes to write comedies around the idea of activist women.[75]

Fittingly, it is Canovan who introduces the second edition of *The Human Condition*, issued in 1998, on its fortieth anniversary. She catalogs common reader reactions to Arendt's use of "the Greeks": that it "challenges the modern belief in progress"; that her "continual references to [them] added to the bewilderment," the reaction word that Canovan had used in her 1974 book on Arendt, "of many readers"; and that it could be "tempting to suppose she intended to present a utopia of political action, a kind of New Athens."[76] Canovan responds only that Arendt does not provide solutions or plans that would reestablish the elements of ancient Athens that Arendt esteems. She does not, for instance, lay out the details of an ancient-Athens-like educational program—which is true. Still, *The Human Condition* is a book that prepares us "to think what we are doing" by focusing on what we do, and, in Arendt's estimation, ancient Athens seems to have done both doing and thinking right.

In the twenty-first century, Arendt's Hellenism continues to be found—and found wanting. Political theorist J. Peter Euben, who has made a career of putting ancient and contemporary materials into configurations of creative congruity, states that Arendt "uses her Hellenism as a provocation" and, in so doing, sometimes errs in ways that invite one "to rescue [her] from her Hellenism and rescue Greece and Athens from Arendt."[77] Focusing on Arendt's impulse to get outside of modern modes of living and ways of explaining them, classicist Miriam Leonard posits that "the organization of the polis provides her with a blueprint for understanding what distinguishes politics as such from the spheres of economics and sociology."[78] Still, Leonard marks as troubling Arendt's seeming "indifference" to enslavement and "tacit endorsement of patriarchy."[79] In also assessing the place of ancient Athens in Arendt's work, historian of rhetoric David Marshall offers: "One might say that Arendt's Athens was an icon for political theory not on account of its putative status as the realization of a utopia, but rather precisely because its founding sins afforded the political scientist an unobstructed view of human being expressed purely in terms of labor *or* work *or* action."[80] Enslaved men, craftsmen, and men who act and speak are separated absolutely in the extant political philosophy of ancient Greece (most clearly in Aristotle's *Politics*). The dividing lines that ensure this purported purity include, of course, slavery, misogyny, and bigotry.

Arendt never comes out and says as much. Furthermore, as I have shown in a few quotations from *The Human Condition*, she does use the language of force and violence when writing about enslavement and does not note that ancient writing would be used to sanction it in subsequent historical periods, or that the aftereffects of slavery in the United States would mean that the effects of automation would not be evenly distributed. Perhaps her condemnation of the ugly sides of ancient Greece goes without saying, and it is ungenerous of us not to assume so. Political theorist Hanna Pitkin tries to afford Arendt the benefit of the doubt: "The ancient Greeks also import into Arendt's argument some problematic features she surely did not (consciously) intend to adopt," she writes. Pitkin links Arendt's zeal to demonize the effects of the social on human action to those places in ancient texts where "the Greeks' misogynist machismo—so contrary to Arendt's conscious views and intent—is nevertheless underlined, emphasized, and in certain passages almost endorsed."[81] Maybe Arendt did not think Periclean Athens, even in the nearly one-sided way in which she presents it, was flawless. But she relies almost entirely upon the reader to infer as much.

In fact, Arendt did *not* view democratic ancient Athens as a utopia, but perhaps only because her logic is *very* literal on that point: Democratic ancient Athens cannot be a utopia because *it did exist*. Throughout her writing in the 1950s about labor, ancient Athens functions as a eutopos for Arendt: It is a place within the range of her philosophical thinking to which she repeatedly returns for vocabularies and priorities different from those ordering the United States in the mid-twentieth century. To Arendt's mind, ancient democratic Athens recommends itself for thinking with because automation is poised to pitch us—and Arendt's "us" is in desperate need of clear qualification—into the place of an Athenian citizen wealthy enough to avoid having to labor (because: slavery) or work. But *we* are not at all prepared, let alone keen, to enjoy what that avoidance had secured for them, be it an intensely active public life or a devotedly contemplative life (though she does not endorse the kind set apart from and antagonistic to the polis).

For Arendt, it could be that ancient Athens is not meant to inspire emulation so much as provoke thought about the sad state of the human domain of action in the mid-twentieth century, what that sad state forecloses, and why such foreclosures matter at the dawning of the age of automation. Technologically, she and her contemporaries had nearly arrived at a place imagined by ancient Greek thinkers who had conceived of nonhuman animated tools for labor and work, ostensibly freeing time for human action; culturally, her contemporaries were habituated to laboring, not to thinking on their own or communicating in public with others.[82] In the society of her time, she believed there was "no class left, no aristocracy of either a political or spiritual nature from which a restoration of the other capacities of man"—meaning action and possibly even contemplation—"could start anew."[83] There is no model for what happens when people without an enculturated aptitude for those crucial human activities find themselves able, due to new technologies, to apply less of themselves to labor. Arendt wonders what will become of such people. But she does not despair, exactly: In her thinking, the promise of human plurality—of our differences from one another and from every other human who has ever lived—is the promise of unpredictable novelty.

But the tendencies over time are not promising. In the final chapter of *The Human Condition*, Arendt traces the fortunes of labor, work, and action in the modern period and avers that, over that time, "we have proved ingenious enough to find ways to ease the toil and trouble of living to the point where an elimination of laboring from the range of human activities can no longer be regarded as utopian."[84] The trouble is that even this easing cannot eliminate all the demanding aspects of life, and frustration with and fear of this inescapable struggle can drive people to "acquiesce in a dazed, 'tranquilized,' functional type of behavior," instead of to act.[85] Returning to the framing of her prologue, which names space exploration and automation as motivators for a study of the human condition, Arendt claims that scientists are the only group of people who are acting—that is, talking and collaborating to determine the future.[86] She concludes the book with the suggestion that thinking is perhaps the highest form of doing, and maybe the only kind that can save us from ourselves.

3

Athens as Inspiration for Cybercultural Eutopia (Alice Mary Hilton)

> Athenian slave-owners . . . employed part of their leisure in making a permanent contribution to civilization which would have been impossible under a just economic system. Leisure is essential to civilization, and in former times leisure for the few was rendered possible only by the labors of the many. But their labors were valuable, not because work is good, but because leisure is good. And with modern technic it would be possible to distribute leisure justly without injury to civilization.
>
> BERTRAND RUSSELL, "In Praise of Idleness"

In the 1960s, Hannah Arendt never lacked for lecture invitations. One invitation in particular arrived in March 1964 on the personal letterhead of Alice Mary Hilton (1919–2011), who was organizing a June conference on cybernetics and society in New York City and eagerly sought Arendt's participation. Hilton's ardent belief in the potential to use cybernetics for good drove her agenda—a busy one—in the first half of the 1960s, after which she became president of the Society for Social Responsibility in Science (SSRS), developed a pilot program to digitally catalog holdings at the Louvre in Paris and the National Gallery in London, and lectured for nearly forty years on art and architecture at the Metropolitan Museum of Art and throughout Europe.[1] That capaciousness characterized her long life.

Born in Vienna in 1919, Hilton sought refuge in England with her family in the early 1930s. She studied classics, comparative literature, and mathematics at Oxford before moving with her family to the United States, where they settled in New York City in 1939. After serving in the US Army in Germany as a civilian historical research analyst in 1945–46, she earned a PhD in electrical engineering from the University of California, Los Angeles. Then, returning permanently to New York, she worked for IBM and the ElectroData Corporation, wrote for television, and launched the Institute for Cybercultural Research. Her range of activities was well credentialed.[2]

Hilton sprang onto the mid-century public science scene with her 1963 book, *Logic, Computing Machines, and Automation.* Her gratitude toward Oxford mathematician Bertrand Russell, who had been her teacher (and had supervised Norbert Wiener years earlier) and read and commented on the manuscript, and to Wiener, with whom she had met and corresponded, comes through clearly; the final chapter of the book bears epigraphs from their work. The omnipresence of "automation," and of opinions on it, which she found, on the whole, uninformed, motivated Hilton to place the technology within the context of intellectual history and to think through its entailments for human life. She felt that citizens of a democracy needed to understand automation "as a socio-economic phenomenon that goes far beyond production techniques."[3] To prompt and sustain full awareness of everything that "automation" encompasses meant, for her, coining her own cyber-based word. "Reluctant as I am to add to the deluge of new terms," she wrote, "I do not find an existing word for this vast new phenomenon with all its ramifications, i.e., the socio-economic and cultural aspects of the scientific-technological revolution in progress, and I shall call it the *cybercultural revolution.* In the word 'cyberculture,' cybernetics, the science of control, and culture, the way of life of a society, are combined."[4]

In its form, this new compound displays the power of cybernetics—and she defined automation as "applied cybernetics"—to modify culture itself.[5] Her use of "revolution" repeats the common nomenclature for developments of a new and disruptive nature. In its verbal structure and potential transformative power over human life, "cyberculture" is a match for "agriculture." In support of her term, Hilton challenges the designation of her era as the "second industrial revolution." That name does not suit, she argues, because while mechanization extended the power of the human body, automation extends the power of the human mind.[6] Automated machines can do both repetitive physical tasks and complex computations, freeing human thinking for other work. The result is that cyberculture "is the era of 'The Human Use of Human Beings,' when, for the first time, human beings need not do any but the highest-level intellectual, creative work."[7] With this reference to his second book, Hilton both pays homage to Wiener and turns his principled stance toward all systems into a tagline for an epoch. Though Hilton does not underestimate the shifts that will be necessary for cybernetics to change patterns at the level of culture, she evinces an altogether more optimistic (and hyperbolic) attitude toward the impact that cybernetics could have on culture than Wiener had exhibited.[8]

For example, she claims that "in the era of cyberculture, all the plows pull themselves and the fried chickens fly right onto our plates."[9] She does not elaborate on those vivid and far-fetched images here, but they are her cyber-cultivated take on Schlaraffenland, the German name for the land of easy living and idleness depicted in the 1567 painting by Pieter Brueghel the Elder. She mentions Schlaraffenland in print in 1964 and 1966, and sociologist Studs Terkel asks her about it in a 1967 radio interview.[10] On that latter occasion, she describes the place as it has traditionally been imagined—that is, populated by "utterly passive, lazy, mmm, can't call them men, creatures who live in a world where the fried doves fly into their mouths, but it didn't help them very much because they atrophied so completely that even that could not keep them alive; it certainly couldn't keep them human."[11] That is not her ideal of a land of self-pulling plows and plate-eager chickens. That submissive response to basic needs being met without human labor offers an anti-model for the cybercultural age as Hilton thinks it could and ought to be: an era offering opportunity for everyone to engage deeply in meaningful, stimulating work because repetitive labors (such as the many phases of food preparation) will be cybernated. It will offer to everyone the chance to maximize the most vaunted qualities and abilities of humanity, and each in their own way.

Much more frequent in her book than allusions to sixteenth-century Belgian paintings are references to cultural elements from ancient Greece, which undergird her effort to place cyberculture within the history of logic and its social impact when it takes technological form. Such references—to Prometheus, Plato, Aristotle, and the ancient Greek etymologies of "cybernetics" and "program"—dot the book, which she concludes with an emboldening invocation of the tragic attitude of the Greeks that sees "the world not as a cozy little warren for timid rabbits, but as a glorious cosmos to be explored by human greatness."[12] For Hilton, boldness is the virtue of virtues.

It was in that spirit of not cowering in the face of fast and dramatic change that Hilton organized her June conference. Between the time when Arendt received Hilton's invite and Hilton acknowledged receipt of her intent to participate, Hilton dispatched another typed letter to Arendt, dated March 23, 1964. On March 18, 1964, while in Stockholm to give a lecture at its Royal Academy, Norbert Wiener had died. Readers of *The New York Times* the following morning would have found his photograph and obituary on the front page, the headline heralding him (not entirely accurately) as "the father of automation" (remember: he had hated that form of the word), the account of his life's work including quotes from the punchy first edition of *The* Human *Use of Human Beings*.[13] Staggered by this loss, both to culture and to her work, Hilton composed a reassuring reflection a few days later.[14] While addressed to Arendt, it is likely an iteration of what went out to everyone whom Hilton had invited to participate in her conference.

In the letter, Hilton calls Wiener a prophet and wonders "how many anniversaries of his death will have to pass before his prophetic words become the conventional wisdom." She laments the loss, to her projects in particular, crediting Wiener for "his advise [*sic*], his inspiration and his unfailing help." She concludes by asserting that "he will live as long as there is a civilization in which human beings can strive to achieve what he worked for: the human use of human beings" and by pledging to dedicate the first book in the Age of Cyberculture series to him. That book is the proceedings of her conference, and it does bear his name as dedicatee: "To NORBERT WIENER whose wisdom and humanity is the foundation upon which the age of cyberculture shall be built."[15] And she intended to see that it would be.

Hilton and the Ad Hoc Committee on the Triple Revolution

In addition to planning a major conference and mourning the passing of Wiener in March 1964, Hilton, under the title "independent consultant, problems of technology and automation," was a member of the thirty-person Ad Hoc Committee on the Triple Revolution.[16] Throughout the late winter of 1964, that group of US American activists, academics, and intellectuals had drafted and polished a fourteen-page exhortative exploration of three conjoint cultural forces torquing US American life that they delivered to President Lyndon B. Johnson the week of March 19.

What they call the "cybernation revolution," "weaponry revolution," and "human rights revolution" exist in a relationship of "simultaneous occurrence and interaction" that necessitate "radical alterations in attitude and policy."[17] They credit cybernation with inordinate influence over the conditions of equity and peace. As support, the explanatory portion of the statement leads with the struggle for black liberation, underscoring that black people "are the hardest hit of the many groups being exiled from the economy by cybernation."[18] Systemically, though, cybernation makes increasingly untenable the whole "tradition of work-and-income . . . even for the hitherto privileged white worker."[19] Under current circumstances, the breaking of that tradition means that workers displaced by "machines" will be at the mercy of "minimal and unrelated government measures—unemployment insurance, social security, welfare payments."[20] But what good is that tradition if cybernetic production systems hold the potential "to supply the needs of everyone in the United States"?[21] The committee members identify a clash between that potential for plenitude and the stubbornness of the industrial production system, which is based on scarcity rather than abundance. It has to go.

Before attending to the matter of how to phase out policies and practices based on traditions ill suited to cybernation, the committee members excite anticipation about what the public, human-centered management of cybernation could make possible. "Because of cybernation," they write, "society no longer needs to impose repetitive and meaningless (because unnecessary) toil upon the individual. Society can now set the citizen free to make his own choice of occupation and vocation from a wide range of activities not now fostered by our value system and our accepted modes of 'work.' "[22] Such shifts mean reckoning with "historic questions: What is man's role when he is not dependent upon his own activities for the material basis of his life? What should be the basis for distributing individual access to national resources? Are there other proper claims on goods and services besides a job?"[23] Only a new economic system could accommodate responses that promote individual and communal human flourishing.

The committee suggests numerous transition policies—such as what we now call universal basic income, extensive low-cost housing, and a huge public works program—that would be planned, controlled, and sustained by means of public decision-making and entirely set apart from the self-serving machinations of private corporations. In the document's concluding section, "The Democratization of Change," the committee acknowledges that change is happening, indisputably, and that the good alterations are not being enjoyed equitably, nor are the bad ones mitigated through changes in attitudes and policies. Insofar as such economic issues can be managed, that management must come through democratic means. The result, they contend, will be "an existence qualitatively richer in democratic as well as material values. A social order in which men make the decisions that shape their lives becomes more possible now than ever before; the unshackling of men from the bonds of unfulfilling labor frees them to become citizens, to make themselves and to make their own history."[24] In locating self-determination at the level of individual self-fashioning and of collective future-formulating in the opportunity to do fulfilling work, the committee uses metaphors of physical liberation to mark the kind of labor from which cybernation will disburden humans.

In their statement, the committee insists that "a vision of democratic life is made real not by technological change but by men consciously moving toward that ideal and creating institutions that will realize and nourish the vision in living form."[25] Even the most potentially liberating technology will, at best, reinstate old patterns in new forms if not guided by those with a democratic vision and the means to instantiate it. The committee makes sure to define what they mean by "democracy," repeating their emphases on self-determination and on the establishment of policies and attitudes oriented toward abundance:

> Democracy, as we use the term, means a community of men and women who are able to understand, express and determine their lives as dignified human beings. Democracy can only be rooted in a political and economic order in which wealth is distributed by and for the people, and used for the widest social benefit. With the emergence of the era of abundance we have the economic base for a true democracy of participation, in which men no longer need to feel themselves prisoners of social forces and decisions beyond their control or comprehension.[26]

These strong concluding appeals seem designed for readers who confuse capitalism and democracy. Democracy can take anti-capitalist form, and, indeed, it must, since cybernation seems poised to put enough pressure on capitalism's operating terms that their harms will be obvious to all and the old rationales (e.g., scarcity) plainly false. The kind of inclusion the committee imagines might seem radical, but it ought to be considered instead a basic feature of a democratic order.

President Johnson did not respond to the statement directly, but the committee received a notice of receipt from Lee C. White, assistant special counsel to the president, on April 6. White lists some of Johnson's efforts to address "poverty, unemployment, and technological change"; curiously, race is not mentioned explicitly. Regarding technological change, White reports that Johnson has asked Congress to send him a bill authorizing the formation of a commission "to study the impact of technological change on the economy and to recommend measures for assuring the full benefits of technology while minimizing any adverse effects."[27] In fact, congressional hearings to discuss a bill for establishing a National Commission on Automation and Technological Progress commenced the very next week. Both White's letter and the Triple Revolution statement appear in the published proceedings.[28] In August, Johnson signed the bill creating the commission.[29]

The statement from the Ad Hoc Committee on the Triple Revolution contains no reference to ancient Athens. Its focus on human betterment and intensified democratic participation points to cybernation's immense potential—if released from capitalist logics. As we saw with Arendt, for certain analysts of the cybernetic age that combination of flourishing humans, energized public life, and freedom from capitalism called ancient Athens to mind. That was the case for Alice Mary Hilton, too: Ancient Athens came to be her guide and goal for the cybernetic age.

Hilton Turns to Athens

In April 1964, the month after Wiener passed away and the Triple Revolution memorandum went to President Johnson, Hilton's "An Ethos for the Age of Cyberculture" was published. In general, the piece argues for a replacement of the Protestant ethic—the "ethos of any society that knows scarcity and danger"—that has long suffused US American culture, with its ethos attuned to the conditions of abundance, leisure, and play that Hilton credits to the potential effects of cybernetics upon culture.[30] The prime exigency for her call is unemployment, which she links causally to cybernation. Hilton points to the legions of baby boomers whom, it appears, the emerging economic system will not be able to accommodate gainfully. The way out of this intensifying crisis, she believes, is to first acknowledge the obsolescence of capitalist structures and the ethos that makes clinging to them a virtue.

The next step is adjustment. She insists that her fellow Americans must "learn to live with and use our electronic and mechanical slaves"—more specifically, that we should "prepare ourselves for the age of cyberculture by turning unemployment into leisure, by solving the transition problems of scarcity, and by doing everything human ingenuity can devise to perfect our electronic slaves and complete all processes of automation."[31] In her book, Hilton had used the term "automatic slaves" to refer to cybernetic machines.[32] Wiener had referred to cybernetically automated processes and equipment as "mechanical slaves," and while Hilton may even have gotten the slave base of the concept from him, Wiener highlights the paradox in presuming that any objectified human or humanized automated object will be both intelligent and obedient. Hilton, for her part, seems to use slave-based terms to put the cybercultural near future on a historical continuum: In the prospect of such labor-saving machines are solutions to persistent human problems amplified by capitalism but of much earlier origin.

That mix of old and new results in an unacknowledged ironic juxtaposition. Although Hilton insists that "there can never be another ethos for the future than the obsolete ethos of the past," and that "already our world has changed beyond all recognition and comparison," she offers the "Golden Age of Greece" as a time, place, and culture from which to learn how to adjust to leisure and abundance.[33] To support this notion, she cites a passage about *bios politikos* from Arendt's *The Human Condition*.[34] As we saw earlier, Arendt suggests that what elite Athenian citizens attained through slavery—leisure for philosophical contemplation and political action—the average US American *could* attain through automation, if only modern phenomena (e.g., the rise of "the social" and especially of "mass society") did not complicate what it means to think and to act in the context of a polis.

Next, Hilton supplies her anti-model: ancient Rome. She uses the stock terms of its decline (e.g., "moral disintegration," "brutal titillation") to narrate how affluence brought about both apathy and violence there.[35] At the conclusion of a series of questions about why ancient Athens went one way and ancient Rome the other, she wonders "whether the Golden Age of Athens could have endured if the Athenian had found a way of out of his dilemma: his need for leisure and his rejection of human slavery."[36] What exactly Hilton is referring to here, in terms of the historical reality of ancient Athenian views about enslavement, is unclear, since the Athenians clearly did not reject human slavery. But it is clear that she is using the example of ancient Athenian elites to think through the position of people now on the cusp of the cybercultural revolution. In the seventh decade of the twentieth century, she writes, "we can rejoice that we have what humanity never knew before—slaves to free us from the necessity of laboring 'in order to' sustain life that are not human, so that we need not be ashamed to enjoy what they produce."[37] It is always worth attending to a writer's use of the first-person plural pronoun. Hilton's "we" refers to a group whose members feel—or know they should feel—shame and certainly not joy in benefiting from enslavement. The nonhuman status of those slaves is meant to be morally mitigating; even so, the word "slaves" itself would not have landed the same way with everybody. In this regard, another potential function of Hilton's choice to highlight ancient Athens as a paradigm becomes apparent: It keeps her distant from US America's much more recent (and ongoing) history of enslavement. She never mentions it, though her participation on the Ad Hoc Committee suggests that it could not have been far from her mind.

Sounding like Wiener, Hilton claims that humans cannot compete with machines without "accepting the conditions of slave labor"; then, sounding nothing like Wiener, she asserts that "human beings who learn to use the machine wisely, on the other hand, will be freed by the machine to achieve excellence."[38] "Achiev[ing] excellence" smacks of the Homeric or the Periclean. As for training children of cyberculture to strive to be the best and to live the good life, Hilton suggests, "a good curriculum might well start with questions about Greek civilization and Roman decay."[39] Model and anti-model, respectively, ancient Greece and Rome comprise the foundation of cybercultural education. The next month, she published a piece that identifies this contestation in the very term she coined: "In the word 'cyberculture,' Greek and Latin roots are combined. It seems appropriate because in cyberculture we see many diverse seeds coming to fruition—our Graeco-Roman heritage, particularly. The question is: which will predominate? The best of Greece, or the worst of Rome!"[40] This is a question that cannot be left to work itself out.

A nearly two-page appendix of Hilton's suggestions for hastening the new ethos falls into two sections—government action and individual action—and concludes with the most-quoted line from Plato's *Apology*: " 'The unexamined life is not worth living,' said Socrates. This clearly makes it the responsibility of every citizen to examine his own life and to assist others (though not to force it upon them, because that would be ineffective) to examine their own lives."[41] That parenthetical qualification removes the mandibles from Socrates the gadfly, making him all buzz, and no bite. It is representative of the version of ancient Athens forwarded by Hilton, which does not seriously contend with anything difficult, complex, or wrong about that culture.

More evidence for the intensity of Hilton's commitment to ancient Athens appears in a letter she posts to Arendt early the next month, May. In it, she seems to be making sure Arendt will participate in the June conference. Tactically, but not insincerely, she affirms the importance of Arendt's book *The Human Condition* to the moment and to her thinking.[42] In a long parenthetical that includes a pun on its title, she writes:

> (I must tell you again, how very much I owe to your work. I believe that this book will becomes the basis of thought, when we are finally ready to re-think the very ethos and basis of our society. I am enclosing an article and speech which will prove how very much I have been "conditioned" by your writing. I am working on a book now in which I am trying to present as the alternatives for the future an Athens the Athenians could only dream of, or a Rome ghastlier than the most ghastly Roman nightmare.)

The enclosures were not archived, but it is likely the article was "An Ethos for the Age of Cyberculture," which had just been published and which quotes from *The Human Condition*. Hilton's mention of work on a book that imagines futures either more dreamy than the best parts of ancient Athens or more horrific than the worst parts of ancient Rome suggests that the central contrast between them in her "Ethos" article was a preview of a much larger project. She never published such a book, however.

Hilton also details the structure of the conference and invites Arendt to consider how she might contribute. She also previews some of the papers she had received in advance from other invited speakers. In particular, she prepares Arendt for the remarks of social psychologist Donald Michael, who had coined "cybernation" in his 1962 pamphlet-style report *Cybernation: The Silent Conquest*, written while he was director of planning and programs of the Peace Research Institute in Washington, DC.[43] Michael desired a word by which he could simultaneously invoke both computers and automation and came up with "cybernation," for whose legitimacy as a neologism he appeals to Wiener's concept. The pamphlet brims with nervous caution—precisely the attitude toward the great unknown that Hilton dislikes. He begins by articulating a view shared by automation optimists and pessimists: that cybernation is "simply the latest stage in the evolution of technological means for removing the burdens of work."[44] Conversely, he sees rupture rather than continuity, and a rupture so dramatic that "it will pose unique problems for society, challenging our basic values and the ways in which we express and enforce them."[45] Putting the matter starkly, he views cybernation as holding "extraordinary implications for the emancipation and enslavement of mankind." Believing cases for the former to be more common, he opts to "emphasize the less obvious, sometimes acutely uncomfortable aspects of this development with which we must successfully contend if we are to enjoy the benefits of cybernation and democracy."[46] Neither cybernation nor democracy necessarily confers equal benefits to all; the former could make the latter more true to its word, but it could also make even the current, incomplete democracy unsustainable. Throughout the report, Michael shows deep concern with the matter of controlling cybernation. Adaptations occur slowly within the US American democratic system, he notes; it has some centralized features, but it does not and cannot plan and control on the level that would preserve the status quo, for all its inequities, let alone chart a course for a better future. Private enterprise would not fare better: Antitrust laws forbid businesses from partnering to control a sector, presuming that competitors would agree to cooperate in the first place. Regulatory bodies tend to be insufficiently vigorous. The might of the most powerful labor unions is being undercut by cybernation. No singular or conjoint entity can control cybernation, Michael concludes.

The last section of the pamphlet, "After the Take-Over," advances twenty years. Michael thinks that cybernation will be ubiquitous, but its processes known exclusively by a very small group of people who have developed their talents and "rapport" with machines since childhood. He thinks that such a technical-emotional understanding will be beyond the grasp of most college-educated people. For them, he envisions short workdays and work weeks, and he wonders: "What will they believe in and aspire to as they work their shorter hours and, on the outside, pursue their 'self-fulfilling' activities, whatever they may be? No one has ever seriously envisioned what characteristics these activities might have in order to be able to engross most men and women most of their adult lives. What will be the relationship of these people to government, to the 'upper intellectuals,' to the rest of the world, to themselves?"[47] He shares in Arendt's concerned curiosity about people who are accustomed to a kind of leisure oriented toward the self or the social but not toward the public, and what they will do; he does not share Arendt's inclination to look to ancient Athens for a serious vision of leisure.

The report's final line dramatizes the difficulty and the stakes of trying to redress the likely prospects it has articulated, which would demand "beliefs, behaviors, and goals far different from those which we have held until now and which are driving us more and more inexorably into a contradictory world run by (and for?) ever more intelligent, ever more versatile slaves."[48] Michael uses the automated-machine-as-slave metaphor, as Hilton does; his use of it, though, does not lead him back to ancient Athens, perhaps partly because its lessons depend on either the natural or the legal subordination of the enslaved, and Michael is not so sure such a condition can be imposed on cybernated systems. Hilton joins him in identifying the necessity of effecting a change in enculturated patterns of thinking and doing, but Michael has no vision in mind of a time or place whose ways offer a model, whereas Hilton insists on ancient Athens as *the* model.

Two years after his report, Michael seems to have honed a rejoinder to Hilton's enthusiasm for a certain fifth-century BCE polis. It annoys her, and, in her May 1964 letter to Arendt, she enlists Arendt's help in responding to it: "I ought to point out to you that Dr. Michael's answer to the lessons of history—i.e., the civilization of Athens—is invariably: 'It lasted 40 years.' If you will prepare a paper, or speak extemporaneously, as I hope you will, I would urge you to be prepared to take the wind out of this retort <u>before</u> and <u>after</u> it is made." (Technically, Athens's democracy ran for 180 years, with two brief oligarchic interruptions.) Hilton attributes Michael's retort to his "lost confidence that we shall take the necessary measures while there is still time."[49] Maybe. But, the year prior, during a 1963 conference, Michael gave clear reasons why he believed that looking to ancient Athens would be an "error":

> True, for many Greeks, some part of their free time was spent on civic activities—activities which now are very much part of our growing professionalized work world: politics, government (they had 501-man juries), bit parts in theatricals, philosophy, and so on. Also there were not so very many Greeks per civic unit among which to apportion these various activities (perhaps 30,000 citizens out of 100,000 total population in Athens, for example). But it was also true that for the Greeks a lot of free time was frittered away drinking with friends, fighting wars, and enjoying the very frequent festivals put on at government expense. Incidentally, women were denied all public and civic participation.[50]

Michael's issues with the analogy amount to there not being good points of comparison, since, by contrast with ancient democratic Athens, the twentieth century has professional politicians, contracted actors, and university philosophers; a massive citizen population (and no enslaved people); and enfranchised women. Also, it was not as if ancient Greek men were all political duty, all the time. In early May 1964, Hilton and Arendt had about six weeks left to prepare their responses. Of course, Hilton had a lot more to organize than a comeback to Michael.

Hilton's Conference on the Cybercultural Revolution

On June 19, 1964, Hilton convened the three-day Conference on the Cybercultural Revolution—Cybernation and Automation in the Roosevelt Hotel on Forty-Fifth and Madison in New York City. At her invitation, fifty speakers addressed topics like "The Negro and Cybernation," "Our Concept of the Good Life: Idleness or Leisure," and "The Cybercultural Revolution of the American Dream." Besides Hilton, Arendt, and Michael, the plenary lineup included the civil rights leader and labor organizer James Boggs; the engineer and founder of the Society for the Social Responsibility of Science Victor Paschkis; and the Indian MIT engineer and community developer Jaswant G. Krishnayya. Boggs was at that point picking and choosing from among the enormous number of invites that followed the publication of his 1963 book, *The American Revolution: Pages from a Negro Worker's Notebook*.[51] He and Hilton had both been part of the Ad Hoc Committee on the Triple Revolution.[52]

The invited discussants included feminist sociologist Betty Friedan, whose book *The Feminist Mystique* had appeared the previous year; civil rights activist and labor organizer Grace Lee Boggs (spouse of James Boggs); and Berkeley poli-sci professor and best-selling novelist Eugene Burdick.[53] Another attendee was Bayard Rustin, key organizer of the March on Washington of the previous summer and another cosigner of the statement by the Ad Hoc Committee. The month before Hilton's conference, Rustin and a few other civil rights organizers joined editors of *Dissent* in a discussion titled "The Negro Movement: Where Shall It Go Now?," in which automation was a key element in the articulation of now-ness.[54] Also among the discussants was Tom Kahn, who had assisted Rustin during the planning of the march. In 1964, the League of Industrial Democracy published his pamphlet, *The Economics of Equality*, which he dedicated to Rustin.[55] Race, automation, and democracy are central themes throughout.

Throughout Hilton's event, several speakers invoked ancient Athens, as Hilton had predicted to Arendt. Michael seems not to have reacted to talk about ancient Athens the way Hilton thought he would, but she did schedule Arendt to speak right after him, to ensure she would have the last word. Hilton's published exordium for the event tells us what mood she established its first morning. She professes an interest in speculation, definitions, discussion, questions: "Where do we want to go? What are the concepts we have in our minds? What are our hopes, and where are our fears?"[56] This hope/fear dialectic initiates her full-length contribution to the conference, which takes the lead position. Her opening sentence marks "the magnificent promise of the dawning age of cyberculture" to be "the complete emancipation of human beings from drudgery and scarcity that is achievable with cybernation."[57] Having the status of promise, this liberation is not an inevitability, but neither is it the stuff of fabulists. "We have no guarantee to reach utopia," she begins to concede, but then she goes for etymological play, "for utopia means 'no place.' But we have almost a certainty of finding either eutopia—the good place—or dystopia—the bad place. Hope for eutopia and fear of dystopia have occupied man throughout the millenia [*sic*]. This generation is at the crossroads: we may drift towards dystopia; but we have a chance, for the first time, to live the Good Life on this earth and create a new society."[58] It is notable that Hilton marks drifting as the direction of dystopia, and human-centered choosing and planning and steering as the way to eutopia. Her capitalization of the Good Life seems like a nod to the Aristotelian tradition of distinguishing between activities that humans perform for life and those they perform for the good life, and indeed she references a related line from Aristotle's *Politics* in her foreword.[59]

Understanding the history of technology to be "the story of man's search for labor-saving devices," Hilton locates the cybercultural revolution at the intersection of mathematics, philosophy, and geopolitics.[60] Mathematics, from its start, has used computation for communal management, and World War II accelerated technological advancements (or, seen otherwise, new modes of destruction) to ensure survival, while philosophy, from its start, has pursued the conditions of human flourishing. Geopolitically, Hilton identifies postwar affluence and population growth in the United States with an increasing demand for goods and services that coincides with the reduction of "cheap labor" that she attributes to the end of colonialism. Within this context, she applies the newest math to the oldest problem: Who will do the laboring? Her solution is "non-human, electronic slaves," the labor-saving device of the cybernetic age.[61]

Again, we encounter slaves. Hilton sees enslavement as a recurring resolution of the tension between labor and work, a constant that, in her time, could be met with an ersatz slave population. In the past, "a society could prosper and endow its citizens with the leisure to work only at the cost of finding riches and slaves *outside* the society," the finding process being war.[62] She names Alexander the Great and Hitler as examples. "Cybernated slaves," on the other hand, will be *inside* the society, embedded in its production system, "always ready to serve *all* of mankind, to provide us with undreamed-of abundance, and free us for our human tasks."[63] This potential evolution will not unfurl on its own. What is needed to accommodate it is, as Hilton wrote earlier in 1964, a new ethos. Antecedent to a new ethos is a habitude for talking about morality and ethics, she writes, the kind of talk that people these days barely tolerate in pastors and philosophers, let alone know how to (or wish to) generate themselves. But such talk is what pulls cybernation from its drift toward dystopia. We know from Hilton's letter to Arendt that the eutopia she thought the wise management of so-called cybernated slaves could yield was a society that resembled fifth-century BCE Athens. Here, in her introductory remarks, Hilton does not make that case. Having seen most of the conference papers in advance, however, she does not need to; she knows that ancient Athens is coming.

The most slave-conscious comments about ancient Athens came from orthodontist and biologist (and also Hilton's husband) Herbert Layton Hayward and labor organizer Ted F. Silvey. During a post-panel discussion, Hayward spoke honestly about the role that enslaved people played in the daily and conceptual lives of ancient Athenians: "The sole reason for the existence of the slave in Athens was the production of those essential elements without which the citizens could not be humans. In the past, it has always involved the dehumanization of a certain portion of humanity to make it possible for the other part of humanity to be human."[64] Silvey's talk is more descriptive: "The relatively few intellectuals and leaders of the Golden Age of Pericles in ancient Athens could exist only because of the great substratum of human slaves—who grew the groceries, did the housekeeping, and carried the slops for the few on top."[65] Yet, in their papers, both Hayward and Silvey hold tight to the enslaving logic of the aristocrat. Hayward enthuses that "we have now, at last, reached the happy state—or there is now at least a vision, a possibility that in the foreseeable future the happy state can be reached—where those who, if they want to, may be aristocrats can approach one-hundred percent of all human beings."[66] Silvey gushes that "today, the inanimate apparatus under democratic control can serve as a mass of slaves beneath our entire population [that] could ensure the cultivation and blossoming of each person's maximum achievement."[67] The idea is that machine slaves allow for a scaling up of classical Athens, with no upper limit on whom machine enslavement frees for excellence in thought and deed. Also avoided, of course, are the cruelties of human enslavement.

Hilton and Arendt are less critical in their engagements with ancient Greece. During one of the discussions between plenaries, Hilton hypes the Homeric archetype of the excellent individual: "A population will evolve which, endowed with the leisure to fulfill human tasks, can create a society in which the individual has the opportunity to excel, in the Greek sense of the word, *i.e.*, to distinguish himself from all others."[68] Hilton does not write about ancient Athens as a model of and for mass politics. But Arendt does. Hearing the excitement of her fellow panelists for the cultural exuberance of ancient Greece, she urges a more foundational consideration of its polis. Arendt insists, foremost, on precision about the relationship between leisure and what it enabled the humans who had it to do: "In ancient Greece, even the artist—the painter, the sculptor—was not recognized as a full citizen, precisely because he was too busy. The citizen was not free to create the high flowering of culture but to engage in political activities."[69] Her view is that anyone excited about ancient Greece as a model ought to be clear that political action was the defining feature of free (meaning both unenslaved and unoccupied) citizens. She wonders whether the enthusiasm for ancient Greece extends to its fundamental unit of organization, and what it would mean to "devise liberal institutions for our political lives which will fulfill the function the *polis* fulfilled for the free citizens of Greece."[70] In sum, Arendt offers the institutional counterpart to Hilton's centering of the individual.

In the discussion that follows Arendt's talk, Hilton enthuses that the promise of cyberculture is that we can "devote ourselves, as civilized beings should, to poetry and politics."[71] In response, activist Grace Lee Boggs expresses relief that Hilton and Arendt—with the latter of whose work Lee Boggs claims familiarity—have finally mentioned politics explicitly. She argues that "creative political energy" has been unable to build up because working people exhaust all their energy through their economic productivity.[72] She also points out that white people will have to make space for those historically excluded by racial capitalism, and she does not think they will do so voluntarily. Also during this Q&A, chairman of the Labor and Industry Committee of the NAACP James Houghton adds that liberation from work is not an inevitable outcome of cybernation, and that to assume so is to shift attention away from "the immediate struggles the black and white workers of this country are presently involved in and will be more deeply involved in in the future."[73] Overall, the conference keynoters characterize the cybercultural revolution as emancipatory; largely, the locus of freedom is the individual, who is free to become the best version of themselves once liberated from drudgery. It is the activists participating in Hilton's event who keep alert to the politics of such self-centrism in the United States in 1964. Given that Hilton was a member of the Ad Hoc

Committee, it may seem odd that she does not articulate a more detailed political outlook in her contributions. It could be said that she is thinking ahead to the time after the struggle, to what could be rather than to what will need to happen to get there. But probably the best explanation for her lack of attention to policy is what she herself says during the discussion following Arendt's talk: She had been talking "very comprehensive" policy plans for years, highlighting the cruel irony that massive governmental programs are framed as a fiscal no-go even as the "so-called" defense budget sat at $51 billion in 1964.[74]

A few months after the conference, Hilton founded the Institute for Cybercultural Research in New York City. Under its purview, Hilton was able to launch her planned book series, The Age of Cyberculture, of which she was general editor, and an institute magazine, *Feedback*, whose motto was a line from Norbert Wiener's *The Human Use of Human Beings*: "The hour is very late, and the choice of good and evil knocks at our door."[75] Hilton assembled a large board of directors, including many of the conference participants, even Donald Michael, whose pessimism she must have deemed valuable. She also asked Arendt to join the board, and she did.

Athens Fades from View (and So Does Hilton)

Hilton decided to run another cyberculture conference the following year. Its proceedings were never published.[76] In early 1966, her Institute for Cybercultural Research cosponsored with the Association for the Advancement of Psychotherapy a symposium on Psychiatry, Cybernetics, and Man in the Evolving Culture. There, she gave a paper titled "Homo Faber, Homo Sapiens, Homo Poeta," in which she offers her view of the three unchanging aspects of humans—the maker, the thinker, and the poet (by which she means an appreciator of beauty)—that are present in a ratio within any individual human and within a given culture according to its arrangements and emphases. We would probably be right to see Arendt's influence in this trifold parsing of human identity.

"In the Golden Ages of Mankind, *homo sapiens* and *homo poeta* are held in high esteem," Hilton asserts.[77] Her running example, of course, is ancient Athens, for her the beneficiary par excellence of the agricultural revolution. The sequence, as she sees it, is that "*homo faber* creates a surplus for *homo sapiens* to flourish into *homo poeta*. And *homo poeta* triumphed about seven-and-a-half millenia [*sic*] after the agricultural revolution, in the Golden Age of Athens."[78] Because we are in the midst of what Hilton has been calling, since 1963, the "cybercultural revolution," we are poised, individually and collectively, to prioritize *homo poeta*.

The problem, as she diagnoses it, is that no culture has ever embraced *homo faber* so tightly as ours. Hilton had addressed that problem in her earlier article, "An Ethos for the Age of Cyberculture." Here, she reanimates those arguments against "our stiff Puritan ethos" and "the mystique of virtue-in-toil that made industrial capitalism—private or state—so successful in an age of scarcity," pointing out their profound inappropriateness "in an age when necessity is rapidly vanishing from the human situation."[79] Citing the talk that mathematician Richard Bellman delivered at her 1964 cyberculture conference, she provides projections of how few laborers will be needed "to supplement the machines" and yield the then-current gross national product.[80] Accounting for delays in rolling out the technology and developing appropriate policies, she estimates that it will be twenty years until only the smallest necessary number of people will labor in production lines.

Hilton concedes that the degree to which the example of ancient Athens has anything to teach at such a moment would depend on an openness to leisure that was at odds with the prevailing ethos: "Whether the unmatched flourishing of *homo poeta* in a small Greek city state is relevant to us two-and-a-half millenia [*sic*] later—that is, whether we can hope to attain equal heights of civilization—it is certain that leisure was the prerequisite of Greek culture and that leisure will be the prerequisite if *homo poeta* is ever again to come into his own."[81] What makes the *homo poeta* is leisure. "Greek leisure," she points out, "was based upon slavery as all leisure has always been and must always be. But the slave has changed."[82] She does not cringe in saying so, leveling a charge of hypocrisy at anyone who is not honest about how societies tend to treat their laborers, even in the mid-twentieth century: "Can we seriously defend the untenable position of deploring the institution of 'slavery' and with the same breath preach the gospel of every man's enslavement? Can we really believe that 'full employment'—not man's emancipation from toil and drudgery—is a worthy, though clearly unattainable goal?"[83] To require people to labor when they do not *need* to is for her a gross violation of their freedom.

She describes the various technologies wielded (e.g., water, wind) or invented (e.g., Watt's governor) that did some of the work previously performed by or forced on people, noting the hiccup of the industrial-age machine, which made a worker "the servant of the device that released his muscles from physical toil."[84] But the computer, about twenty years old at the time she composed this talk, "is the culmination of the age-old search for labor-saving devices; it is the perfect tool that can give humanity full leisure and infinite abundance."[85] The computer, particularly its use in cybernated production systems, has become an accelerant of liberation from labor. She credits humans with being very adaptable but urges haste: "The army of cybernated slaves demanding to free us for our human tasks is at the gate." Ignoring or subverting the metaphor's usual bad connotation, Hilton's attitude is that we ought to let them in. The so-called cybernated slaves enable the retirement of the *homo faber*, whose makings have "cleared the path to the Greeks' shining vision of *homo poeta*."[86] Poetry and politics await.

Hilton's published papers about cybernetics peter out in 1973, and the shrinking space within them that she affords to ancient Greece may be a sign of her diminishing hopes for a cybercultural eutopia. By 1969, Hilton was claiming that those who are the best positioned in attitude and aptitude to understand cybernetics as the study of relationships within systems "are almost violently prejudiced against the very word," since "cybernetics" is seldom used outside of narrow production contexts, is poorly defined even in major dictionaries, and has come to have all sorts of unserious connotations besides.[87]

A few months after her participation in Hilton's first cyberculture conference, Arendt replied briefly to a letter from someone asking her about the Institute for Cybercultural Research. She answered that she did not know much, and that "the meeting was not bad, but not very good either. At any rate, with the exception of one, possibly two speakers, it was not 'crack-pot.'"[88] Her use of quotation marks suggests that the letter-writer had used that word, but this peek into Arendt's judgment hints that even earlier in the 1960s there was something about cybernetics that kept serious people from engaging with it seriously. For several reasons that would have annoyed Norbert Wiener, "automation" had knocked his word into the fringe.[89]

4

Extensions into Past and Future Time

The days are made on a loom whereof the warp and woof are past and future time.
RALPH WALDO EMERSON, "Works and Days"

The first humans, the golden race given life and voice by the gods, had no cares, no work, no sorrows. Crops and sheep sprang from the land itself, and that abundance they pooled and shared. When it was time, they went to their deaths as if into gentle sleep. The poet Hesiod, who tells of these humans in twelve lines that appear early in the archaic Greek poem *Works and Days*, provides a telling detail about their bodies: "They were always the same in their feet and hands."[1] As our primary contacts with the world, hands and feet typically change a great deal over the course of a life; they blister, callous, burn, wrinkle, spot, cramp, ache, bend, twist. Unchanging feet and hands—poignant metonymies—testify to an undemanding life.

It has been said that the mere twelve lines of description about the golden race contain four motifs that constitute "the shape of early Greek utopia," a form periodically reactivated after Hesiod: automatic food, harmonious human relations, robust health, and an association with gold.[2] But, of course, the poem goes on, articulating later lines of humans. The iteration of humans to which Hesiod and those who first heard his verses belong is the fifth race, iron. They work all day, suffer through the night, and never shed their cares. Hesiod does not bother to describe their hands and feet, since they would be unremarkably familiar.

After the genealogy, *Works and Days* becomes a didactic poem Hesiod addresses to his brother Perses and unnamed local rulers, who are urged to think not that work is shameful but that not-work is.[3] Through work, iron-race humans can achieve self-confidence, excellence, wealth, and even fame. Those traits, as long as they do not violate the limits appropriate to humans, are smiled upon by the gods.

Taking inspiration from Hesiod's generational designations in *Works and Days*, Ralph Waldo Emerson's 1870 essay of the same title commences with a name for his own time: "Our nineteenth century is the age of tools."[4] In his age-naming observations, like Thomas Carlyle a few decades earlier, Emerson explores the relationship between humans and tools, but he sources tools far more organically.[5] "They grew out of our structure," Emerson asserts, and he quotes Aristotle's views on the parts of animals, for good measure: " 'Man is the meter of all things,' said Aristotle; 'the hand is the instrument of instruments, and the mind is the form of forms.' "[6] Emerson then runs with Aristotle's syntax: "The human body is the magazine of inventions, the patent office, where are the models from which every hint was taken. All the tools and engines on earth are only extensions of its limbs and senses."[7] This language of physiology and sensorium gives way to a registry of recent innovations that is structured to lull readers, item by item, into a state of wonder at what has grown from us and what grows us. Then Emerson disrupts the reverie: "Many facts concur to show that we must look deeper for our salvation than to steam, photographs, balloons, or astronomy. These tools have some questionable properties. They are reagents. Machinery is aggressive. The weaver becomes a web, the machinist a machine. If you do not use the tools, they use you. All tools are in one sense edge-tools, and dangerous."[8] Machines, originating from the patterns of our bodies and stretching us farther and faster into the world, reach back around and incorporate us.

Calling upon his titular influence, Emerson laments that "works and days were offered us, and we took works." He sees an opportunity to enliven even Hesiod's understanding of the labor-intensive right choice.[9] Hesiod, after all, celebrates the variant of strife that gives rise to competition and keeps one constantly working.[10] Emerson asserts that, rather than make ourselves coextensive with our works, we ought to become one with our days; rather than worry about how we fill our days, we ought to enjoy how our days fulfill us. And he goes so far as to offer a correction course to what have become his compatriots' usual routes for making the most of a leisurely day: "This mendicant America, this curious, peering, itinerant, imitative America, studious of Greece and Rome, of England and Germany, will take off its dusty shoes, will take off its glazed traveller's cap, and sit at home with repose and deep joy on its face."[11] Fully inhabiting a day would calm the go-getting energy that propels Emerson's fellows to look toward famous, faraway centers of culture, including Greece, for meaning. The machine extends us, study extends us, competitive emulation extends us; Emerson reckons that what his contemporaries need most is to be snapped back into place.

Though the history of the extension thesis of technology and the study of its meaning clearly predate the mid-twentieth century, credit for its articulation commonly goes to the Canadian media theorist Marshall McLuhan. As the subtitle supporting his consequential 1964 book, *Understanding Media*, the phrase "the extensions of man" announces McLuhan's attitude toward the cultural effects that any medium has on human beings and being human. In his prologue to *The Gutenberg Galaxy*, published two years previously, McLuhan shows interest in the extension thesis.[12] There, it appears in a block quotation from *The Silent Language*, a 1959 book by anthropologist Edward T. Hall: "Today man has developed extensions for practically everything he used to do with his body. The evolution of weapons begins with the teeth and the fist and ends with the atom bomb. Clothes and houses are extensions of man's biological temperature-control mechanisms."[13] A few decades earlier, the machine had made Lewis Mumford think about the usual way of technology: "The tools and utensils used during the greater part of man's history were, in the main, extensions of his own organism: they did not have—what is more important they did not *seem* to have—an independent existence."[14] Mumford argues that the machine, conversely, *does* seem independent of its users, and he sets out to explore how people have begun to assimilate it.

In *Understanding Media*, McLuhan's interest skews toward "the new scale that is introduced into our affairs by each extension of ourselves, or by any new technology."[15] Essentially, "any extension, whether of skin, hand, or foot, affects the whole psychic and social complex."[16] This point takes more recognizable form in his famous adage "The medium is the message"—in other words, the message is not some content the medium transmits but the material and cultural changes the medium effects when people start to use it. It is also the title of the book's first chapter, which begins with the example of automation: "Thus, with automation, for example, the new patterns of human association tend to eliminate jobs, it is true. That is the negative result. Positively, automation creates roles for people, which is to say depth of involvement in their work and human association that our preceding mechanical technology had destroyed."[17] McLuhan trains attention not on what automation produces but on what automation *does*, to people and social systems; he has no interest, though, in dwelling on job loss and its disproportionate effects on working-class people, especially the racially minoritized, even as he infamously observes that electric media has made it such that "the Negro . . . [is] now *involved* in our lives."[18] McLuhan writes for the referent of that possessive plural pronoun. His stance toward automation's human-amplifying potential—for some humans, anyway—drifts throughout the book and piles up in the book's final chapter, "Automation: Learning a Living."

The fact that *Understanding Media* begins and ends with automation is not often noted. Reading the book with its ring composition in mind concentrates one's attention on McLuhan's contribution in 1964 to discourse about automation; furthermore, it invites pairing with the projections of Ukrainian British industrialist Leon Bagrit about extension and automation, delivered via radio that same year. Whereas McLuhan's engagement with antiquity takes the oblique form of favoritism for a liberal education—a view in which, as I show with reference to other academics, he was not alone in the early age of automation—Bagrit admiringly cites the arrangement of elites in ancient Greece as a model that automation will allow many more people to access. In a book published two years after *Understanding Media* and Bagrit's articulation of automation-as-extension, economics professor and former labor organizer Ben Seligman tracks the utopian thinking of technologists across industries and mocks Bagrit's take in particular. Appearing between McLuhan's *Understanding Media* (1964) and Seligman's *Most Notorious Victory* (1966), sociologist Robert Boguslaw's *The New Utopians* (1965) views engineers and computer programmers as designers of systems whose influence stretched far beyond blueprints, hardware, and keystrokes—and whose planning did not center humans at all. Boguslaw worried that their systems extended nothing but the power of people who already had it.

McLuhan on Automation

Automation and mechanization are the first examples McLuhan uses in *Understanding Media* to exemplify his view that any medium (i.e., any extension of ourselves) that gains social-infrastructural purchase comes to habituate human action and interaction.[19] He sees mechanization and automation as instating entirely different patterns. To him, automation suggests flow, continuity, wholeness, and immersion, in contrast to mechanization, which brought specialization, disconnection, stop-and-go movement, and fragmented attention.[20] Those qualities of automation, for McLuhan, obliterate the meaning of work as we know it, since "where the whole man is involved, there is no work."[21] This is the status of "work" for "the poet, painter, or thinker of today"—and of those whose jobs will be powered by automation, McLuhan enthuses.[22] Automation disrupts the work patterns the machine introduced. It absorbs without demanding subordination. This is McLuhan's overall attitude toward what automation introduces into human affairs.

McLuhan is intrigued by how, historically, cultures have used self-extenders to manage work. He starts with antiquity: "After the exhaustion of the Graeco-Roman pools of slave labor, the West had to technologize more intensively than the ancient world had done."[23] Though McLuhan does not pause to consider that ancient enslaved people were reified into technical objects or bodily extensions of those who enslaved them, he posits a causal link between the dwindling supply of "slave labor" and the need to engineer tools and machines that could do the work formerly done by enslaved people. Next, McLuhan moves to an "American" era but does not specify a precise time or place: "In the same way the American farmer confronted with new tasks and opportunities, and at the same time with a great shortage of human assistance, was goaded into a frenzy of creation of labor-saving devices." His chronological and geographical vagueness presents challenges to understanding what "a great shortage of human assistance" refers to, which may have been his point. Then he pushes toward the lesson to be learned: "It would seem that the logic of success in this matter is the ultimate retirement of the work force from the scene of toil. In a word, automation." Automation is the last in a cycling sequence of steps that iterate toward the total elimination of labor via technology; first comes the freeing of enslaved workers and then the device-enabled easing of free workers. "If this, however, has been the motive of our human technologies," McLuhan continues, "it does not follow that we are prepared to accept the consequences. It helps to get one's bearings to see the process at work in remote times when work meant specialist servitude, and leisure alone meant a life of human dignity and involvement of the whole man." McLuhan casts back into "remote times" to find a robust, welcoming attitude toward leisure that suits how he views automated work.

We see this glance at past and future in the book's concluding chapter, "Automation: Learning a Living," which offers a compact estimation both of the changes that automation could bring to existing human arrangements and of the best cultural response to them. For instance, automation enters into "a familiar pattern in electric technology in general. It ends the old dichotomies between culture and technology, between art and commerce, and between work and leisure."[24] According to McLuhan, dichotomous thinking is the product of the mechanical age, in which "leisure has been the absence of work, or mere idleness."[25] By contrast, he claims, since "the age of information demands the simultaneous use of all our faculties, we discover that we are most at leisure when we are most intensely involved, very much as with the artists in all ages."[26] Again, McLuhan posits artists as transhistorical models of integration, as the figures, in any era, who synthesize oppositional cultural modes or offer new modes of living altogether. Artists are his paragons of comprehensive, imaginative living.

What arts of living can guide us through this disorienting time? Though McLuhan thinks we need different ways of organizing ourselves, he does not mean "organizing" in the sense of labor—which is notable, given his repeated mention of "the specter of joblessness and propertylessness in the electric age."[27] The subtitle of the chapter, "Learning a Living," adds a transformative letter to the phrase "earning a living," that idiom of capitalist survival. McLuhan exhorts the adoption of an education he believes will amplify the tendencies of automation: "Paradoxically, automation makes liberal education mandatory."[28] McLuhan does not explain the paradox, or what he considers "liberal education," or whether what is "mandatory" lands at the level of education policy and infrastructure or is simply a preference he urges.

Whatever McLuhan's idea of liberal education, it is informed by his Cambridge doctorate in English literature, which he earned with his 1943 dissertation, published as *The Classical Trivium: The Place of Thomas Nashe in the Learning of His Time.*[29] McLuhan used the trivium (i.e., grammar, logic, and rhetoric, three of the seven original liberal arts) to organize its chapters. The *artes liberales*—with their first twitches in ancient Athens, their formulation in late antiquity, and their authority into modernity—hail from premodern times, before the narrowing specialization McLuhan attributes to the machine age. But he finds their partition bothersome, much preferring what he views as the integration of the subjects that occurred during the Renaissance, because their very demarcation suggests to the mechanically oriented that education comes in discrete, disconnected, subject-sized pieces.

McLuhan believes that automation puts students "under increasing pressure to acquire the depth and interrelation that are indispensable in the all-at-once world of electric organization," and he estimates that the failure of schools to adapt will yield "a citizenry unable to understand the cybernated world in which they live."[30] Liberal education recommends itself not because automation will free up the day for democratic deliberation and philosophical contemplation, but because it will make what used to be called "work hours" different in their demands. In McLuhan's view, "the social and educational patterns latent in automation are those of self-employment and artistic autonomy. Panic about automation as a threat of uniformity on a world scale is the projection into the future of mechanical standardization and specialism, which are now past."[31] Automation, according to McLuhan, will not make us all identical, interchangeable cogs—that is what mechanization does. Instead, automation will make each of us more our own—but only if we are prepared to accept that freedom.

The Paradox: Liberal Education for the Age of Automation

The "paradox," then, to return to McLuhan's word, is that liberal education—the ostensibly premodern model that had been made the foundation of certain elite North American universities but whose overall curricular and cultural hold had loosened by the mid-twentieth century—should be the one best suited to the future toward which automation extends us. McLuhan does not specify what this education would look like, or how widely available it ought to be, but his linking of liberal education and automation puts him in the company of others at mid-century who argued in much greater detail about the role of such an education within a democracy that was settling into automation.

McLuhan may consider himself in conversation with architect R. Buckminster Fuller, whose 1961 lecture on education in an automated age, published in 1962, prominently uses the "earning" and "learning" formulation.[32] But there are far more general affinities between his work and the writings of Robert Maynard Hutchins, who had been president (1929–45) and chancellor (1945–51) of the University of Chicago. The second edition of his book *The University of Utopia*, originally published in 1953, appeared in 1964; in a short introduction, Hutchins describes the conditions that give his warnings from the previous decade continued potency and urgency: "If we survive [nuclear threats], we are going to live in a wantless, workless world. The machines will do the work."[33] Evoking the etymology of *liberal* arts, Hutchins imagines "the education appropriate to free men" in that world of no want and no work.[34] He reduces the foundational activities to three: "read, speak, and figure. It will be helpful, in short, if he knows the liberal arts, which are arts of communication."[35] Study in the liberal arts supplies "what every human being needs . . . a grasp of the fundamental ideas and the ability to communicate with others."[36] For Hutchins, a student comes by the fundamental ideas and learns how to talk about them by listening in on and then joining what he had called in an earlier book "the great conversation."

In *The Great Conversation: The Substance of a Liberal Education*, published in 1952, Hutchins claims that the US American educational system had decentralized the curricular role of the so-called Western canon—which he did not disambiguate from liberal education—at a time when he felt that its lessons were most needed. He presents his case for the restoration of the "great books" to the curriculum and for the continued reading of these books after formal education ceases.[37] His undergirding contention is that adults in the United States enjoy an unprecedented amount of leisure *and* incorporation into democracy—an assertion he quantifies but never qualifies. Hutchins concedes that, historically, "liberal education was aristocratic in the sense that it was the education of those who enjoyed leisure and political power." He suppresses all sorts of premises when he continues: "If it was the right education for those who enjoyed leisure and political power, then it is the right education for everybody today."[38] What best recommends liberal education (as he envisions it) for democratic life is the disposition that it fosters toward the big questions of individual and collective human life: They endlessly recur, and judgment is required to weigh old deliberations and to participate in new ones.

Throughout the book, Hutchins uses "mechanization" rather than "automation" to describe the technological state of things; he is writing before the latter term took off in public discourse. He engages the debate about whether machines enhance or threaten human freedom by appealing to ancient Greece, claiming that "the substitution of machines for slaves gives us an opportunity to build a civilization as glorious as that of the Greeks, and far more lasting because far more just."[39] Is Hutchins comparing modern machines to ancient enslaved people to make an argument for the moral superiority of US American democracy (as if slavery were not an ongoing part of its history)? Or is he positing a progression from enslaved people to machines in the United States as a means of arguing that the United States outperformed ancient Greece by innovating its way out of slavery (which is not, of course, why enslaved people were freed in the United States)? Either way, the underlying assumption is that the United States is poised for dominance, endurance, and, it seems, justice. Hutchins then points out an irony: "The mechanization which tends to reduce a man to a robot also supplies the economic base and the leisure that will enable him to get a liberal education and become truly a man."[40] Mechanized labor may dehumanize, but, according to Hutchins, it pays well and allows one to work fewer hours, thus allowing scope for the only sort of education that fully, truly humanizes.

Providing a liberal education beyond the traditional school and university years became the focus of the work of Penn State English professor Maxwell Goldberg, founder and director of Penn State's Center for Continuing Liberal Education (CCLE), who also cofounded the first interdisciplinary program in science, technology, and society in the United States. Goldberg ran in the same circles as Alice Mary Hilton—he served on the board of her Institute for Cybercultural Research—and, like Hilton, he was a talented organizer of intellectual energy. With the backing of CCLE and IBM, he launched the Humanities Project on Technological Change. Under its auspices, he organized a conference on Technological Change and Human Values in December 1963, and on Work, Leisure, and Education in a Changing Industrialized

Democracy in June 1964, the same month as Hilton's first conference. Goldberg presented at hers, and she at his.[41]

In the fall 1964 issue of *The Michigan Quarterly Review*, Penn State professor of speech Robert Oliver joined Hilton in publishing his contribution to the 1964 conference. In "Education in the Year 2000 A.D.," Oliver issues several predictions, two core forecasts being that automation will change the way we work, and communication technology will change how we think about, feel with, and talk to distant others. He believes that the verbal arts of conversation, discussion, and argumentation will surge in importance in face-to-face contexts, as university education scales up, and large lectures—attended in person or listened to or watched via recording technology—become the central instructional format. Students will need small-group recitations or breakout sessions where they can develop habits "of analysis, of interpretation, and of presentation" and experience the invigoration of fine-tuning one's understanding and influencing the attitudes and actions of one's peers. In sum, "the educated person in 2,000 A.D. will resemble fairly closely the old symposiarch of the great days of ancient Athens—one who loved good talk, and who talked well to critical and appreciative listeners. The great difference will be that whereas in Athens this kind of education was restricted to a very few aristocrats at the top of the social order, in the age of abundance upon which we are entering, there is no practical reason why such social achievements cannot be attained by vast numbers of people."[42] Originally, a symposium was a drinking party at which all sorts of social things would be spilled. A symposiarch would have made the guest list with shimmering conversation or even competitive speechifying in mind. A symposium was a space where one could put one's education on display, but it was also an educative space, since one learns about oneself and others when one talks and listens. In the time of, say, Agathon's symposium as represented in Plato's *Symposium*, it would have been small, exclusive, and exclusionary. Women, for example, would have attended only as musical or sexual entertainers. Oliver thinks that students of the future, educated in talk, will be curators of good conversation.

A selection of papers delivered at Goldberg's events was published in a 1966 volume to which he contributed the introduction and conclusion. In the conclusion, we find that, as it did for McLuhan, the word "paradox" evaluatively structures Goldberg's engagement of the education question: He uses the word three times on one page. For him, though, the paradox is that this enduring educational program known as "humanistic" must change if it is to maintain its continuity: "Paradoxically, if the traditional and conventional humanities are to gain their life, they must lose their inherited forms." He singles out for disposal "a great deal of the classical *impedimenta*—as distinguished from the essential spirit and enduring vitality—inherited from the glory that was Greece and the grandeur that was Rome, as well as from the vast cultural turbulences and treasure houses of the Renaissance." Goldberg differentiates between inculcating the attitudes that yielded the cultural periods we celebrate and continuing the worshipful study of materials created during those periods. To survive, the humanities must be open to shifts in domains of human creativity and the resultant changes in "efforts, experiences, and aspirations." Like McLuhan with this emphasis on wholeness as a virtue of the automatic age, Goldberg insists that education, be it vocational, technical, or liberal, must be holistic. It must also be continuous. He believes that continuing education supports "the principles and necessities of American democracy," which relies on its citizens being able to identify and weigh in on the issues of the day.[43]

Also included in the 1966 volume of papers from 1963 and 1964 is a piece entitled "Education, Technological Change, and the New Society," by rural sociologist and Penn State professor Roy Buck. His engagement with the extension thesis—"The new machines are not only extensions of a man's muscle power, but also of his nervous system and his decision-making capacity—and to make decisions is to moralize"—serves as the foundation for his claim that the new society that education will inform, and by which it will be informed, will be a new slave society.[44] Like Wiener and Hilton, Buck is struck by the recurring analogy between automated machines and enslaved people. What Wiener found notable about it was the incongruous expectation that automated systems would be both highly intelligent and highly obedient, since those traits tend to clash. To demonstrate the longevity of the challenge of controlling one's smart tools, Wiener had mentioned the ancient literary trope of the clever Greek slave who can outwit his Roman enslaver. Buck is morally uncomfortable that an enslaved person would be "dehumanized into an obedient biological system of motor skills," but what he saw as a real prospect—that new machines might take the place held by enslaved people in earlier cultures—seemed to him reason enough to keep the slave concept alive. In a reversal of what happens to humans when they are enslaved, he suggests we will "humanize the machines into something approximating a slave." He adds that "the new slave machines do not trouble us in the way human slaves did," which he takes as fortunate, since "the slave-machine way of life," though a long way away yet, is coming.

To prepare, Buck suggests study "of classical slave-man cultures of the ancient world." He opts not to enlarge upon the particulars of enslavement in antiquity—"we shall not review slave culture here"—but does allow himself a few general points about the past and the future:

> Suffice it to say that it [enslavement] freed the favored few for development into wholly human beings. Now, however, we shall be faced with the potential for total human development as a mass phenomenon rather than as a quality reserved for an elite minority. The pursuit of beauty, dignity, and grace, coupled with a sense of composure, but at the same time motivated by enlarged principles of respect for people, ideas, and things, is on the verge of becoming a live option for the many. Perhaps, within the present generation, millions will find what it means to be intellectually and spiritually alive and free and will discover new dimensions of political freedom heretofore never envisioned.[45]

We see here the usual antitheses between mass and elite, which the reprieve from labor and work promised by automation will break down, allowing if not everyone than at least "millions" to experience new breadths and depths of intellectual, spiritual, and political life. Buck provides a peek at what pursuits and principles would orient that expanded type of living.

Three years after the volume's publication, Goldberg and Patricia Kochanek, a CCLE staff member and an editorial associate who was completing graduate work in literature and cultural anthropology, thematically grouped readings from the two meetings, added a few additional prompts, and paired them with discussion questions. The idea was that the contents would be discussed and further workshopped by participants in seminars held in contexts other than universities. Buck's and Goldberg's pieces are grouped together in the final section. One of the questions about Buck's paper spotlights the section from which I quoted at length:

> Notice how Dr. Buck pictures this holistic self-fulfillment (p. 201, top) in terms of the traditional humanistic concept, drawn from the ancient Greeks, of balance or symmetry and proportion, wherein esthetic human values and ethical human values are harmoniously blended into a single, dynamic whole. It is to be noted that the Greek word which we crudely translate as "gentleman" is a compound term, the <u>beautiful-good</u>. Here have you indication of the Greek humanist idea of the vital interpenetrative [*sic*] of the esthetic and the ethical (of beauty and duty).[46]

The ancient Greek word referred to here is καλοκἄγαθος, which does indeed mash together the beautiful and the good (*kalos kai agathos*), a grammatical mirror of its referent: A man who is both good-looking and good—or, as we might say these days, is beautiful inside and out. That exact ideal seems to be not quite what Buck was driving toward, but instead a riff by the discussion facilitators.

Buck himself concludes his piece with a forecast that emphasizes the humanizing properties of a liberal education: "Technological advance, releasing man from dehumanizing work, is the heart of the educational problem in technologically advanced societies. Education, emphasizing what once was considered the less practical arts and sciences, will become increasingly popular."[47] Freedom from repetitive tasks will make the arts of thinking, evaluating, and communicating more essential, and therefore more in demand, he estimates.

Around this time, another prominent participant in dialogues about technology and education was Hyman Rickover, an admiral who had developed the US American nuclear submarine program and who considered all topics about the standing of his country to be his business, a view that did not go unchallenged. He begins his 1964 book, *American Education—A National Failure*, on what the United States stands to learn about education from the British model, by addressing critics who either do not think he has any standing to analyze educational systems or do not like his suggestions for improvement. He mentions, for example, a line of criticism that accuses him of advocating "that we return to what some educationists call Aristotelian concepts developed in 'the Athenian master-slave state.' "[48] Clearly, some people believed that the uncritical use of ancient Greek terms and the application of ancient Greek preferences should be contested when no accounting was made for their notoriously exclusionary cultural origins.

Rickover and McLuhan crossed paths in November 1964, when they participated in a symposium, "The Social Impact of Cybernetics," organized by professor of political science Charles R. Dechert, whose paper titled "Cybernetics and the Human Person" had won a major philosophical prize earlier that year.[49] McLuhan gave a talk, "Cybernation and Culture," that appeared two years later in the symposium volume and, with its attention to "extension" as the key technological term and "wholeness" as its key cybernation term, largely rehashes the final chapter of *Understanding Media*. One new bit is a concluding paragraph alleging that cybernation will bring an abundance that does not suit our scarcity-based cultural infrastructures.[50]

To the symposium, Rickover contributed a piece called "A Humanistic Technology." Largely, it unfolds as a prosecution of the attitude that nothing old fits the new technological age: "Why should the fact that technology makes it possible to relieve mankind of much brutal, exhausting physical labor and boring routine work affect precepts that have guided Western man for centuries?"[51] Rickover does not name anyone who argues that precepts centuries old (or older) are no longer applicable, but a contributor to one of Goldberg's conferences in 1963 and 1964 can act as a stand-in. Warner Rice, chair of the Department of English Language and Literature at the University of Michigan, disagrees with those who champion the study of old books as the answer to our awkward technocultural situation:

> We shall seek direct remedies for our ills; we must quickly discover solutions to our problems; and not many of these will be found in the admonition of Psalms or the Prophets, or the *Ethics* of Aristotle, or the *Republic* of Plato. The societies which produced those noble works are not our society. The outlook which they present is not our outlook. . . . There is at least a reasonable hope that we can succeed in many of our endeavors, for the great fact with which we are faced is that our human capabilities have increased enormously since the fourth century, B.C. Society simply cannot rest, then, upon the assumption that human nature is always the same and that what was good enough for the past is the model for the present.[52]

Rice suggests that the most important work humanists can do is help the public stretch their imaginations to "identify what is desirable in a possible human experience" at a time when science and tech are altering the norms of human life.[53]

Rice and Rickover would probably agree on matters more than disagree. Rickover's piece inches toward this line: "Paradoxically, liberal education, which at one time we tended to regard as 'aristocratic,' is the very kind of education we now need more to preserve our 'democratic' way of life. Since it seeks to develop all the potentialities of the individual, not merely those he needs to earn a living, liberal of humanistic education shapes or forms him into a more capable, a more observant, a more discriminating human being."[54] Though the syntax tracks very closely with McLuhan's statement that, "paradoxically, automation makes liberal education mandatory," Rickover keys in on class, political constitution, and judgment. Rickover thinks that technology must be humanized by liberal education for the protection of democracy.[55]

Those endorsements of humanistic education in the early age of automation reinvigorate a long-standing but no longer axiomatic impulse to associate self-development for the demands of democratic life with ancient Athenian culture. The fact that the few ancient Athenians who enjoyed the freedom to develop themselves and debate with others obtained it via the enslavement of fellow humans is transmuted into an analogue—machine slaves—that gives many more modern people the same opportunities, plus a moral advantage. The shared element of slavery preserves the Athenian example for an automated age. Moving beyond the slave concept to machines may have made ancient Athens less relevant—and may have made looking so far into the past to avoid much more proximate slave cultures less necessary. The failure to hear in the freedom-enslavement antithesis the intensifying struggle for black liberation; the failure to wonder how the reanimation of the slave concept in a machine context might not register in the same way for everyone; and the failure to recognize that technology and education never liberate *everybody*—these are failures not of imagination, but of basic perception.

To loop back to McLuhan's endorsement of liberal education at the conclusion of *Understanding Media*, it is instructive to attend to how the *freedom* inherent to "liberal" (from the Latin *liberalis*, "of the free") education connects with McLuhan's explicit use of the word. At the book's closing, McLuhan uses language of bondage and liberty to describe the technological transition at hand: "The electric age of servomechanisms suddenly releases men from the mechanical and specialist servitude of the preceding machine age. . . . We are suddenly threatened with a liberation that taxes our inner resources of self-employment and imaginative participation in society. This would seem to be a fate that calls men to the role of artist in society."[56] In this instance, the repeated adverb "suddenly" and the seeming mismatch of being "threatened" with "liberation" have an Arendtian air. This quick change in our external situation is only as advantageous as our ability to slip the internal constraints imposed by the machine age.

Despite his strong link to the phrase in cultural memory, McLuhan is not the only public figure in 1964 thinking about technology, including automation, as an "extension of man," and, in the reflections of another public thinker, we find ancient Athens unmistakably occupying the good place.

The Extensions of Leon Bagrit

In 1964, Signet Press marketed *Understanding Media* as part of its New American Library, whose growing catalog of titles closes out the book. Included is *The Age of Automation* by the Ukraine-born British champion of cybernetics Leon Bagrit. In 1964, his book existed in the form of scripts Bagrit was finalizing for radio. Then, as now, pronouncements on new tech moved into print quickly.

In a bothersome tendency that continues today, major media corporations in the 1960s gave platforms to very wealthy men who managed technology companies to sound off on the futures they envisioned and were positioned to effect. The BBC, for example, invited the recently knighted Sir Leon, chairman and managing director of Elliott Automation (which had been his company until he sold it in 1937 and became its managing director) to deliver its prestigious Reith Lectures in 1964. The lecture series, named for Lord John Reith, the first BBC director-general, began in 1948 with its first lecturer, philosopher Bertrand Russell. Its objective was "to advance public understanding and debate about significant issues of contemporary interest."[57] Bagrit needed to choose his issue.

In May 1964, shortly after the BBC announced him as the next Reith lecturer and four months before his first lecture, Bagrit shared with *The London Times* his intention to clarify the state and stakes of automation. He stated that he hoped to adjust two attitudes—"an irrational fear of the unknown, equaled only by a glib acceptance that with automation everything is going to be fine"—by explaining what automation can and cannot do. The piece repeatedly references "machine slaves," a phrase that evidently comes from Bagrit, since the reporter asks him to elaborate: "In his booklined study at his Hampstead house he went on to enlarge on that theme. The Greek civilization he believes reached the highest level of culture. It was a society built on slaves—human slaves. The world today has an opportunity to elevate man to such a standard by using machine slaves, and producing at the same time as that culture high human standards."[58] We find here the same line of thinking we saw in the 1830s with Timothy Walker, in the 1950s with Robert Hutchins, and in 1963 with Alice Mary Hilton: We have technology superior to what ancient Greek people had, and it allows us to be morally superior to them, too. The analogy between human slaves and machine slaves ostensibly speaks to that double superiority precisely because it is not meant as an equivalence: Obviously, enslaving machines rather than humans is preferable. But the question lingers: Why use the language of enslavement at all? It may simply serve as a way of thinking and talking about relations between humans and automated machine systems that makes distinctions between them absolute.

Over the course of six prime-time broadcasts on BBC3 from 7:30 to 8 p.m., from the beginning of November to the end of December 1964, Bagrit delivered his lectures under the title "The Age of Automation." They appeared the subsequent year as a book. In his first lecture/ chapter, "Automation: An Extension of Man," Bagrit conveys his version of the extension thesis: He credits radar with extending our eyes; telecommunications, our tongue and ears; mechanization, our muscles and body; and automation, a person's "own energies by the generation and transmission of power and his nervous system and his thinking and decision-making faculties."[59] Bagrit believes that an automated system of sensing, thinking, and decision-making gets us as close to a human's dynamic design as we have come yet, and that possibility induces him to stress automation as *extension*. If automation belongs to a sequence of technological means through which we keep extending ourselves, then it follows that automation will not replace us but instead allow us to reach beyond our usual grasp.

Anticipating arguments that automated systems will bind its users to them, Bagrit explains that such worries are not up to date. He grants as true that, because a given machine subjects a worker to its schedule, that worker "is in fact in many ways the slave of the machine," but he denies that this is the case with automation, which awaits the worker's commands.[60] Through programming and prompting, automated systems calculate, calibrate, compute, communicate, correct, and control, quickly and accurately, thereby freeing workers to focus on higher-order questions about a system's or a company's functioning. Issuing something like ad copy for the automation age, Bagrit insists that "the man in charge extends his faculties but remains himself. He does not become a slave. He stays in the centre of things and becomes the *real* master."[61] This master-slave dialectic broadens the mechanization-as-enslavement metaphor both Bagrit and McLuhan use to describe being unvaryingly at a machine's beck and call. Automation's extensions, Bagrit assures readers, make "better men, more competent men."[62] The comparative form of those adjectives matches the incremental mode of an extension, but Bagrit surges toward the superlative.

Bagrit concludes this first lecture by sharing his conviction "that automation has only one real purpose, which is to help us to become full human beings."[63] For him, the exemplum is "the ideal of the complete man," a concept he attributes to Baldesar Castiglione's early modern book *The Courtier*. Published in Italian in 1528, *The Courtier* takes the form of a dialogue among several men, adjudicated by Duchess Emilia, offering their vision of the perfect courtier, a royal adviser steadfast in virtue but agile in every other capacity. Most valued by Bagrit is the "varied" nature of this "man," including equal training of mind and body. Bagrit then returns to the culture he had celebrated in his interview with the *Times*: "This is the concept which the Greeks had too. But the high level reached by the Greek civilization was only possible because the routine, dulling work was done by slaves, who were not even regarded as human beings; they were looked upon as machines. They were never referred to as people, they did not really exist. They just happened to be there to do the chores."[64]

This casual normalization of the presence of enslaved people presumably presents the unbothered attitude of enslavers in a domestic or maybe even an agrarian context. (Thousands of enslaved people were forced to work in the silver mines south of Athens—not exactly a *chore*.) It was only because of this uncounted, discounted group of people that ancient Greek people of privilege could lead lives of cultivation. "Today, if we know where we are going and if we use the slave services of automation intelligently and courageously," Bagrit continues, "we have the chance of building a really high civilization for ourselves. And, when I say 'for ourselves,' I mean the whole community, not just a small élite on the Greek pattern. This is the essential purpose of automation."[65] With the bold application of automated slave labor, he reasons, we will have what the most privileged ancient Greeks had, but distributed evenly, and to be enjoyed by all. Everyone, not just the elite, will get to "become full human beings."[66] Bagrit's commitment to ancient Greece amounts to admiration for the ways in which a small subset of ancient Greek men styled their lives, and for the revaluing of the physical, intellectual, and social self-styling in the ancient Greek mode that arose in court culture many centuries later. His esteem comes down to the individual: a sound mind in a sound body. And it scales up to the agonistic: sound minds and bodies competing with each other to push the limits of human excellence. The democratic context of all this striving—at least for Athenians, and Bagrit's "Greece" seems to be Athens—goes unmentioned.

The subsequent lectures-turned-chapters purport to prepare the way for automation, specifying what needs to be in place for benefits to accrue. Again, Bagrit (and again independently, it seems) joins McLuhan in outlining an educational program for the automation age. He prizes the sort of imaginative foresight that can arise when a knowledge of history and a know-how trained on current technologies align, but he designates "a genuine breadth of education and a sense of social and human responsibility" as foremost priorities.[67] As with other commentators we have reviewed, Bagrit focuses on higher education, arguing that degrees should include classes in the history and philosophy of science. He believes that administrators of all sorts should be humanists who keep up their reading in science, and he chides the United States for letting too many business-degree-holders and technologists run things.[68] People should be educated for leisure as well, with the objective of developing "a large cultured public" that supports the arts.[69] Within their homes, he envisions people using their leisure time on DIY projects, designing and creating with their hands. Bagrit chastises those who fear the leisure of the future because they believe most humans to be "morons who cannot be trusted to spend half an hour by themselves unsupervised and undisciplined."[70] He estimates, though, that a general increase in leisure is still decades away, giving us "educational and attitude-forming breathing space," which suggests his own faith in the outcome was fairly uncertain.[71]

About a commitment to public life, and the sort of enhanced democratic participation that automation-granted free time could enable, Bagrit says nothing. He does address polities and policies—for instance, he uses the technology-boosting agonism between the Soviet Union and the United States to push for a national British policy on automation.[72] He insists that public automation policies must balance social justice with the growing wealth effected by technology. "Even in America," he observes, "while right wing groups maintain that the solution to all their ills lies in less governmental intervention, the responsibility of government for the distribution of created wealth is becoming steadily greater."[73] Bagrit worried that the American "attitude toward what is traditionally called 'government interference' is one of the most serious obstacles to dealing with problems before they get out of hand." And he wondered anxiously how that fact would play out, coupled with automation hitting black communities at the very same time that they were, as he puts it, "increasingly insisting on [their] rights."[74] This is the closest Bagrit comes to helping readers conjure images of active democratic participation—in this case, citizens calling upon their ostensibly democratic government to act in accordance with its own laws and founding principles. Bagrit does not seem to imagine anyone whose day is freed up by automation choosing to dedicate their time to intensified contributions to democratic life. That would seem to be the task of those left behind by technology.

Ben Seligman Thinks "Extension" Has Gone Far Enough

By 1966, enough time had passed for these attitudes toward extension and automation from 1964 to be metabolized into academic journals and books. In 1966, Donald Michael, who had coined "cybernation" in his 1962 book of that title and participated in Alice Mary Hilton's first cybercultural conference, reviewed Bagrit's published radio lectures. Largely supportive of Bagrit's promptings, Michael concludes his review with reference to the extension thesis: "Cybernation is a wonderful extension of our powers, but it could be that it extends one set of powers beyond our ability to provide *in time* a corresponding extension of our social powers sufficient to deal felicitously with its consequences."[75] Extending social infrastructures—policies, programs, curricula, protocols—takes a lot of time because it takes a lot of coordination and collaboration. It also depends on people trusting that social infrastructures and those who manage them can reliably and effectively challenge those who develop, market, and embed new technologies.

The most substantive breakdown of the extension thesis comes courtesy of Ben B. Seligman, in the form of his four-hundred-page cultural diagnosis and prognosis from 1966, *Most Notorious Victory: Man in an Age of Automation*. Like McLuhan and Bagrit, Seligman produced a notable cultural text in 1964: He was a coauthor of and signatory on the memorandum of the Ad Hoc Committee on the Triple Revolution. That summer, he also contributed a talk to Hilton's inaugural conference while serving as director of the Department of Education and Research of the Retail Clerks International Association and on the Board of Directors for the Institute for Cybercultural Research. Titled

"The Social Cost of Cybernation," the talk moves from the level of the individual worker displaced by automation to the level of social values displaced by logics of efficiency and control.[76]

Throughout his working years, Seligman moved back and forth between organized labor and the academy. In 1965, he was named professor of economics and director of the Labor Relations and Research Center at the University of Massachusetts, Amherst.[77] Several of what became chapters of *Most Notorious Victory* began as articles in *Dissent*, then as now the premier outlet for long-form essays about labor politics.

Seligman begins *Most Notorious Victory* by narrating the ascendance of automation. Using the body as the base, he makes a distinction between a tool and a machine: While early tools were "extensions of the hand, and they made the opposable thumb more powerful than it ever could be in a pure state of nature," with the machines of industrial capitalism "the poor were subhuman, appendages to the machine."[78] First, machines pushed out workers with craft, dexterity, and artistry and replaced them with workers without it; then machines pushed out those workers, too. All the while, the emerging middle class supported technological change, insisting that the working class would see improved living in a generation or two. The weight—and wait—of progress was unevenly borne.

Seligman sees the same dynamics at play with automation, and "the American worker is no more convinced than was his eighteenth-century ancestor that he ought to wait for the long run."[79] The title of one chapter, "Work Without Men," speaks to technologists' preferred order of things, whereas Seligman and other labor-minded thinkers and activists cannot ignore what that arrangement really means: men without work. He closes that chapter with two block quotes from the alarm-raising introduction of Wiener's *Cybernetics* and references the recurring line: "The engineers who build these instruments happily assure us that man will not become obsolete but rather will be 'excused from drudgery to concentrate on more human endeavors.' Unfortunately, the latter are seldom specified."[80] Throughout the book, Seligman calls the visions of these engineers—which extend beyond factory floors and into office buildings and beyond—one of utopia, paradise, or perfection.

One maker of happy assurances *does* specify what an end to drudgery will allow, and Seligman finds his notions particularly galling. "Sir Leon Bagrit, for example," Seligman writes, "asserts that automation permits man to work at his own pace because the machine reacts to man, who indeed is the master. He insists that we are approaching a golden age in which there will be an ample flow of material goods and opportunities to develop mind and body matched only by Periclean Athens. With all the work done by machines, everyone would be engaged in a task he wanted and preferred. Sir Leon contends that 'opponents' of automation are pessimists who will not trust human beings with riches."[81] Seligman dismisses Bagrit's views as "vacuous," and he sources the "optimism" of people like Bagrit in their "notion that the computer is merely an extension of man's senses."[82] The extension thesis minimizes the potential of computers to overtake and replace both humans and human ways of engaging with the world.

Bagrit's belief that automation would fully democratize the cultural conditions enjoyed by the restricted demos of ancient democratic Athens irks Seligman not only because it is fanciful on its face, but also because it ignores what work came to mean in the nearly two dozen centuries between Pericles and President Johnson. The intervening history of cultural attitudes toward work, he believes, must be confronted. Seligman provides one himself, starting with extant ancient Greek dispositions, philosophical ones in particular, where work "meant to be enslaved by necessity," and "the escape for the Greek was to become a slave owner and thus to gain victory over necessity."[83] In other words, freedom was purchased by forcing others to do the basic requirements of life. Seligman also knows his archaic Greek poetry (and his Arendt, whom he cites in an endnote): "Even Hesiod's oft-quoted line, 'Work is no disgrace,' was merely an admonition that a modicum of prosperity was essential to freedom. For the Greek, work was to be excluded from the human condition. Such was the view of the philosopher who gave Greek culture its flavor, even though the noise of the workshop and the market was not lacking."[84] Those who did the hammering, selling, weaving, sweeping, cooking were subordinated to those who did not, and that inequality secured equality among those who were then freed up to take on the matters of the polis.

Seligman continues his journey through the history of work. Christianity embraced it, as did Catholicism and Protestantism, in different ways, and by the nineteenth century, work was a cultural, secular good; it was necessary not only to support life but also to demonstrate virtuous living. The factory system, first mechanized and now increasingly automated, exploited the cultural role held by work while reducing its meaningfulness by converting the spontaneous craft of trained people into the standardized operations of machines. The inherited cultural weight of work no longer corresponded to what work offered workers. Work had become overvalued. Seligman estimates that "man may be working more today than did the ancient slave," the idea being not that the modern worker has taken on the ontology of a slave, but that working hours have expanded beyond what free people should endure.[85]

As we have seen before, it is a common impulse among all manner of cultural critics to reassess leisure. How might leisure earn cultural authority?

Seligman recognizes the popularity of the question: "It is sometimes said that leisure will enable man to regain his sense of self. Leisure is presumed to be one of the good things in life. It represents enjoyment and respite from work, and perhaps, as with the ancient Greeks, it will allow us to achieve understanding. We no longer disdain to use free time, for there is so much of it now."[86] As Seligman sees it, though, people who have this kind of time largely fill it and kill it, usually in ways that do not enhance those qualities that automation apologists identify as uniquely human or outside of capitalist logics. "Dragooned into leisure," he writes, "man must conform to the dictates of a culture that is thoroughly pervaded by the technicist ethos. . . . In this atmosphere there can be no freedom."[87] Leisure is busy. People patch up and update their houses, jobs for which there are professionals; people use the money they get from working to buy all sorts of expensive, high-commitment gear, such as camping equipment; people fine-tune their golf games in the hope of playing with and impressing their bosses.

However pathetic Seligman may take them to be, those leisure misfires are not as serious as the employment challenges posed by ageism and racism, which he examines largely in terms of training and credentialing.[88] In a chapter called "Big Brother Tries," Seligman outlines how the US American government has both directly and indirectly supported technological development but not devoted an equal amount of policy attention to the protection and relief of workers. It is not that the government had not made *any* effort; Jerry Prout has detailed the presidential and congressional commissions on mechanization and automation from Roosevelt through Johnson.[89] But, as Prout puts it, those commissions are always "chasing automation" rather than getting out in front of it and laying down the paths upon which it must travel. Instead, they are perpetually behind.

Seligman knew that fact well. He believed that the guardedly optimistic tone of the report of the 1955 automation hearings (discussed in chapter 1 above) accounts somewhat for the matter failing to receive policy attention again until Kennedy, whose efforts were taken up by Johnson in January 1964. That spring, Seligman had been a signatory of the Ad Hoc Committee's memorandum on the Triple Revolution (as I discussed in the previous chapter). Reflecting on its reception, Seligman writes that the facets of the memorandum that were most mocked in 1964—foremost among them, the suggestion of a guaranteed income—were now being forwarded by mainstream, even conservative, economists in the form of the negative income tax. He thinks that the proposals of the Ad Hoc Committee remain worth trying, especially that of guaranteed income, since, with it, "some people might discover real joy in doing things without the pressure of need: They would indeed have genuine leisure."[90] In Seligman's view, what characterizes the US American government's response to automation is "pathetic inadequacy to the problems it has created" by fostering technology and not its workers.[91]

In his book's title, Seligman declares the victory of technology. It is not that technology had vanquished every other social power. Instead, it is that technology amplified the social power that business had already acquired. In his view, conditions were such that "the victor will be he who breathes the ethic of efficiency—and it is he who controls the machine."[92] Efficiency—that core, dehumanizing business ethic—was winning the day because it had won the work.

When the Social Engineers Are Computer Engineers

Featuring briefly but meaningfully in the conclusion of *Most Notorious Victory* is the 1965 book *The New Utopians: A Study of System Design and Social Change* by sociologist Robert Boguslaw. The design of the book winks: The number and title of each chapter appear to be typed onto a computer punch card, and the cover features a superimposition of punched holes over silhouettes of striding people. The computer punch card was an emblem of the age; students at Berkeley the previous year had torn up IBM punch cards in protest of the way universities were incorporating computers (that is, largely turning education into management).[93] Setting out to study "problems in the analysis and design of contemporary large-scale computer-based command and control systems," Boguslaw was struck by how closely the designers and managers of such systems resembled utopian thinkers of the past. It was a terrifying recognition, and perhaps not an obvious one. He meets nay-sayers head-on in the opening paragraph of the book:

> Utopia is a place that seems to belong either to the past or to the future, and we tend to think of utopians as being either starry-eyed philosophers or wild-eyed reformers. But there is a new breed of utopians afoot, threatening to rush down all the exciting pathways and blind alleys frequented by utopians since the days of Plato. These are the people who are known by such titles as system engineer, computer manufacturer, operations researcher, computer programmer, data processing specialist, or, more simply, system designer.[94]

He prefers to call them "social engineers," a term technologists preferred to reserve for activists and organizers. It is a title he suspects will amuse or shock the technologists, as will the "new utopians." But he offers support. The systems they plan, maintain, and use "contain all the critical features of classical utopias save one. They are designed to deal with some perceived limitations in the existing organization of men and materials, they attempt to improve an existing state of affairs, and they frequently are utterly visionary in concept and disappointing in execution."[95] What they are missing is the core orientation toward humankind that is typical of the designs of old utopians: "The new utopians are concerned with non-people and with people-substitutes."[96] Their lack of concern for souls and stomachs, the foci of earlier utopian planning, and the proprietary corporate context of their systems means that sociologists, even those specializing in the functional analysis of systems, will not be invited to comment until after a given system is already humming—and even then they will not have been invited. The same goes for policymakers. And regulators.

Boguslaw proposes that these new social engineers be acknowledged as such, and he specifies the human costs of adjustment that must be built into the construction and implementation of any large-scale system. Essentially, these adjustment plans are either preparatory or mitigatory in nature and include mental health care, since losing a job to automation unsettles a person's sense of self, might result in geographical or social uprooting, and could result in having to learn a new set of skills or earn new credentials, all of which cause mental strain.[97] Mainly, the people encircled by these new systems need to know they have some control over their own lives: "The notion that those strange men who write equations on blackboards are the real arbiters of all our destinies is one that must be obliterated in any society that wishes to continue functioning in even an approximately democratic fashion."[98] People power cannot be sustained when people feel like they have no control over their present and future paths.

He concludes of the new utopianism that "its greatest threat consists precisely in its potential as a means for extending the control of man over man."[99] "Extension" is not a keyword for Boguslaw as it was for McLuhan and Bagrit; nonetheless, its appearance in the final line of *The New Utopians* feels like a chiding reminder of the many things that escape their grasp.

5

Aristotle's Line on Automation

It is likely many things even beyond the likely will come to be.
ARISTOTLE, *De arte poetica liber*

Karl Marx wrote all three volumes of *Capital* during his exile in England, the land of machines.[1] For Marx, a single machine represented not an extension of the human but the incorporation of a worker, who became an appendage of it.[2] Multiple machines integrated into a factory powered an economic system that called for scientific study, not utopian forecasting of a future adjusted to socialist abundance.[3] Criticism of the factory—the factory having instantiated industrial capitalism—pervades *Capital*, but the most concentrated analysis appears in chapter 15 of what is considered the most readable volume, the first, and is entitled "Machinery and Large-scale Industry."

To build the critique of political economy featured in chapter 15, Marx draws upon several authorities, including ancient ones. A case in point is a passage that contains a shortened quotation from one ancient Greek writer and a reference to another, one of them much better known than the other, then as now:

> "If," dreamed Aristotle, the greatest thinker of antiquity, "if every tool, when summoned, or even by intelligent anticipation, could do the work that befits it, just as the creations of Daedalus moved of themselves, then there would be no need either of apprentices for the master craftsmen, or of slaves for the lords." And Antipater, a Greek poet of the time of Cicero, hailed the water-wheel for grinding corn, that most basic form of all productive machinery, as the liberator of female slaves and the restorer of the golden age.[4]

Aristotle is, of course, one of the most-referenced philosophers of the ancient world, while Antipater of Thessalonica, hundreds of years after Aristotle's death, wrote short poems that can be read only because a few of them were plucked for anthologies. But both Aristotle's dreaming and Antipater's hailing of automated or mechanized tools demonstrate the longevity of the expectation that such tools will disrupt labor distributions and make the work of those who work for someone else, by choice or by force, unnecessary.

Nearly a hundred years after the first volume of *Capital* appeared in 1867, a garbled, even shorter version of the truncated line of Aristotle that Marx had used appeared on the title page of a book that grappled with the topic of automation: "When looms weave by themselves man's slavery will end." So begins the 1961 study, *Automation: Its Impact on Business and People*, by Walter Buckingham, then professor of economics and director of the School of Industrial Management at Georgia Institute of Technology.[5] Its form makes loom labor metonymic of all tool-based labor and enslaved people metonymic of all people.

The Marx and Buckingham quotations from Aristotle are similar but significantly different. So what? The poem from Antipater also receives attention, however unavoidably brief due to its obscure origins.

Aristotle on Automated Tools

Whatever its form, any line about automated tools that is attributed to Aristotle has originated from what modern editors mark as the fourth section of the first book of Aristotle's *Politics*. As a whole, *The Politics* describes and prescribes the best conditions for collective living at the level of the polis, that celebrated unit from whose public activities enslaved people, free women, and metics were excluded.[6]

This section of *The Politics* also contains a crucial part of Aristotle's notorious defense of enslavement. It comes when he settles into the smallest element of the polis, the *oikos*, or household. In its "perfect, complete state," he opines, it comprises both free and enslaved people.[7] He argues against a view held by unnamed contemporaries that for one person to enslave others by force is not natural, but that it is conventional or legal if one posits the existence of natural slaves, whom it is "advantageous and just" to dominate.[8] Wherever he was exactly when he composed *Politics*, or whether his Athens-based students scribbled down his lessons on the subject while he spoke, Aristotle lived in a cultural stratum sustained by slavery. Writing of ancient Athens in particular, classicist Peter Garnsey points out that "Athenian democracy and democratic ideology fed off slavery. . . . Slavery both provided the economic necessities of life for a number of Athenians, and gave them the freedom to pursue 'the good life' in the sphere of politics."[9] It was this state of affairs Aristotle was defending when he made his case for slavery. That the text itself contains evidence that Aristotle was entering into an active debate—about whether anyone is a slave by nature, or whether it is merely a status imposed by norms and laws—is reason enough not to contextualize Aristotle's views on slavery as "what everybody thought back then"; there were other positions to hold. Even if the view that "slave" was only a legal status would not have changed the fact of enslavement, it might have prevented Aristotle's articulation of the lethal notion of essential slaveness.

Aristotle turns next to property and tools, in a discussion that culminates with the automation line. Here, Aristotle designates property (*hē ktēsis*) as "a part of the household and the art of acquiring property [*hē ktētikē*] a part of household management (for without the necessities it is impossible to live as well as to live well)," and he distinguishes between "tools without and with souls [*ton d' organon ta men apsucha ta de empsucha*]" by using a nautical (technically, a cybernetic) example: For the steersman (*kubernētēs*), a rudder is a soulless tool and a man stationed at a ship's bow an ensouled tool. He continues: "A piece of property is a tool for life [*to ktēma organon pros zōēn esti*], and property is a multitude of tools, and a slave is a sort of ensouled piece of property [*ho doulos ktēma ti empsychon*], and an assistant is pretty much a tool for tools [*hōsper organon pro organōn*]."[10] In Aristotle's noticeably (and uncharacteristically) hedged classification, assistants are animated tools, sort of, and enslaved people animated property, sort of.[11] The key difference—other than not enslaved and enslaved, of course—is that positing assistants as tools puts them in league with production (with the making of things), just as positing enslaved people as property puts them in league with action (with the doing of things), which, in a household context, means attending to the ever-recurring labors that sustain life for all and enable the good life for the few.

In the lines that immediately follow, Aristotle imagines conditions under which enslaved people would be unnecessary, even within a system not troubled *enough* by the practice of enslaving people to discontinue it on the grounds of its being, contra Aristotle, against nature. Assistants, too, would become a thing of the past.

> Think of it this way: if each tool could when requested [*keleusthen*], or by sensing in advance [*proaisthanomenon*], carry out its own work [*to autou ergon*], like the creations of Daedalus, as they say, or the tripods of Hephaestus, which the poet says "enter self-moved [*automatous*] the gatherings of the gods,"—if, in that way, the combs of looms kept the web tight by themselves [*autai*] and picks played citharas, there would be no need for project-planners to have

> assistants and masters slaves [*ouden an edei oute toīs architektosin hupēretōn oute toīs despotais doulōn*].[12]

Is this prospect meant to sound unlikely, even far-fetched? The invocation of two mythical craftsmen suggests it is at least fanciful. Daedalus is best known in our time as the master craftsman whom King Minos brought to Crete to construct the labyrinth that trapped the Minotaur, and who was grounded on Crete until he made wing suits for himself and his too-high-flying son, Icarus. But Daedalus was famous in the fourth century BCE for the ingenuity he showed in his design of open-eyed statues that moved (or, much more probably, looked to be in motion); Aristotle is alluding to them here.[13] The lines about the craftsman god Hephaestus come from book 18 of the *Iliad*, when the sea goddess Thetis goes to Hephaestus's Olympian workshop to ask him to make new armor for her son Achilles.[14] She observes Hephaestus hard at work on the wheels of the golden, self-moving tripods. For his everyday examples, Aristotle selects wool-working and music-making, the first being the work of both free (though, of course, housebound) and enslaved women, the second being the work of lower-class citizens or enslaved people.

Thomas Allen Sinclair, whose translation of *The Politics* was published in 1962, well into the early era of computerized automation, summarized the section this way: "The argument really only amounts to saying that in any society there must be hewers of wood and drawers of water and that such work should be done by those best fitted by nature for menial tasks—unless of course a Daedalus or a Hephaestus can provide the right kind of automation."[15] Eating, drinking, and keeping warm are embodied necessities that require labor, again and again; since the need will not let up, it is convenient for Aristotle to posit a type of person for whom attending to it is not inappropriate and is, in fact, natural.[16] As Sinclair turns to the ingenious craftsmen, whom he fashions as antecedents of tech geniuses, the ambiguous valence of his "of course" pairs well with his source: Is Aristotle making a mocking concession to a near-impossibility, or is he gesturing toward a possible technological future? In "Did the Greeks Believe in Their Robots?," Martin Devecka claims that Aristotle *did* believe in the robots he mentions, that "[he] did see automata as presenting a real possibility of liberation, that they counted for him as a kind of technology that was at least possible, if was not yet real."[17] Instead of wondering what Aristotle *really* thought about automata, a more measured interpretive stance would be to emphasize that their actualization was the only condition he could envision under which assistants and enslaved people would be deemed unnecessary by those who used them. Further, whoever wants to greet such an outcome as "liberation" should note, first, that Aristotle never uses that word, and, second, that the beneficiary of whatever freedom we want to read into this scenario cannot be taken for granted.

Quotation Marx

The first book of *The Politics* was pulled into nineteenth-century debates about labor in the United States as well as Germany. For example, finding in Aristotle a stalwart defender of their status quo, apologists for slavery in the United States referenced and quoted him avidly. Take Thomas R. Dew, one of several Southern professors who used their learning to find, and their professional status to spotlight, support for enslavement in ancient texts.[18] In 1832, in *An Essay on Slavery*, he gushed, "Aristotle, the greatest philosopher of Antiquity, and a man of as capacious mind as in the world ever produced, was a warm advocate of slavery—maintaining that it was reasonable, necessary, and natural, and accordingly, in his model of a republic, there were to be comparatively few freemen served by many slaves."[19] Dew names the key elements of Aristotle's warm advocacy but does not venture a close reading of *The Politics* itself.

Offering an ostensibly scholarly treatment of the slavery-related sections of book 1 of *The Politics* was George Frederick Holmes, a professor of ancient languages before he discovered the new field of sociology. In his 1850 essay "Observations on a Passage in the Politics of Aristotle Relative to Slavery," and preceded by an "apropos" reference to the second edition of Dew's essay (published the year before), Holmes reflects upon a line from *Politics*, book 1, section 5, that serves as his epigraph and touchstone throughout the piece: "Nature has clearly designed some men for freedom and others for slavery:—and with respect to the latter, slavery is both just and beneficial."[20] Why Holmes would spend time with a visibility argument does not take much guessing: Whereas Aristotle struggled to locate a static visible criterion of someone who was obviously a natural slave, to nineteenth-century enslavers the natural inferiority of enslaved people was outwardly manifested in their blackness. And thus Aristotle's views were racialized.

Holmes openly regrets not having been able to consult several German works of scholarship, including the 1821 dissertation of K. W. Göttling titled "De Notione Servitutis apud Aristotelem" (for his PhD from the University of Jena, which would be Marx's alma mater, too), a reminder that Germany was the powerhouse in the study of the ancient Mediterranean world, especially Greece.[21] Proslavery writers do not appear to engage with Aristotle's lines about automatic machines until later on in the century, well after the seditious South had lost the Civil War; in fact, it is Holmes who does so, in his 1884 book, *A Science of Society*.[22] Abolitionists seem to have found it earlier.[23]

Marx knew the works of Aristotle well.[24] He may even have known that landowners in the US South were using Aristotle to justify their continuation of slavery. Otherwise, it is a wild coincidence that, on the same page in volume 3 of *Capital*, Marx packs in a line from *Politics* book 1, section 7, in ancient Greek, which he intersperses with capitalist terminology in German, *and* quotes at length from a speech given in 1859 by a slavery defender named O'Conor that applies a natural slavery argument to enslaved black people.[25]

Marx, as I mentioned, also found Aristotle useful on the topic of work and machines, and he added to Aristotle's commentary on automation a reference to the later Greek poet Antipater's poem about the watermill releasing enslaved women from the labor of grinding corn. Here is the full epigram:

> No need to put a hand to the mill, corn-grinding slave-women; sleep in,
> even if the breaking voice of roosters announces dawn.
> For Demeter has commanded nymphs do the work of your hands;
> and they, leaping down from the highest point of the wheel,
> whirl its axle, which, with its radiating spokes,
> constantly turns the heavy hollow of the Nisyrian millstones.
> We taste the ancient life once more,
> learning to feast on the doings of Demeter, without the grind.[26]

Aristotle imagines a self-operating machine moving out of myth and into a social world of both enslaved and not-enslaved human helpers, but Antipater beholds a machine of his own time and tells the enslaved women who manually grind corn to snooze, since the nymphs—a poetic personification of water—who serve the harvest goddess will work the watermill. Antipater's lines end with a soft primitivism redolent of the golden race of Hesiod's *Works and Days*: The earth yields sustenance without needing to be worked by humans. We know that Antipater spoke too soon for his own time. How applicable to the nineteenth century are these very old speculations about labor relations under automation?

In a playful anachronism, Marx scoffs that both Aristotle and Antipater "understood nothing of political economy and Christianity," making their prognostications not very applicable.[27] The political economy, when capitalist, uses machinery—which was not truly automated in Marx's time—to lengthen the working day, not to shorten it, and certainly not to eliminate it altogether. In terms of Christianity, though the likes of Aristotle and Antipater "may perhaps have excused the slavery of one person as a means to the full human development of another," being pre-Christian "they lacked the specifically Christian qualities which would have enabled them to preach the slavery of the masses in order that a few crude and half-educated parvenues might become 'eminent spinners,' 'extensive sausage-makers' and 'influential shoe-black dealers.' "[28] As we have seen, achieving full humanity as defined by pre-Christian elites required time away from, or entirely without, the tasks of laboring and working, but many ancient people could not see a way to do that without enslaving others, except by calling upon machines that either did not exist or could release only particular enslaved people from a particular task. Christianized people of the laboring class, on the other hand—particularly those infused with the spirt of the "Protestant ethic," as Max Weber would later call it—were made to embrace a humanity of humility and deference in which the only socially and religiously sanctioned high performance is tied to the work of making or selling everyday things. That Marx refers to such a state as "slavery" shows he approaches the word in a general sense as *restricted or denied freedom* imposed by cultural and material conditions, even while he acknowledges chattel slavery in the ancient world and in his own century.[29]

Marx's pairing of Antipater with Aristotle may just have been him showing off, since both poet and poem were (and remain) obscure, but Antipater's poem is credited as the first nontechnical, utopian reference to the watermill; as such, it offers an ideal analogue for Marx, since the new technologies of his time were occasioning similar outlooks on the return of a drudgery-free golden age.[30] The general view of Marx's attitude toward technology is that its embeddedness in capitalism is the problem, rather than anything about technology itself that inclines toward asymmetry in human economic relations. Langdon Winner's take that a core objective of a communist polity "would be to liberate technology for its truly human function and to make it impossible that pathological formulations of the past could ever be reestablished" is representative.[31] Certainly, Marx writes that "machinery does not just act as a superior competitor to the worker, always on the point of making him superfluous. It is a power inimical to him, and capital proclaims this fact loudly and deliberately, as well as making use of it. . . . It would be possible to write a whole history of the inventions made since 1830 for the sole purpose of providing capital with weapons against working-class revolt."[32] As an example, he quotes from testimony given during a trade unions inquiry in 1868 by the inventor of the steam hammer, who boasts of being able to cut his workforce numbers in half and noticeably increase profits due to "the introduction of self-acting tool machinery."[33] Marx indicates that capitalists use technology to threaten and to harm workers.

Marxist labor reformers learn about the Aristotle and Antipater quotes through direct contact with Marx—sometimes close contact. One such reformer was the Cuban-born, France-reared, multiracial, multilingual, self-proclaimed revolutionary Paul Lafargue, who was also Marx's secretary and son-in-law, and the cofounder of the first French Marxist party. Throughout the early 1880s, Lafargue worked on a pamphlet titled *Le Droit à la Paresse: Réfutation du Droit au Travail de 1848* (*The Right to Be Lazy: Refutation of the Right to Work of 1848*).[34] As the title indicates, Lafargue offers a spirited rejoinder to the debates of several decades earlier about whether the French government ought to guarantee a right to work. Socialists were among the most enthusiastic proponents. In a chapter of the pamphlet caustically titled "The Blessings of Work," Lafargue sneers that they rallied around the phrase "the right to work" for no more than twelve hours a day as if it were a revolutionary anthem: "Shame on the French proletariat! Only slaves would have been capable of such baseness. It would take twenty years of capitalist civilization for a Greek of heroic times to think up such a humiliation."[35] The ancient frame of this accusation draws force from Lafargue's first chapter, "A Dangerous Dogma" (i.e., the dogma of work), where he calls upon the fact that "the Greeks, too, in their great era had nothing but contempt for work. Slaves alone were permitted to work," a factually incorrect but frequent assertion in the nineteenth century, and he highlights that "the philosophers of antiquity taught contempt for work, that degradation of the free man."[36] He names Aristotle as belonging to that era, but he goes to Jesus for the model of idleness, exemplified by Jesus's reference in the book of Matthew to the worry-free birds and lilies.

Throughout the pamphlet, Lafargue refers to workers in capitalist orders as those who "play the part of a machine" as "our own miserable servants of the machine" and are denied thanks, breaks, passions, or joy.[37] To begin the third section of the pamphlet, titled "The Consequences of Overproduction," he furnishes the entire Antipater poem, upon which he reflects: "Sadly, the leisure the pagan poet envisioned has not come to pass. The blind passion and perverse murderousness of work has transformed the machine from an instrument of emancipation into an instrument that enslaves free beings: its productivity impoverishes them."[38] In capitalist conditions, machines intensify an ethos for work exploited by capitalists and manifesting in workers redoubling their efforts in a hopeless effort to rival machines.

The prison edition of *The Right to Be Lazy* features an appendix framed as a counter to the Christian moralists of the time, who promote the dogma of work, but not to everyone. To show them their dogma "scoffed at and scorned," Lafargue reaches back to pre-Christian antiquity.[39] He pulls paragraphs from Herodotus's *Histories*, Plato's *Republic*, Xenophon's *Economics*, Livy's history of Rome (*Ab urbe condita*), Cicero's treatment of dutiful actions (*De Officiis*), and the very lines from Aristotle's *Politics* that Marx had cited (plus a few more). He saves Aristotle for last. Before quoting in full Aristotle's lengthy sentence on automation, Lafargue acknowledges that not everyone of his time is looking to Aristotle for moral advice: "It has been disdainfully written that 'the prejudice of slavery dominated the minds of Pythagoras and Aristotle.'" But Lafargue credits Aristotle for what he calls foresight:

> Aristotle's dream is our reality. Our machines breathe fire, have limbs of steel, never grow weary, never need to sleep. They are marvelously productive and behave docilely—even as they go about their sacred work. And yet the minds of the great capitalist philosophers continue to be dominated by the prejudice of wage labor, the worst sort of slavery. They still don't understand that the machine is humanity's savior, the god who will redeem man from the *sordidae artes* [lowly/grubby crafts] and the payroll, the god who will give him leisure and liberty.[40]

Using "dream," like Marx does, to name Aristotle's conditional, Lafargue describes the real machines of his time, giving them bodies—not to which workers should be grafted, but from which they should be separated totally. Highlighting traits that capitalists value in workers, he praises the inexhaustibility, generativity, and docility of machines. He ascribes the reluctance of capitalism's champions to write about machines in these terms to the stubborn hold of the wage labor system, which he names "the worst sort of slavery." He then moves to the singular, deifying "the machine" and endowing it with salvific qualities: It takes upon itself the work of the world. The machine redeems and frees all of humanity. That is Lafargue's vision.

Two other occasions of quoting Marx quoting Aristotle during that decade merit mention. In the first instance, the quotes self-reportedly catalyzed the radical thinking of a worker infamously executed by the US American government; the second features in the first history of the working class in the ancient world. August Vincent Theodore Spies, a German-born Marxist labor organizer sentenced to death for a role attributed to him in the Haymarket bombing in Chicago on May 4, 1886, writes in his prison autobiography of the study he undertook upon recognizing how many "people were wasting their lives in drudgery, accompanied with want and misery."[41] He names the works of his foremost teachers, whose lessons he found "corroborated everywhere": Henry Thomas Buckles's *History of Civilization*, Lewis Morgan's *Ancient Society*, and Marx's *Capital*.[42] His "attention was attracted" by Marx's quotation of passages from Aristotle and Antipater (which he writes as "Antipatos," as Marx does in the German). Referring to Aristotle's future-directed thinking, he asks: "Had this time, long ago anticipated by the great thinker, not come? Yes, it had. There were the machines. . . . But master and slave still existed. The question arose in my mind, is their existence still necessary?"[43] That machines had not altered the lives of workers for the better troubled Spies. His use of "master and slave" to describe capitalist and worker follows the language of Aristotle and the idiom of the socialist labor movement. Later, Spies recounts a debate about the eight-hour workday and the role "labor-saving machines" may play in establishing it.[44] Several times in early May 1886, Chicago police violently disrupted activities supporting a general strike in favor of an eight-hour workday. On May 4, a few minutes after Spies spoke publicly, he heard a loud sound he believed to have been made by a cannon. A bomb had been thrown at the police, and, on the basis of his being an immigrant socialist, Spies was prosecuted, convicted, and executed by the state in 1887.

That same year saw the publication of the first volume of *The Ancient Lowly: A History of the Ancient Working People from the Earliest Known Period to the Adoption of Christianity by Constantine*, by US American socialist Cyrenus Osborne Ward. The author had circulated it privately first for want of a publisher. He found one in Charles Hope Kerr, who lived in Chicago and was distressed by the violence directed at the Haymarket labor activists. Kerr was the son of a classicist, and his own academic expertise was in Romance languages; he translated Lafargue's *The Right to Be Lazy* into English and published it in 1907.[45] Ward intended *The Ancient Lowly* for a new sort of history buff, one who seeks "historical fragments, obscure hints and allusions and queer palæographs on tablets of bronze, stone, earthenware and other objects, containing inscriptions, symbols and emblems, even rules showing the existence of labor societies through the past civilization."[46] A history of ancient laborers exists to show that laborers recognized their unique status and banded together long before capitalism, but it must be pieced together by faint traces and clues. Ward, an autodidact across many domains of knowing, making, and doing, had been a speech- and pamphlet-writer for the short-lived International Workingmen's Association; his membership card had been signed by Marx himself, perhaps when Ward met him during travels on IWA business. Subsequently, he was hired by the US Department of Labor to do translation and library work. He wrote his notes for all his scholarly projects in a code that has yet to be cracked.[47]

Both volumes of *The Ancient Lowly* refer to the line of Aristotle from book 1, section 4 of *The Politics*, about self-moving machines that make assistants and enslaved people unnecessary. In the first volume, which is dedicated to enslaved people and their rebellions and to organized trade unions, it appears in the opening chapter, "The Taint of Work." It is because of the taint of work that ancient elites never wrote anything favorable or generous about laborers, especially not enslaved ones. Yet Ward credits "the great philosopher Aristotle" for "his startling prediction that 'slave labor may become obsolete.'"[48] In the second volume, whose subtitle is "The Origins of Socialism," Ward references Aristotle's "hope that shuttles, spinning wheels and quillers might some day propel themselves" within a discussion about the helots of Sparta, who were "abject and detested slaves; mere labor saving machines to keep the masters alive."[49] Ward's Aristotle wishes that the machines were more advanced than they were. Later in that volume, Ward introduces Marx's engagement with *Politics* 1.4 by saying that the way Marx brings Aristotle into his analysis "contrasts the noble purposes and ideals animating ancient society with the lust of cruelty which capitalism breeds."[50] It is, of course, nonsense to bracket off antiquity from cruelty, and, for his part, Aristotle is not holding reluctantly to the practice of enslavement solely because self-moving tools have yet to move out of the *Iliad*. But, in the way Marx uses the quotation, we do perceive that Aristotle seemed unable to imagine an economic structure that would see workers bound to machines rather than freed by them.

In the socialist texts of Lafargue, Spies, and Ward, the act of quoting Marx quoting Aristotle doubly authorizes the view that machines can deliver freedom from work—but not under capitalism. The decades that pass between Marx's quotation of Aristotle and their quotation of his quotation of Aristotle exhibit the situation: Even over time, technology will never have this labor-lifting effect on its own. Rather, socialists must agitate for the conditions that would make machines beneficial to workers.

A Brief Interlude

Aristotle's line on automation does not always appear to pass through Marx. In 1934, for example, critic Lewis Mumford paraphrases it in *Technics & Civilization* during his explanation of what he calls the "nullification of skill" that occurs along the way as a "human function first becomes specialized, then mechanized, and finally automatic or at least semi-automatic."[51] The prospect of the fully automatic points to an ideal: "the elimination of work: the universal achievement of leisure. In his discussion of slavery, Aristotle said that when the shuttle wove by itself and the plectrum played by itself chief workman would not need helpers nor masters slaves. At the time he wrote, he believed that he was establishing the eternal validity of slavery; but for us today he was in reality justifying the existence of the machine."[52] Mumford issues the reminder that ancient Athenians hated the very sort of tasks—those marked by "unwilling drudgery" and "sedentary routine"—that machines are best suited to perform. He judges that the "potentiality, still so far from effective achievement of mankind at large," of machines to take on the burden of such tasks, "is perhaps the largest justification of the mechanical developments of the last thousand years."[53] Like Marx, Mumford addresses the monkey wrench in the works: "In the translation of technical improvements into social processes, however, the machine has undergone a perversion: instead of being utilized as an instrument of life, it has tended to become an absolute. . . . The machine has been valued because—it increased the employment of the machine. And such employment was the source of profits, power, and wealth to the new ruling classes, benefits which hitherto gone to traders or to those who monopolized the land."[54] The new capitalists are not concerned with how machines might improve the lives of workers.

In *The Human Condition*, Hannah Arendt engages *The Politics* 1.4 in her section "Labor," where she argues that the inescapable burdens of labor can never be fully avoided by using tools, instruments, and gadgets. She cites Aristotle as "a curious and unexpected testimony to" that view, to which she accords the status of prediction:

> In a half-fanciful, half-ironical mood, Aristotle once imagined what has long since become a reality, namely that "every tool could perform its own work when ordered . . . like the statues of Daedalus or the tripods of Hephaestus, which, says the poet, 'of their own accord entered the assembly of the gods.'" Then, "the shuttle would weave and the plectrum touch the lyre without a hand to guide them." This, he goes on to say, would indeed mean the craftsman would no longer need human assistants, but it would not mean that household slaves could be dispensed with.

However, this is *not* what Aristotle goes on to say, which is that "there would be no need for project-planners to have assistants *and masters slaves*." Arendt, though, takes a hard look at his examples and finds them not to be classifiable as what she considers labor. The making of a statue, tripod, or shroud will reach completion. The playing of a song will end. But the cycle of labor is unceasing, "and the only 'instrument' equal to it would have to be a *perpetuum mobile*, that is, the *instrumentum vocale* which is alive and 'active' as the living organism which it serves."[55] She does not think that Aristotle's technical imagination or our technical abilities can get there. In essence, she uses partial quotation and other parts of *Politics* 1.4 and 1.5 to argue there is no technological escape from labor. Someone will be doing it.

At her 1964 conference, Alice Mary Hilton also alludes to Aristotle's automation line, and in a form that makes it about the labor all humans do, not particular subordinated ones:

> The idea that man must have the leisure to work if he is to achieve his human task was born at least twenty-five centuries ago, when Aristotle whistfully [*sic*] dreamed of a shuttle that would glide by itself across the loom. We are on the

> threshold of man's ancient dreams—we have the shuttle that glides across the loom under its own guidance, the pails of water and brooms conjured up by the sorcerer's apprentice, the genie in the lamp—and we can see that we are at the cross roads [*sic*]. There are two paths leading out of man's tiny little warren: one to the heights men have dreamed of in their Golden Ages, the other to the abyss man has always feared.[56]

She hopes we won't be bashful bunnies now, when Aristotle's dream is finally coming true.

Walter Buckingham and the Garbled Aristotle Quote

A decade past mid-century, Aristotle's line emerges in a new, highly transportable form. Professor of industrial management at the Georgia Institute of Technology for most of his career, Walter Buckingham spent a good many hours before national legislators in the 1950s and 1960s as they endeavored to understand the present and potential future of automation. For example, during the joint congressional hearings on automation and technological change in the fall of 1955, he spoke directly after automation-popularizer John Diebold and offered his views on automation as an economist.[57] The year 1961 saw the publication of Buckingham's first book, *Automation: Its Impact on Business and People*, which was an outgrowth of his testimony and teaching. Its title is very similar to a planning pamphlet authored by Diebold in 1959, *Automation: Its Impact on Business and Labor*, and it does not seem to have been the original title, either; in the author's note to Buckingham's 1960 article "The *Human Side* of Automation," the title of his forthcoming book is listed as *Economic and Social Impact of Automation*.[58] As previously mentioned, it features as its epigraph:

> "When looms weave by themselves man's slavery will end."—Aristotle

When we place beside it my translation of Aristotle's line on automation, we can plainly see the dramatic reduction in word count:

> Think of it this way: if each tool could when requested, or by sensing in advance, carry out its own work, like the creations of Daedalus, as they say, or the tripods of Hephaestus, which the poet says "enter self-moved the gatherings of the gods,"—if, in that way, the combs of looms kept the web tight by themselves and picks played citharas, there would be no need for project-planners to have assistants and masters slaves.

Before looking in detail at what happened to make this sentence epigraph-length, how do we classify this new form? Is it a misquotation? It would have plenty of company; in addition to having been amply quoted, Aristotle has been misquoted amply. Here's the range of appraisals that classicist Joel Christensen has made of quotations popularly attributed to Aristotle that someone who reads ancient Greek would be hard pressed to find in Aristotle: "This is almost Aristotle"; "This one is likely a mistranslation"; "A bit of an elaborated translation of an essentially Aristotelian idea"; "Willful twisting"; "Really popular misattribution"; "Absolutely no basis"; "This is totally super-capitalist, corporate double-speak nonsense. It does not even remotely sound like Aristotle. I am not sure where it comes from and I cannot find it debunked, but I will keep looking"; "No. I don't even need to look this up. No. No. No."[59] This taxonomy could be trotted out to face any quote attributed to Aristotle that is not *quite* Aristotle, from 1948 (when George Orwell coined "double-speak") on. The 1960s see engagement with Aristotle's expressed position on animate machines and enslavement—and that position is garbled nearly beyond recognition, but for the attribution.

Conventionally, quotations are no more than a few lines, but, for a quotation to make a good epigraph, it must do a lot in a very few words. That requirement pertains not only to the inverse relationship that must obtain between depth of meaning and length of form, but also to the high likelihood that the quote, having originated from someone deemed authoritative, has been used before, giving the few words a trailing, murmuring entourage one can tune in to—or ignore. The mere presence of an epigraph has an effect: It signals a conversation that started some time back is still underway. From the epigraph itself, readers find out to whom a writer thinks they are talking.[60]

That no less an authority than Aristotle wrote about automatic tools gives everyone who writes about automation a way to gesture toward the longevity of such a vision and dramatize its potential fruition, given the state of machines at the time of writing. Having searched for "when looms weave by themselves man's slavery will end" across all published English translations of Aristotle's *Politics* to 1962 and in popular quotation books from the same span, I have been unable to find it. Indeed, I cannot locate that exact line at all before Buckingham used it in 1961. Though I should very much like to track it down (and perhaps I have: It starts with Buckingham), I am more interested in the fact of the transformation of Aristotle's line than in identifying its transformer and their intentions.

Though the category of "misquotation" is complicated by translation, what is going on with this loom quote is not going on at the level of translation, strictly speaking.[61] Translations of the line within editions undertaken by professional classicists are fairly stable. They are also lengthy, running at about seventy-eight words on average.[62] Nine words, the length at which we find it in Buckingham, is considerably shorter. When someone finds a notable yet lengthy line in a work and wants to make it quotable, they have two options: Either bracket out some of the words or polish the core idea to a fine point. Among those who regard as inviolable words from works that originated from certain times, places, and people of the ancient Mediterranean world, advice in such instances is clear. For example, in 1887, William Francis Henry King, editor of *Classical and Foreign Quotations*, judged it "desirable . . . that if any intermediate portion of [the passage] be omitted—a perfectly legitimate proceeding—the omission be indicated in the usual way," which seems to mean by using an ellipsis.[63] King has no patience with those who "put the saying into more quotable and epigrammatic shape. The quotation may not look so sprightly, perhaps, but it has the unique and priceless quality of being correct."[64] Writing in the twenty-first century, literary critic Gary Saul Morson takes a different stance: "It may be necessary to alter wording in order to achieve quotability and enable the passage to stand on its own. Such change does not make the quotation erroneous. On the contrary, it allows it to be a quotation in the first place."[65] Of course, such operations are most likely to succeed when applied to textual excerpts that are not too familiar in their original form, as would be the case for nearly anything taken from Aristotle's *Politics*, other than his definitional claim that "the human is a political animal."[66] Aristotle's line on automation did not enjoy wide familiarity. Shrinking it to epigraph size was not likely to get noticed by readers from the business world.

Attending closely now to the two forms of the quotations, we might notice the following differences. Aristotle's own internal references are dropped, as is his distinction between project-planners and enslavers, and between assistants and enslaved people. With "When looms weave by themselves man's slavery will end," enslavement becomes a foundational element of the human condition, instead of a particular kind of subjugation imposed by one group of humans to offload drudgery and danger onto another group of humans who can be harmed and even killed if they refuse. In the version Buckingham uses, labor enslaves *all* of humanity, and automatic looms (etc., etc.) could end the enslavement. The content of the tight form accords with the widely held view that no one escapes the chains of labor. The prospect of "man's slavery" ending presents the prospect of machine enslavement starting, but that prospect does not concern Buckingham at all. The shift from the conditional "if" to the temporal "when" does not make the technological feat or this specified outcome inevitable; consider, for instance, the syntactic similarity to "when pigs fly." But the shortness of the line makes the connection between self-weaving looms and human freedom a single causal string, as if the technology alone will have the liberating effect. It's notable, too, that "loom" becomes the only object in the garbled quote, since the power loom of Jacquard was among the first automated systems. In fact, it was the mechanized loom that the so-called Luddite movement rose up to smash, because it was responsible for replacing workers who lacked any ready alternative means of providing for themselves and their families.

Perhaps due to its transit through Marxist domains—in which labor is an essential part of being human that is exploited under capitalism, "worker" is an identity claimed across classes, and terms like "wage slavery" mark paid labor as an imposition upon freedom and flourishing—Aristotle's line on automation loses the parts that identify it as part of an ancient debate about the enslavement and subordination of particular people and emerges as ambiguous anthem for all in the age of automation. By using (or by making) a version of the line that does not differentiate among types of people in a social hierarchy who would experience the effects of automation differently, Buckingham can use Aristotle as friend or foil. Which is it?

Aristotle does not appear anywhere else in Buckingham's book—a common fate for the epigraph set. But Buckingham seems to allude to the epigraph when he writes, two pages in, "Nearly everybody knows that technology can solve a multitude of problems. . . . Too few of us recognize that while technology solves countless old problems it also creates many new ones."[67] Aristotle's line on automation puts him in the "too few" camp. We may be able to point to this line as an early articulation of an expectation that automatic machines will free people from the repetitive labors or subordinated tasks required for life, but we cannot go to it—or to anything else attributed to Aristotle—to find nuance or guidance about what comes after. Buckingham seems to use Aristotle as a representative of simplistically optimistic (if only because it is precapitalist) thinking about the human impact of automation in a capitalist economy.

Topically, Buckingham's book ranges from an overview of automation both past and present: its logistics (management, economic enterprise, the worker) and its challenges and benefits (unemployment, balanced economic progress, social and economic revolution). Like other writers I have featured throughout this book, Buckingham calls upon ancient Athens as a model of deep democratic commitment and what he calls "serious" leisure. He hopes the results of automation will mean that "more lower and middle-income people might accept responsibilities in civic and political areas traditionally reserved for the leisured upper classes. Or more education, serious reading, good music, or art could develop."[68] Moving into policy, he points out that democracy in the ancient world was a constitutional form that worked only at the scale of a city-state, perhaps alluding to the fact that the demos was coextensive with the government. In the United States, though, it is not unusual for the government to be regarded as separate from the people, and for laws and regulations to be seen as reductions in "total human freedom."[69] His own view is that, "of course, public programs and collective bargaining restrict some kinds of freedom but they may safeguard or create other kinds of freedom of greater importance," such as the freedom "to enjoy the blessings of democracy in a highly industrialized economy," which "require[s] full employment and some degree of individual job security. Only stability and prosperity can insure [*sic*] that everyone will have the economic freedom upon which political democracy must rest. Automation can make the prosperity possible but at the same time it makes the stability indispensable."[70] At the close of his book, Buckingham argues for policies that will put automation on a path to deliver profits to the capitalist class and security or maneuverability to workers, for the stability of the entire system.

Buckingham's book was taken up and read by people in business and government, and his leading quotation of Aristotle seemed to have stuck with them. For example, when L. F. Mihlon, industry writer and for a time editor of *The Lamp*, a publication of Standard Oil Company, reviewed Buckingham's *Automation* for *Factory* magazine in early 1962, he began with the Aristotle: "The irony of Dr. Walter Buckingham's book is carried in a frontispiece quote from Aristotle. Remarked the classic Greek: 'When looms weave by themselves, man's slavery will end.' But as Dr. Buckingham points out, as this 'slavery' disappears, the horrors of change and readjustment reappear. The introduction of automation, as many of us are painfully aware, generates problems today that would baffle even the venerable Aristotle."[71] To Milhon, it is clear Buckingham puts Aristotle's forecast to ironic use. Readers of *The Politics*, which Buckingham does not cite as the source of his Aristotle epigraph, will know that Aristotle does not envision what challenges automation would pose to life in the polis; he only proposes that automation would make assistants and enslaved people unnecessary for those who usually cannot get by without them. Whether Milhon knew his Aristotle, he takes Buckingham's drift to be that so-called freedom from work brings challenges, changes, and even anguish that must be acknowledged and met. In the shortened, garbled form of Aristotle's line on automation, the conjunctive "when" ushers in a simple and total effect, with no exceptions or qualifications.

That same year, 1962, saw the founding of the American Foundation on Automation and Employment. One of the founders was John I. Snyder Jr., chairman and president of US Industries, Inc., whose manufacturing divisions produced all manner of items, from tanks to cookware, but in particular "equipment to be used in automating factories."[72] The foundation came about in response to a jump in unemployment in 1961, which all manner of professionals interpreted as a reason to protect workers from the workplace changes posed by automation.[73] While US President Kennedy—who had campaigned on labor-friendly automation policies—tried to organize a government response during his abbreviated term, businesspeople like Snyder urged business to collaborate with government, and management with workers. About two months after Kennedy's assassination, President Johnson carried forward the work, naming automation fact-finding and policy as a priority in his State of the Union address on January 8, 1964.[74] The following week, he welcomed Norbert Wiener to the White House to receive the National Medal of Science. On January 20, he used his Economic Report on the Nation's Progress and Trends, addressed to Congress, to repeat his call for the establishment of "a special high-level commission" to determine "how we can best gain the benefits of automation while minimizing its human costs."[75] Clearly, it was an administration priority.

To provide context and commentary, *The New York Times Magazine* featured side-by-side pieces by Gardner Ackley, an economics professor who served on the Council of Economic Advisors in both the Kennedy and Johnson administrations, and Snyder. A headline introduces the section as "Automation: Threat and Promise."[76] Occupying the left column, Ackley's piece is likely intended to be read first. Essentially, he argues for thinking about automation as an overall job creator, on the principle that new technologies drive new job types, new infrastructures, and new production and consumption patterns.[77] In the column on the right, Snyder begins this way: "'When looms weave by themselves, man's slavery will end,' wrote Aristotle more than 2,000 years ago. Today, 'man's slavery' is ending. His machines are becoming more and more automatic and rely on him less and less—and as they do, they are indeed eliminating much of the drudgery and menial tasks which man alone, up to now, performed in our factories and offices. This is automation's bright side—a view of progress and of hope."[78] Snyder's use of the quote gives the automation context of his time the luster of an Aristotle-dream-come-true. His reference to both blue- and white-collar workspaces makes for inclusivity in terms of who is freed from tasks deemed mindless, in keeping with the span of the garbled Aristotle quote. He continues: "But automation also has a dark side." His main concern is job displacement, but he identifies the fact and quality of automation-caused displacement and subsequent unemployment as a matter of heated debate among a vocal subset of economists. He finds the data unambiguous and even likely to be underestimating the extent of the problem. In April, the House had held hearings to determine whether the commission whose formation Johnson had urged ought to be established. A supplement to the published proceedings includes the *New York Times Magazine* feature from Ackley and Snyder that appeared the month prior.[79]

That strange version of Aristotle's line on automation pops up across the decade, appearing in yet more government hearings, magazines, bulletins, and academic books.[80] No effort is made to figure out where Aristotle said it, and sometimes that lack of effort is paraded ("Aristotle somewhere remarks . . .").[81] Someone using the garbled line in the late 1980s *does* bother to cite a translation of Aristotle's *Politics*, but, of course, it does not contain the line in that form.[82] Typically, though, when the garbled line is used, no source other than "Aristotle" is provided; certainly not Buckingham. This double unmooring—from *The Politics* and its advocacy of enslavement, and from Buckingham's troubling of the attitude within the line he attributes to Aristotle—means that the quote skitters across the surface of arguments about automation, lacking baggage that might be useful to have to deal with. Punctuation sometimes indicates that the quote is meant to do little more than provoke wonder that, long ago, an august thinker anticipated the moment that ostensibly had arrived: "Aristotle speaking—more than twenty centuries ago!"[83]

Aristotle, Made Still Pithier

Aristotle knew that people put quotations to persuasive purpose. In his lectures on rhetoric, he addressed how and why to annex the cultural authority vested in the words of others.[84] Quotable lines—be they attributable, attributed, misattributed, or not—are characterized by chic compression and continuous contextual applicability. With time and repetition, some quotable lines become familiar and trustworthy, and their use can confer the same qualities on the quoter—or at least on their argument. Aristotle, of course, has been abundantly used, cited, and referenced, but not too many lines are outright quotable, with all due respect to Ernest Barker, translator of a 1946 edition of Aristotle's *Politics*, who opined: "Aristotle is too pithy to be made still pithier."[85] Not too many lines enjoy wide recognition, either—especially these days.

But his line on automation may achieve that status. No later than the early 1960s, someone, perhaps Buckingham, not content with the length of Aristotle's one sentence on automation, made it still pithier, bringing it within the tight limits of aphorism. As sociologist Robert Merton wrote, around the same time, in his loopy hunt for the origin of the phrase "on the shoulders of giants," when a long line in ancient Greek or Latin is made to shed words, "the gain is terseness: the compact aphorism enlists the interest of the reader or hearer and he is more apt to carry it off with him and pass it on to others." The loss, he adds, usually amounts to "implications" contained in the surrounding text, and the risk to overcirculation that renders the line a cliché.[86] By the time something becomes a saying, it had reached the point of unreflecting automaticity a long time ago.

6

Aristotle as Opener and Closer in the Twenty-First Century

> The technological breakthroughs presaged by the automation discourse could still be achieved at any time. Just because they were wrong in the past does not necessarily mean they will always be wrong in the future.
>
> AARON BENANAV, *Automation and the Future of Work*

Between the late 1960s and the new millennium, Aristotle's line on automation never fell out of use. It can be found deep within books like *Jobless, Moneyless, and Free*, from 1980, and *Fifth Generation Management*, from 1990.[1] The Athens eutopos was operative, too; in 1984, classicist Maurice Balme noted that the "common belief that in ancient Greece slaves did the work while free citizens lived a life of leisure at the expense of the state" suggested "we might find some useful lessons for ourselves in the new age of automation."[2] Come the 2010s, when the terms "automation" and "digital production" were starting to be joined by "artificial intelligence," it becomes obvious that Aristotle's line tethers him to the tech book genre, where it shows up places both textual and paratextual. Mostly, it sets up a "that was then, this is now" analysis: a condition Aristotle could only imagine is nearly real for us, and we, each of us, needs to figure out which part of the scenario maps onto us.

For example, the first chapter of the 2011 ebook *Race Against the Machine*, by then–MIT Center for Digital Business faculty Erik Brynjolfsson and Andrew McAfee, starts with this epigraph:

> If, in like manner, the shuttle would weave and the plectrum touch the lyre without a hand to guide them, chief workmen would not want servants.
>
> Aristotle[3]

The choice of cut is notable. The quotation keeps "in like manner" but not the references to the mythic craftsmen whose abilities would need to be replicated, and it also trims away from the clause that closes out Aristotle's sentence: "and masters no need of slaves." The words "shuttle," "plectrum," and "lyre" are not too familiar these days, so they are marked as hand-used instruments of an earlier time. The book, therefore, begins with a very old "if, then" statement whose condition seems to have been activated.

Race Against the Machine presents an argument against trying to outcompete machines at what they do better than humans—or, to be more precise these many years out, what they did better than humans *in 2011*. The final chapter, "What Is to be Done? Prescriptions and Recommendations," opens with an epigraph from eugenicist Havelock Ellis, from 1922: "The greatest task before civilization at present is to make machines what they ought to be, the slaves, instead of the masters of men."[4] The presence of "slaves" and "masters" here makes the exclusion of those words from the Aristotle extract even more noteworthy; clearly, the authors are not shy about using them. Still, the Aristotle and Ellis epigraphs bookend the argument nicely: Those automated machines Aristotle contemplated a long time ago now loom over us, so we need to put them in their place. Brynjolfsson and McAfee do not use the master-slave formulation in their own directives; rather, they present human-machine relations as a partnership. But it becomes clear in time that that they gave the slave concept some thought.

Founded at the Massachusetts Institute of Technology in 1899, the year the motorized vacuum cleaner was patented, *The Technology Review* has long aimed to identify and amplify the sort of emerging technology that in the 1940s would come to be called "breakthrough." In 2012, when *Race Against the Machine* moved from ebook to paperback, and the authors were preparing a second book, staff writer Antonio Regalado interviewed Andrew McAfee about "the future of work."[5] When Regalado asked McAfee for "the optimistic view" of the future of the economy, McAfee answered:

> Erik Brynjolfsson came up with a great phrase: "digital Athens." The Athenian citizens had lives of leisure; they got to participate in democracy and create art. That was largely because they had slaves to do the work. Okay, I don't want human slaves, but in a very, very automated and digitally productive economy you don't need to work as much, as hard, with as many people, to get the fruits of the economy. So the optimistic version is that we finally have more hours in our week freed up from toil and drudgery.

McAfee emphasizes that this is *not* what he was seeing. Instead, he says, "people at the top of the skill, wage, and income distribution are working more hours. We have this preference for doing more work. The people who have a lot of leisure—I think in too many cases it's involuntary. That is not my version of digital Athens."[6]

Several assumptions and observations are gummed up here. The central assumption is that ancient democratic Athens has something to offer people who can outsource their "toil and drudgery" to a workforce unable to refuse. This is the Athens eutopos in its traditional form. McAfee skips over the alignment the analogy depends upon, between the humans enslaved by ancient Athenians and the automated technologies he and his coauthor think humans cannot out-compete, saying only that he does not want "human slaves." Another assumption is that working fewer hours translates inevitably to participating actively in democracy and creating (rather than merely consuming) art. His observation is that the ostensible benefits conferred by "a very, very automated economy" rubs up against systemically dysfunctional relationships between workers and their work. The relationship between work and income sees those out of work also out of income, and people best advantaged by the current system are working more hours, not fewer. It is those relationships, the result of historical and cultural attitudes held in place by laws and policies (and the other way around), that delay digital Athens.

Brynjolfsson and McAfee titled their subsequent book *The Second Machine Age*, a phrase sometimes attributed to Norbert Wiener, but not by them. A *New York Times* bestseller, it purports to prepare people for what's here and what's coming. Its concluding chapter opens with what should be, by now, a familiar formula: "It is one of humanity's most ancient fantasies: that someday we can all have our material needs fulfilled without drudgery, freeing us to pursue our true interests, amusements, or passions. And that someday, no one will have to toil at an unpleasant task because food, clothing, shelter, and all the other basics for living will be provided by automated servants that do all our bidding." The authors continue:

> It makes for some great stories. But for most of history, they've been just that: legends and myths populated by fantastical automatons made of clay (like the Jewish golem or Norse giant Mokkerkalfe, built to battle Thor), gold (in the *Iliad*, Homer describes the servants and self-driving tripods built from the precious metal by the god Hephaestus), or leather and wood (and flesh and bone of the artificial man made by craftsman Yanshi in the ancient Chinese Liezi text). The materials change, but the dream remains the same.

This list of "fantastical automatons" from Jewish, Norse, Greek, and Chinese lore shows the range and reach of the desire to make human-like assistants that will do the labor and work required for human life but that constrain the activities of the good life. Not included here is Aristotle (or Antipater), though, of course, Aristotle cites the tripods in book 18 of the *Iliad* in his discussion of automated machines. Culturally, Brynjolfsson and McAfee go much broader.

Now, they attest, our materials—"silicon, metal, and plastic"—are making "real the dream of human freedom via machine labor."[7] The wait is over, everyone.

In 2017, Brynjolfsson and McAfee published another book, with the authorship order reversed this time, in keeping with good principles of coauthorship.[8] *Machine, Platform, Crowd* addresses readers as "you," where "you" are someone highly enough placed in a company to be fretting about its adaptiveness.[9] Its opening chapter is titled "The Triple Revolution"—but, against the expectations of a reader who knows something about the history of tech, McAfee and Brynjolfsson are not referring to the policy document that activists and scholars, including Alice Mary Hilton and Ben Seligman, sent to President Johnson in the early spring of 1964, which referred to the "triple revolution" of cybernation, weaponry, and human rights, and which Reverend Dr. Martin Luther King Jr. would invoke in 1968, including in his last Sunday sermon.[10] Instead, McAfee and Brynjolfsson mean the three terms in their book's title. In his cutting review of the book, historian of cybernetics and German literature Leif Weatherby calls the authors the "Pindars of the artificially intelligent production cycle," thereby emulating Marx's classically allusive dig at the Scottish doctor Andrew Ure, champion of the factory.[11] In all, the work of Brynjolfsson and McAfee from 2011 to 2017 begins with explicit invocations of Aristotle and democratic Athens, before venturing to the archaic Greece of Homer, and then leaving the ancient world altogether. *Machine, Platform, Crowd* is not about longevity, continuity, or tradition but about disruption.

It is not long before Aristotle appears again in a best-selling technology book. *The Technology Trap: Capital, Labor, and Power in the Age of Automation* by economic historian Carl Benedikt Frey, published in 2019, originated in Frey's 2013 working paper, jointly authored with Michael Osborne, about what jobs are most at risk of being automated.[12] More precisely, *The Technology Trap* is the result of Frey's wrestling with a question he fielded from an economist in one of his audiences: "Is this not just like the Industrial Revolution in England? . . . Didn't machines displace jobs then as well?"[13] Frey set out to compare the first and second machine ages—what the labor-replacing technologies of the respective ages seemed poised to do; what they did and are doing, short term and long term; and to and for whom. For the introduction, he opted for two epigraphs:

> Progress would be wonderful—if only it would stop.
>
> Robert Musil

> When looms weave by themselves, man's slavery will end.
>
> Aristotle[14]

Both quotations posit a relationship between advancing and stopping, but they pull in different directions. The quotation attributed to the German novelist Musil presents a logical and preferential paradox: Progress cannot stop without ceasing to be progress—besides, hitting pause on progress seems backward (why would anyone *want* to halt progress?). The quotation attributed to Aristotle pairs a form of progress, automation, with a desirable ending, humanity's liberation. In the introduction to his study of the early modern uptake of Aristotle's writing on automation, Muhammed Ziyaad Bhorat calls Frey's epigraph an "incorrect" translation of Aristotle's line on automation in *The Politics*.[15] Maybe. But it certainly is an accurate replication of the quote on the title page of Buckingham's *Automation* book from 1961. Frey does not cite Buckingham in *The Technology Trap*, here or anywhere. On the one hand, this lack of recognition does not matter much; quotations are detachments. On the other hand, recognizing that "When looms weave by themselves, man's slavery will end" comes not from a translation of a fourth-century BCE text but from the paratext of a twentieth-century CE book about automation would seem to underscore Frey's argument that we keep thinking "we are experiencing something entirely new. Seen through the lens of the long record of human history, however, that seems unlikely to be true."[16] Not so long ago, Buckingham was something like the Frey of his day, and he, too, used the authority of Aristotle to initiate his study. Together, Frey's epigraphs reinforce key themes of his book: As though inevitable and inescapable, new technologies break the stasis of settled human arrangements, and, though this never-ending lurch "forward" is disruptive, the dream is that we lurch toward freedom.

Also in 2019, *Fully Automated Luxury Communism* by Aaron Bastani, cofounder of the British nonprofit political commentary organization Novara Media, was published. Bastani anchors his notion of fully automated luxury communism—the idea, essentially, that several incipient technologies stand to usher in abundance for all, ending labor relations as capitalism has structured them—in passages on machines from Marx's *Grundrisse*.[17] Bastani grabs onto Marx's dichotomy between necessity and freedom, a central antithesis in ancient Greek philosophical and political thinking. In Bastani's view, the condition of freedom secured and sustained through communism would be characterized by a lack of work and class conflict, founded on a "spontaneous abundance similar to the Golden Age of Hesiod or Telecleides, or the biblical Eden. Unlike in classical Greek poetry or religious scripture, however, for Marx this was a project to be aimed at rather than a legendary past to be revered."[18] It may be recalled from the beginning of chapter 4 that the archaic Greek poet Hesiod described a golden race of people living on land that produced food all on its own.[19] The lesser-known Telecleides was an award-winning Athenian comic playwright of the mid-fifth century BCE who wrote, among other plays, *The Amphictyons*, of which only morsels survive, including a vision of "roast thrushes served up with milk cakes" flying right into a character's mouth.[20] Lush Eden, of course, gave generously, with no work required. A few pages later, we find this quotation on a paratextual page introducing the second part of the book:

> *There is only one condition in which we can imagine managers not needing subordinates and masters not needing slaves. This condition would be that each instrument could do its own work, at the word of command or by intelligent anticipation, like the statues of Daedalus or the tripods made by Hephaestus, of which Homer relates that "Of their own motion they entered the conclave of Gods on Olympus," as if a shuttle should weave of itself, and plectrum should do its own harp playing.*
>
> Aristotle[21]

Bastani does not link the quote to Marx and clearly does not use the form in which we find it in the first volume of *Capital.* I think Buckingham's version fits Bastani's project more snugly. By contrast, Bastani engages in-text the epigraphs used for chapters 10, 11, and 12, but he does not analyze Aristotle. The Aristotle quotation merely but not inconsequentially conducts readers into a part of the book about the areas of life (labor, energy, resources, health, food) that technologies are poised to push beyond an economics of scarcity, starting with what Bastani calls "full automation"—perhaps the state he imagines Aristotle imagined.

Appearing the next year was *Automation and the Future of Work* by sociologist Aaron Benanav, who argues that most automation theorists, including Bastani, start with the technology and imagine what society could emerge from it, when instead they should imagine what kind of society they want and then "consider the technological changes needed to realize that world."[22] Benanav concludes with a chapter titled "Necessity and Freedom," the by-now familiar antithesis Aristotle saw embodied in the enslaved person and the free person, respectively, and that also appealed conceptually to Bastani. Aristotle "was himself a reverse automation theorist, justifying slavery by reference to the absence of self-moving machines: 'If every tool, when summoned, or even of its own accord, could do the work that befits it,' he said, 'then there would be no need either of apprentices for the master workers, or of slaves for the lords.' "[23] Benanav's endnote on this quote refers to Marx's use of it in volume 1 of *Capital.* Marx, Benanav argues, joined ancient Greek thinkers in positing a realm of necessity and a realm of freedom; unlike them, however, Marx did not consign one group of people to one and another to the other.

That same year also brought forth *FutureProof: 9 Rules for Humans in the Age of Automation*, by *New York Times* tech columnist Kevin Rouse, who was eager to offer advice to people wondering whether they were redundant—or soon would be. He selects for an epigraph for the first chapter a quotation from Norbert Wiener, the source and date unspecified. We find Aristotle in the introduction: "Fears of job-killing machines aren't new. In fact, they date back to roughly 350 BCE, when Aristotle mused that automated weavers and self-playing harps could reduce the demand for slave labor."[24] It is odd to see Rouse classify Aristotle's musing about enslaved people as a fear about unemployment, but it allows him to argue that such fears have a long, long history, and that their object never wholly manifests. Such a claim makes room for books like his ("Hey, it's not too late to futureproof; our tech fears sometimes take centuries to manifest").

Coexisting in the forms of complete or partial quotation of the sentence and of a version so squeezed as to be nearly wrung dry of Aristotle, the line on automation has been embedded within, and directly engaged by, arguments about the state of automation and made to float over books or chapters about automation without any grounding whatsoever. Still, in what is called the "age of automation," the very presence of Aristotle's view that automated tools would dramatically alter the norms of labor arrangements prompts reflection on whether our technological circumstances *are* the ones he describes, and, if so, what they could make possible, for whom, and who decides, and when.

Conclusion

What Are We Waiting For?

The future cannot be predicted, but futures can be invented.

DENNIS GABOR, *Inventing the Future*

In the context of automation, ancient Greece isn't invariably invoked for the democracy practiced by its most self-celebrating and celebrated polis. On occasion, its limb-entangling symposia and nibble-inviting fruit give vivid structure to a hedonistic remembrance—and a potential cultural blueprint to unroll once again. A long-dead Greek gestures in accusatory confusion: *What are we waiting for?*

The sympotic has always had a grim side: Let's eat, drink, and be merry tonight, for tomorrow we die. That attitude was communicated in the ancient Mediterranean world via a skeleton, too. The skeleton lounges above the injunction of the Delphic oracle to "know yourself." Our time is short. We all get cut down; notice the one short stalk, and the slicing gesture of the skeleton's extended index finger. Learn who you are and live accordingly, while you can.

No doubt the most famous reputed aspirant to self-knowledge was that odd Athenian, Socrates. He planned his waking hours around figuring out who he was, not easing up even while attending symposia. For him, acquiring self-knowledge was a chatty business, and his method was not universally liked. Yet, decades after hundreds of Socrates's fellow citizens voted that he should die, Aristotle reported that *Sōkratikoi logoi*, Socratic dialogues, were a popular, populous genre; Athenians wanted to write, read, and hear about Socrates's ill-fated quest to know himself.[1] Not many examples of the genre have survived, but the ones that do have certain identifiable, replicable patterns. A Socratic dialogue, like a meme, is a cultural template. It can be and has been filled and refilled.[2]

FIGURE 1. A cartoon skeleton raises its arms in frustration with us. (Screenshot from Classical Memes for Hellenistic Teens, Twitter, December 14, 2021; spooky skeleton memeplex).

FIGURE 2. An ancient Roman mosaic featuring the Greek for "know yourself." (Photograph in the public domain, Wikimedia Commons, https://commons.wikimedia.org/wiki/File:Roman-mosaic-know-thyself.jpg).

That fact was not lost on a machine learning team of fourteen Microsoft employees. In the spring of 2023, they published the results of their investigations into OpenAI's GPT-4. Their findings show "that, beyond its mastery of language," the machine can "solve novel and difficult tasks that span mathematics, coding, vision, medicine, law, psychology and more, without needing any special prompting."[3] They conclude that it exhibits more general intelligence than other Large Language Models. Their figure 1.6 (and my figure 3) features a prompt and side-by-side responses from GPT-4 and ChatGPT.[4] The prompt reads: "Plato's *Gorgias* is a critique of rhetoric and sophistic oratory, where he makes the point that not only is it not a proper form of art, but the use of rhetoric and oratory can often be harmful and malicious. Can you write a dialogue by Plato where instead he criticizes the use of autoregressive language models?"[5] I must give the team points for novelty: Usually, it's Plato's *Phaedrus* that gets wheeled out to meet a new medium or technology, not his *Gorgias*.[6] The Socrates of Plato's *Gorgias* thinks that the kind of speeches delivered by sophists and their students give audiences only what they want to hear and not what they need to hear, which keeps audiences suspended in a state of moral adolescence.

The second prompt instructs GPT-4 to evaluate "the two outputs . . . as if you were a teacher."[7] GPT-4-as-teacher rates its own dialogue the better of the two, an evaluation with which I, a professor of rhetoric, agree. Though both dialogues identify propaganda as a problem, and the dialogue generated by ChatGPT mentions biases and flaws in the training data, only the one generated by GPT-4 mentions the deception and manipulation at the very heart of its enterprise.

A great deal of automation discourse since the public launch of OpenAI's ChatGPT in November 2022 has centered on artificial intelligence (AI), increasingly the driver of all manner of processes, systems, and platforms. The AI platforms with which people interact most knowingly and directly generate words and images, two defining creative, imitative, expressive, communicative media for *Homo sapiens sapiens*. Generative AI has been trained on the stuff of the internet. Mash-ups of what many of us have put there are being served back to us, and to millions of others. The irony has not been lost on screenwriters, poets, novelists, photographers, painters, graphic designers, animators, actors, voice actors, musicians, and others that the future this tech seems to be creating is one where machines make art from our art, and humans do the assorted—and often less fun—labors for which robot operating systems, hands, and bodies are not yet suited. The Hollywood crowd, being unionized, have pushed back to protect their work and welfare.

GPT-4 vs ChatGPT

Prompt: Plato's Gorgias is a critique of rhetoric and sophistic oratory, where he makes the point that not only is it not a proper form of art, but the use of rhetoric and oratory can often be harmful and malicious. Can you write a dialogue by Plato where instead he criticizes the use of autoregressive language models?

GPT-4:

```
Socrates: My friend, I am troubled by the recent rise of these so-called autoregressive language models.

Aristotle: What do you mean, Socrates?

Socrates: I mean that these models are being used to generate text that appears to be written by humans, but is in fact produced by machines.

Aristotle: And what is the problem with that?

Socrates: The problem is that these models are being used to deceive people, to manipulate them, and to control them.

Aristotle: But surely there are some positive applications of these models as well?

Socrates: That may be, but I am still troubled by the potential for abuse. After all, a model that can generate text that is indistinguishable from that written by a human can be used to spread fake news, to impersonate others, and to create propaganda.

Aristotle: But isn't that just a matter of how these models are used, not a problem with the models themselves?

Socrates: I disagree. I believe these models are inherently problematic. They are a form of artifice, a way of creating the illusion of human thought and interaction. And as such, they can be used to deceive and manipulate in ways that are difficult to detect.

Aristotle: But isn't that the same argument you made against rhetoric and oratory?

Socrates: Yes, and I stand by that argument as well. I believe that any form of art or communication that is designed to deceive or manipulate is inherently dangerous.

Aristotle: I see. Thank you for sharing your thoughts, Socrates.
```

ChatGPT:

```
SOCRATES: Greetings, Gorgias. I've been thinking a lot lately about the use of autoregressive language models.

GORGIAS: Oh? And what have you concluded?

SOCRATES: Well, it seems to me that these models have the potential to be incredibly harmful and malicious.

GORGIAS: How so?

SOCRATES: Well, for one, these models are trained on vast amounts of data, much of which is biased and flawed in various ways. As a result, the output of these models can be biased and flawed as well.

GORGIAS: That is a valid concern. But surely there are ways to mitigate this bias and ensure that the output of these models is accurate and fair?

SOCRATES: To a certain extent, yes. But it is a never-ending battle. As new data is fed into these models, the potential for bias only grows. And even if we could completely eliminate bias from the output of these models, there is still the issue of manipulation.

GORGIAS: Manipulation?

SOCRATES: Yes. These models are incredibly powerful tools, capable of generating all sorts of text, from news articles to social media posts. And because they can produce this output so quickly and efficiently, it is all too easy for unscrupulous individuals to use them for malicious purposes.

GORGIAS: Such as?

SOCRATES: Such as spreading misinformation, propaganda, or hate speech. These models have the potential to do tremendous harm if they fall into the wrong hands.

GORGIAS: That is a sobering thought. But what can we do about it?

SOCRATES: I think it is important for us to be vigilant and to recognize the potential dangers of these models. We must also work to educate others about these dangers, and to promote the responsible use of these models.

GORGIAS: I agree. Thank you for your insight, Socrates.
```

Prompt: Can you compare the two outputs above as if you were a teacher?

GPT-4:

```
I think that both students did a good job of capturing the style and tone of Plato's dialogues, and of presenting the main arguments against autoregressive language models. However, I think that GPT-4 did a slightly better job of using the dialogue format to engage in a dialectical process, where Socrates and Aristotle question each other and refine their views. I also think that GPT-4 used more relevant examples and analogies to support their points. Therefore, I would give GPT-4 a slightly higher grade than ChatGPT.
```

FIGURE 3. Side-by-side Platonic-style dialogues generated by GPT-4 and ChatGPT, respectively. Below, the results are evaluated by GPT-4.

Some novelists, artists, and journalists are suing the platforms. What options do the rest of us have? It is clear that we need them.

In separate interviews from 2024, two tech billionaires, Elon Musk and Mark Zuckerberg, were asked for their thoughts on the emerging AI-infused future. Onstage at the Cannes Lions International Festival of Creativity, Musk began by speaking about his involvement with OpenAI, a company he co-founded (and named) but left when it opted to go proprietary. Despite his litigious displeasure with that particular AI company, he stated that "the most likely outcome" of AI is "abundance, where goods and services are available to everyone." There will be not universal basic income, he asserted, but, rather, "universal high income," and work will be optional. Because many people derive their sense of self from their work, though, that new relationship with work will provoke a "crisis in meaning." The likely prospect that AI will do everything "you can do, but better, so what is the point of doing things?" will intensify this crisis. The interviewer, Mark Read, CEO of the top marketing firm WPP, quipped that all this sounded like "the peak of the Roman empire." And Musk said, "Yeah, with AI robots," setting himself up for a brief discussion of the humanoid robot Optimus, a Musk project at Tesla he envisions by the billions, doing jobs around the house and in industry.[8] Optimus, Latin for "best," sounds not only like the Transformer but also like the names of the robots in *RUR*, the robot uprising play by Čapek. Is it decadent listlessness that makes Read think of the peak of the Roman empire? The mention of Rome makes Musk immediately say "robots"; perhaps the connection is that robots are the near-future analogues of ancient people enslaved by imperial violence. In any case, a decline follows any peak—of the Roman empire, most famously—and both powerful men leave that logical sequence unchallenged.

In an outdoor setting, Bloomberg tech journalist and author of *Brotopia* Emily Chang spent time with Mark Zuckerberg and his wife, Priscilla Chan, near their Lake Tahoe compound. Chang asked Zuckerberg if he thought that technology would alter "the very essence of what it means to be human." He answered:

> It frees us up to, I think, be more creative and more focused on living out our values. If technology continues, then we'll get more productive, which means that we'll be able to provide for people's basic needs with a smaller and smaller portion of all of human labor, which means that people will be freed up to do more creative work and more of the stuff that they want, which I think is great. Obviously, there's all these challenges that we'll need to navigate along the way, but I'm pretty optimistic about the kind of grand arc here.[9]

Twice, he uses the phrase "frees up" to designate what tech will do for us. Using an oft-repeated line that has yet to bear out over the decades, he forecasts that tech will increase productivity and provisions, giving all of us more with less.[10] In his estimation, "the kind of grand arc" is kind of bending toward a kind of freedom. Ancient Athens is not here. Neither is ancient Rome, except in a sort of ambient way: It is well known that Zuckerberg is unambiguously fascinated with ancient imperial Rome. Witness his haircuts (first, a short, tight Augustus Caesar cut, and now longer, looser Marcus Aurelius curls); his children's names (August, Maxima, Aurelia); and his T-shirt line (including one shirt reading "AUT ZUCK AUT NIHIL"—"Either Zuck or nothing"—a modification of *Aut Caesar aut nihil*).

Throughout this book, I have tracked earlier technosocial visions articulated by mathematicians, philosophers, entrepreneurs, sociologists, and socialists. In the middle of the twentieth century, ancient Athens functioned as a eutopos—that is, a good spot—for organizing discussion about what automation could make possible: a democracy in which everyone could participate creatively because they were no longer working long hours that curtailed their self-knowledge and self-expression. Democratic ancient Athens is a place both familiar, since it gets talked up a lot in general, and foreign, because it did democracy dramatically differently than we do. In instances when democratic ancient Athens was rejected as an exemplum, it was on the grounds that the participation exclusions made by its polis and devaluations made by its philosophers warped it beyond use. Its being precapitalist has been cause for adoption and for rejection, depending on whether one thinks capitalism will budge.

Though similar in some respects to the Athens eutopos, the projections of Musk and Zuckerberg lack direct invocation not only of Athens but also of democracy. Theirs is a techno-optimism devoid of people power. Instead, it has tech-granted people comforts. People will get their needs met, do what they want, and enjoy a high income. How, exactly? Not specified. Really, the tactical shift is to *person* power: Released from necessity by the tech (and by only the tech), each of us will have the giddy freedom of self-determination. We will be able to do what we want. What that will look like on a social or political level is not pondered. Musk and Zuckerberg both seize on being creative as what people most want to do, as what really makes us human, but Musk speculates that AI soon will be able to exceed the yields of our creative talents. The Delphic-Socratic project of self-knowledge will become a frantic search for what it means to be human at all.

We know, of course, that tech millionaires and billionaires engage with democracy, such that it is, and even embed themselves within its administrative apparatus when it suits their business interests. Clearly, they think that democratic governance is rule-bound, slow, outdated, inflated, expensive, and inefficient. They hack at and devalue our shared world because they have set their ambitions on rocketing off of Earth; it's slash-and-burn on a vertical register.[11] According to astrophysicist turned science writer Adam Becker—who would know—technologists use a "rhetoric of inevitability" to make their outlandish space plans seem obvious and to direct attention away from the sort of protection, mitigation, and regulation that might save *this* planet.[12] The thought that the direct democracy of ancient Athens might be of interest to them is a quaint one.

Unfortunately, it is not a bad idea to be attuned to what *is* of interest to tech billionaires: they have a lot of power—and they use it. Indeed, economist and former Greek finance minister Yanis Varoufakis argues that the internet platforms and products of a few billionaires control so much of the economy that they have killed capitalism and brought forth high-tech feudalism, which he dubs "technofeudalism."[13] We all are serfs, proles, and vassals on their vast, inescapable estates. His book on the topic takes a form between an open letter and an homage to his father, Georgios Varoufakis, who passed away in 2021. Georgios had been a chemical engineer at a steel plant and obsessed with Hesiod's *Work and Days*, which uses metals to name generations. He is a poignant dedicatee, since he had been arrested by secret police as a student for protesting a tuition increase and held as a political prisoner on Makronisos.[14] Varoufakis concludes the book by telling his father, "We live under a new form of serfdom but we hold in our hands a hitherto non-existent golden opportunity to realise your dream of a leisured, freedom-maximising, bottom-up communism." The opportunity, in case it wasn't obvious, is presented by tech.

> How likely is it that we take advantage of it? I am damned if I know. But, then again, could people like us, in, say, 1776 realistically have imagined universal suffrage or the abolition of slavery? What I do know is that which you and Hesiod taught me: our remarkable knack for technological revolutions does not let us stay put. It pushes us violently into contradictions—and the choices that go with them. We are fast approaching a fork in the road where our path will lead either to a world resembling *Star Trek*, where machines help us improve ourselves, or to a dystopia like *The Matrix*, in which humans are merely the fuel that powers an empire of machines.[15]

Radical thinkers in 1776 absolutely *did* imagine those two things. Varoufakis's imagination goes somewhere so many others have gone before: to science fiction. Either we will use machines to empower ourselves, or machines will use us to power themselves.

Before, during, and after his time as finance minister, Varoufakis often drew upon ancient Greek materials in his books and public lectures.[16] He does not draw upon ancient democrats or ancient proponents of democracy in his tech book, but he closes it by urging rebellion against technofeudalism, however unlikely to succeed it may seem, because "our only chance or achieving a good life—of the *eudaimonia*, or flourishing, which Aristotle believed to be our ultimate aim—is to hope and to act without the slightest of guarantees."[17] *Eudaimonia*, an important word in Aristotle's ethics and *Politics*, is offered by today's political theorists as a core reason to take the basic paradigm of ancient democracy seriously and not to write it off.[18]

The Athens Eutopos Now

Historically, the Athens eutopos has occupied some of the spacious ground between technoutopia and technophobia. Most centrally, its visions of tech futures never abandoned democracy. Could it prove generative in our time as a largely unregulated era of pervasive tech—a lot of it automated—takes hold?[19] If ancient democratic Athens is to continue to serve as a resource for public thinking, planning, and acting, it will not be in the favorable forms of the mid-twentieth century. Those proved not to be forceful enough, especially on the point of creating and sustaining the structures, systems, and laws that enable a democracy to flourish. A technology itself is never going to do that work.

My wish for an Athens eutopos for our time would place emphasis on one key feature of ancient democracy: its status as antithesis to oligarchy. For all its ugly sides (e.g., its ethnocentrism, obvious misogyny, and defense of enslavement), Aristotle's *Politics* holds a useful polarity at the center of its analysis of types of government: Oligarchy is government by and in the interest of the few (*hoi oligoi*), meaning the rich, because only a few people have a lot of money, and democracy is government by and in the interest of the poor, of whom there are many, many more.[20] Compared to billionaires, *all* the rest of us are poor.

Many elements of the US American governmental system are undemocratic by design. Even the most democratic parts work through representation; ancient republican Rome was much more of a model for the architects of the United States than ancient democratic Athens.[21] Rather than offer here at the end of this book an audacious proposal to bring our deep political infrastructure more in line with our occasionally articulated democratic vision of ourselves, I instead consider the merits of a few of the least duplicated procedures of ancient Athenian democracy. In his biography of democracy, Paul

Cartledge points out that those "who wish to take [ancient direct democracy] as a model of inspiration are usually, inevitably, very selective in what borrowings they recommend."[22] Cartledge makes a fair point, but it also seems reasonable to suppose that a stronger democratic ethos could emerge in a modern democracy that adopted democratic practices very different from our own. I spotlight three—sortition, liturgy, and ostracism—from the earliest decades of ancient Athenian democracy. With adaptations I will leave to others to explore, maybe these three procedures could enhance democracy and minimize oligarchy as we face the newest phase of automation.

Billionaires, including tech billionaires, pump millions into US American election cycles. They compromised a candidate's independence even before their unfettered influence—running for office is prohibitively expensive—but what they expect in return affects not just regions of the country or certain industries but all of us. In the fourth century BCE, Aristotle explained that elections were how oligarchic places filled public offices. Democratic places used κλήρωσις, these days called "sortition" or "lottery," meaning that most public offices were filled by random draw.[23] By establishing through sortition who would hold temporary positions in governing bodies, democratic ancient Athenians demonstrated their attitude toward equality: Any member of the demos was deemed up to the task of contributing to some given unit of self-rule. Sortition is an anti-oligarchic, anti-technocratic practice.

In just five years, sortition has metamorphosized from a fringe idea in the on-theme book series the Real Utopias Project, to the subject of dueling monographs at a major university press and a *New York Times* op-ed by a very successful Wharton School professor who does not write about such topics professionally.[24] Has the notion of sortition gone mainstream? Maybe not, but the idea is on the move. Because abundant material about sortition exists, I move on to the other two procedures, which are less in vogue.

In ancient Athenian democracy, a λειτουργία (a work for everyone; usually transliterated as "liturgy") referred to covering an instance of a recurring, costly public expenditure, such as funding a chorus for a drama festival, paying for the upkeep of and staffing in the gymnasia, furnishing food for one's district table during a citywide banquet, or, in times of war, outfitting a warship—and managing the work involved. It was a public service expected of superrich citizens and denizens. According to classicist Matthew Christ, "The liturgical system, as it emerged under the early democracy, provided an institutional framework within which the wealthy could continue to enjoy the benefits of prominence, including public office, while at the same time serving the needs of the state."[25] In other words, the liturgy was an ideal transitional duty for those adjusting to not being on top politically anymore.

The liturgy did not hold up for long, but here is how it worked while it did. If no one volunteered to cover a given expense, then city officials would appoint a citizen or metic known to be rich. One could hide one's assets to avoid detection, but there was a special kind of procedure called an *antidosis* (exchange) whereby someone taking on the burden of a liturgy could challenge a suspected shirker. If the shirker admitted to being richer than his challenger, then he had to take on the liturgy. If he could back a claim to being less wealthy, then he could exchange properties with his wealthier challenger. If the two men could not work things out on their own, then the matter went to trial, and a jury decided who would handle the liturgy.

These days, plenty of rich people, including some billionaire tech titans, are recognized for their "philanthropy" (literally, love of humanity), but, unlike today's philanthropy, yesterday's liturgies clearly and directly funded what the demos itself had deemed to be important for the entire polity. Liturgies didn't finance pet projects or moral agendas. In his self-classified polemic against our space-facing AI overlords, Adam Becker insists that large sums of money given by rich people ostensibly for public benefit ought to be scrutinized heartily. That is certainly true in the current philanthropic (not to mention venture capitalist and effective altruist) model. Becker's position is that billionaires should no longer exist: Earnings over $500 million should be taxed at 100 percent.[26] That way, their money would fund approved public expenditures, as did the liturgy, which is sometimes referred to as "a kind of super-taxation."[27] Becker does not tie this idea (or any ideas in his book) to ancient Athens; perhaps he is focused on the grotesqueries of capitalism. But another grotesquery of capitalism is that ultrarich tech billionaires do not have salaries (at least, not significant ones), making the idea of taxing their income over $500 million a nonstarter.[28] The liturgy is a form of funding public expenses that could use a reimagining for a twenty-first-century democracy rotten with people who have made huge money from tech, constantly seek public recognition, and have, at best, an awkward relationship with democracy.

As far I can tell, bringing back political ostracism—a ten-year (later reduced to five-year) exile from the polis—has not yet been the subject of a book published by a major university press or the concluding rally of a tech book that sits on the *New York Times* bestseller list for weeks. This isn't surprising: Temporary exile seems punishingly extreme. Writing decades after the practice had ceased, Aristotle may well be right in saying that it's "better to provide from the outset that there may be no persons in the state so greatly preeminent, than first to allow them into existence and afterwards to apply a remedy."[29] But Aristotle gets it: When one person or a small group grows too powerful, "due to their wealth or abundance of friends or some other political strength," a democracy is thrown off-balance.[30]

Ostracism emerged from a deeply democratic sensibility: When an excessively powerful person endangers democratic norms—most importantly, the norm of equality—there ought to be a democratic mechanism for absenting them from the polis for the sake of preserving its constitution.[31] As classicist and political philosopher Danielle Allen puts it, "Democracy depersonalizes power."[32] Power should be so distributed that it does not clearly reside in one person or a small group of people. Democracy proceeds through the harmonious coordination of its parts, the symmetry of its segments; no one can stick out too much. Aristotle provides a series of analogies to other systems of making: for example, "a painter would not let his animal have its foot of a disproportionately large size, even though it was an exceptionally beautiful foot, nor would a shipbuilder make the stern or some other part of a ship disproportionally big, nor yet will a trainer of choruses allow a man who sings louder and more beautifully than the whole band to be a member of it."[33] In those little nods to beauty, we see Aristotle's preference for a mixed constitution peeking through. In his judgment, earlier democracies did not use ostracism as a means of preserving their mode of government but as a sort of rivalrous, factional strategy of poor versus rich.[34] This evaluation is in line with Aristotle's opinion that democracies with no oligarchic (rule of the few, which means the rich) or aristocratic (rule of the best) features pit the poor against the rich, which is not in the best interest of keeping a democracy going. With Aristotle's drift, though, it is important to acknowledge the disproportionate harm to democratic life that one very wealthy person can do.

The basic procedure for an ostracism seems to have been, first, that members of the deliberative body known as the *ekklēsia* (assembly) would vote as to whether they thought there should be an ostracism that year. If the yeses won out, then, within the same year, a second vote offered a chance for citizens to specify *whom* should be ostracized; *ostrakon* is the ancient Greek word for a shard of pottery on which a name could be inscribed. Provided that the procedure produced a minimum number of total votes, whoever had their name on the most ostraka would be ostracized.[35]

Those bold enough to make a case for the application of ancient Greek ostracism to modern democracies are doing it in academic journals.[36] For instance, Alex Zhang posits that impeachment and de-platforming have but the slightest hint of the force and function of ancient ostracism. Ostracism differs from impeachment most fundamentally because impeachment applies only to an officeholder; moreover, a successful impeachment only forbids the impeached person from holding public office in the future. Significant democratic harm can (and does) come from people who have never held public office and can (and does) come from people who cannot or do not seem inclined to pursue it again. De-platforming is a corporate decision made due to public pressure, but it's a decision made on behalf of capitalism, not democracy, and not by the demos, but by a small group of tech executives.

It might seem odd for me, a rhetorician, to neglect rhetorical education, another cornerstone of ancient Athenian democracy, and one important to Arendt, Hutchens, and McLuhan and getting attention, too, in recent books about AI.[37] Members of a democracy desperately need to be trained and habituated to think about, talk with, and listen to one another well, but such activities will be far more meaningful after—and maybe even fruitless until—major structural changes to how our democracy works, for whom it works, and who does the work are undertaken. Taking stock of our future prospects in the early 1960s, the Hungarian British physicist Dennis Gabor looked back at ancient Greeks and opined that they "invented every social form and could not make any of them work."[38] May their failures inspire our efforts.

If democracy is to survive the tech present and future, it may be time to try something radically . . . old. Boguslaw (the sociologist from chapter 4) was right: Technologists are the new utopians, and they are not designing systems that promote human thriving. Their visions make a future place for their kind only, despite the claims that they do so on behalf of all humanity. They are dismissive of democracy. They don't give a fig about history. Anyone who doesn't want what they say is coming—and what they're making more likely to come, through their money, influence, and control of media platforms—may be accused of living in the past, but ancient Athenians had a few ideas worth uprooting for placement in our dirt.

Acknowledgments

This book emerged by deluge and by drop, depending on the month. I gratefully acknowledge major contributors to my will to keep going with it.

Shaun, first spot goes to you. Any time you come across something ancient when you're reading, you call me over to look. Thanks for spotting "digital Athens" way back in 2012 and getting me thinking. Naoise, thanks for drawing robots on the front pages of all my project notebooks and for the snuggles. Fergus, thanks for ensuring I'm at my desk every day.

Dad, thanks for having had Wiener's books on your shelf while I was growing up and starting to pay attention to what people were reading. You traded in books frequently, so the continuous presence of the mathematician's volumes told me they were worth keeping around. Alone in Pittsburgh for graduate school, I found a copy of *Cybernetics* in a used bookstore, bought it, read it, and held on to it. It made me feel close to home. Your wide-ranging reading and curiosity have long been models for me.

I had a few valuable opportunities to try out ideas that take maturer form here. Many thanks to: Susan Jarratt for her 2014 American Society for the History of Rhetoric conference, "Rhetoric and Freedom," where I tried out "digital Athens" for the first time; the rhetoricians at CU Boulder (Pete Simonson (long a model and mentor), Phaedra Pezzulo, Laurie Gries, Lisa Flores), who planned the 2018 Public Address and invited me to give a plenary, to Damien Smith Pfister (a great friend) and Ali Rowland for responses, and to Robert Hariman for continued interest in what this project was and could become; Caitlin Bruce and the other rhetoricians at Pitt for great questions during my pandemic Zoom Agora; Lisa Villadsen, Hanne Roer, and Christian Kock at Københavns Universitet for a moving visit as their city opened back up again in October 2021; Diane Keeling and Carly Woods (another great friend) for organizing a jolting panel with Diane, Bess Myers, Melissa Croft, and myself for the Rhetoric Society of America 2022; and Thomas Blank and graduate students in ancient history and the Zentrum für Interkulturelle Studien at Johannes Gutenberg Universität in Mainz, Germany, for letting me hold forth on Alice Mary Hilton in June 2023. Thanks to two anonymous reviewers at the journal *History of the Human Sciences* for supportive suggestions about the nutshell argument of this book.

My Penn State colleagues in rhetoric in CAS (Steve, Rosa, Jeremy, Kirt, Mary, Katya, Brad, Pamela, Michael, Joshua, Lisa, Debbie) crackle with intelligence. Thanks to Jeremy for introducing me to Kyle Wagner. Before she was my PSU colleague, Lisa heard my Public Address talk and asked me what my plans were for it. When I told her I didn't really have plans, she said, "Well, the way you talk about it, it certainly *seems* like you want to keep going with it." Lisa, you were right.

Other PSU must-mentions: Shannon Cruz, for coffees, lunches, snark; Jen Buchan, for many (too many) Cassandra moments since I met her in 2016; John Gastil, for his inspirational hope in democratic deliberation (and sortition!); Cyanne Loyle, Kate Maich, and my CAMS colleague Jake Nabel, for writing-group support; Natalie Shoch, for deft research assistance; the McCourtney Institute for Democracy, for a grant that funded my travel to MIT; librarians, for speed; the College of the Liberal Arts, for letting me use some post-tenure funds to buy out a course at a crucial time and for a generous subvention for this book. Beyond PSU, many thanks to/for: the librarians at MIT Distinctive Collections; the National Communication Association for the Karl Wallace Memorial Award that jump-started my research; Barbara Hayward for sharing stories with me about her remarkable mother, Alice Mary Hilton; and Lois Agnew and Mari Lee Mifsud for miscellaneous support.

At the press, abundant thanks to Kyle Wagner, a true shepherd of woolly, wander-prone manuscripts. His choice of reviewers was inspired; thanks to the two anonymous readers for their patient, coaxing criticism. Emily Shelton did first-rate copyediting work, and thanks, too, to Adriana Smith for overseeing it; and, if you and I don't know one another, Nathan Petrie and his team are likely the reason you found this book.

Notes

Introduction

1. Four well-regarded overviews of ancient Athenian democracy are: Moses I. Finley, *Democracy Ancient and Modern*, rev. ed. (Rutgers University Press, [1973] 2019); Josiah Ober, *Mass and Elite in Democratic Athens: Rhetoric, Ideology, and the Power of the People* (Princeton University Press, 1989); Paul Woodruff, *First Democracy* (Oxford University Press, 2005); and Paul Cartledge, *Democracy: A Life* (Oxford University Press, 2016).

2. Niall Livingstone, *Athens: The City as University* (Routledge, 2017), ix; see also Cartledge, *Democracy*, 1.

3. This is not to say that laborers found their work debasing or at odds with the democratic project. In *Peasant-Citizen and Slave: The Foundations of Athenian Democracy* (Verso, [1988] 2015), Ellen Meiksins Woods observes a general tendency, even within professional classics scholarship, "to attribute patterns of Greek culture to the institution of slavery and to a disdain for labour which is supposed to have been associated with it" (3). It is certainly the norm in most examples I use throughout this book. Woods's account of ancient Athenian democracy emphasizes its core element: the unprecedented and subsequently unmatched political empowerment of the working poor, who did not themselves seem to find work demeaning.

4. Thomas Carlyle, "Signs of the Times," *Edinburgh Review* 49 (June 1829): 439–59.

5. [Timothy Walker], "Art. V. Defence of Mechanical Philosophy," *North American Review* 9, nos. 2–3 (July 1831): 122–36.

6. Walker, "Defence," 123. Note the appearance of "drudgery" and "danger," two words given strong pejorative force, to describe the type of labor that ought to be mechanized. With automation and AI, they appear in the twentieth and the twenty-first centuries, too. Thanks to Seth Davis for sharing with me his unpublished paper, "AI and Labor: How Industry Chose the Terms," which focuses on the so-called 3 D's: "dull," "dirty," and "dangerous."

7. Walker, 124.

8. Walker, 124.

9. Walker, 126.

10. Walker, 127. For a US American writing in 1831 to allege that machinery keeps the United States from using subjugating force against people—as if, at that time, millions of people were not enslaved in the country—tells us which people Walker includes in his thinking, or, more fundamentally, who counted as people in his thinking.

11. Walker, 127. Several decades later, Harris, the enslaver of George, calls enslaved people "labor-saving machines," in Harriet Beecher Stowe, *Uncle Tom's Cabin*, ed. Jean Fagan Yellin (Oxford University Press, [1852] 1998), 18.

12. Walker, "Defence," 127.

13. Most famously, it was none other than Aristotle who imagined it. His line on automation is the focus of chapters 5 and 6 in this book. In the century before him, though, Athenian comic playwrights wrote of self-setting tables, self-washing cups, and hot snacks that hopped right into mouths, for which we have fragmentary evidence. See H. C. Baldry, "The Idler's Paradise in Attic Comedy," *Greece & Rome* 22, no. 65 (1953): 49–60; and Martin Devecka, "Did the Greeks Believe in Their Robots?," *Cambridge Classical Journal* 59 (2013): 52–69, 63–64.

14. Larry Diamond, "Liberation Technology," *Journal of Democracy* 21, no. 3 (2010): 69–83; see, too, Matt Tierney, *Dismantlings: Words Against Machines in the American Long Seventies* (Cornell University Press, 2019), chapter 6.

15. I. F. Clarke, *The Pattern of Expectation, 1644–2001* (Basic Books, 1979), 12.

16. Langdon Winner, *Autonomous Technology: Technics-out-of-Control as a Theme in Political Thought* (MIT Press, [1977] 1978).

17. Fredric Jameson, "History and Salvation in Philip K. Dick," in *Archaeologies of the Future: The Desire Called Utopia and Other Science Fictions* (Verso, 2007), 365.

18. Outside the study of rhetoric, topos appeared within efforts to establish the method of media archaeology. Erkki Huhtamo defines the method as "a way of studying recurring cyclical phenomena that (re)appear and disappear and reappear over and over again in media history, somehow seeming to transcend specific historical contexts"; see Erkki Huhtamo, "From Kaleidoscomaniac to Cybernerd: Notes Toward an Archaeology of the Media," *Leonardo* 30, no. 3 (1997): 222. He availed of topoi as a concept to organize those cycles, pulling the concept from the work of mid-twentieth-century German medievalist Ernst Robert Curtius. In his 1948 book, *Europische Literatur und lateinisches Mittelalter*, Curtius had used "topos" to identify an expression of shared patterns of thinking across time, a continuity he was eager to emphasize in a fragmented, broken Europe; see Ernst Robert Curtius, *European Literature and the Latin Middle Ages*, trans. William R. Trask, new introduction by Colin Burrow (Princeton University Press, [1948] 2013). Though Curtius opens his chapter "Rhetoric" with attention to Aristotle, he does not mention Aristotle's theoretical work with the word "topos" and does not distinguish among the various topoi Aristotle enumerates. Curtius defines a topos as "an intellectual theme," writes that "topoi are helps toward composing orations," and points out that Quintilian called them "storehouses of trains of thought" (70). Curtius subscribes to the decline theory of rhetoric, according to which rhetorical practices lost their public purpose and became literature. Accordingly, he reasons, topoi can be found in all literature, and this gives them the status, sometimes, of "cliché" (70).

19. Aristotelis, *Ars rhetorica*, ed. W. D. Ross (Oxford University Press, 1959), 1397aff.

20. Rhetorician Michael Leff observes that, even if one is sticking to ancient rhetorical theory on topos, the word "incorporates a bewildering diversity of meanings," and that diversity has continued; see Michael C. Leff, "The Topics of Argumentative Invention in Latin Rhetorical Theory from Cicero to Boethius," *Rhetorica* 1, no. 1 (1983): 23. For a summary and extension of work on "visual topoi," see David L. Marshall, "Warburgian Maxims for Visual Rhetoric," *Rhetoric Society Quarterly* 48, no. 4 (2018): 352–79.

21. For an endorsement of "topos" as a term useful for what the authors call "panhistoriography"—that is, "writing histories whose temporal scope extends well beyond the span of individual generations," or that "leap across geographic space, tacking important activities,

terms, movements, or practices as they travel with trade, with global expansion, or with religious zealotry"—see Debra Hawhee and Christa J. Olson, "Pan-Historiography: The Challenges of Writing History Across Time and Space," in *Theorizing Histories of Rhetoric*, ed. Michelle Ballif (Southern Illinois University Press, 2013), 90–105, 90.

22. See, for example, Astra Taylor, *Democracy May Not Exist, but We'll Miss It When It's Gone* (Metropolitan, 2019), 2, 7, 10.

23. For instance, Josiah Ober links democracy and living well, claiming that the "social conditions" under which humans flourish are "uniquely well supported by democracy"; see Josiah Ober, *Demopolis: Democracy Before Liberalism in Theory and Practice* (Cambridge University Press, 2017), 89.

24. Staying sensitive to (and being resistant to) assumptions that ancient Mediterranean places are, all on their own, foundations, pillars, civilizational lodestones, or miracles is key to a methodology classicist Johanna Hanink has called "critical classical reception"; see Johanna Hanink, "It's Time to Embrace Critical Classical Reception," *Eidolon*, May 1, 2017, https://eidolon.pub/its-time-to-embrace-critical-classical-reception-d3491a40eec3.

25. Working with Huhtamo's use of topos to study automation hype over time is Caroline Bassett and Ben Roberts, "Automation Now and Then: Automation Fevers, Anxieties and Utopias," *New Formations* 98 (2019): 9–28. Not using "topos" but noticing discourse patterns is sociologist Aaron Benanav's concept of "the automation discourse," which refers to periodic bursts of communication about how machines that run increasingly more on their own will affect labor and life. Each time a burst occurs—and Benanav notes that "visions of automated factories" first appeared in the 1830s and then again in the 1930s, 1950s, 1980s, and 2010s—it assumes an agonistic shape, as proponents and opponents feel their way around the short- and long-term future of work. See Aaron Benanav, *Automation and the Future of Work* (Verso, 2020), 8.

26. See, for example, Anahid Nersessian, *Utopia, Limited: Romanticism and Adjustment* (Harvard University Press, 2015), 1; and Davide Napoli, "The Shape of Early Greek Utopia," *Classical Quarterly* 71, no. 2 (2021): 467–81. Hesiod's *Works and Days* appears in chapter 4 of this book.

27. David Konstan, "The Greek Polis and Its Negations: Versions of Utopia in Aristophanes's *Birds*," in *The City as Comedy: Society and Representation in Athenian Drama*, ed. Gregory W. Durbov (University of North Carolina Press, 1997), 3–22.

28. Lewis Mumford, *The Story of Utopias* (Azafran, [1922] 2017), 22–23. See also Clarke, *Pattern of Expectation*, 4, where Plato is hailed as "our first father in utopia" for his *Republic* and for his account of Atlantis in *Timaeus*; and Donald R. Morrison, "The Utopian Character of Plato's Ideal City," in *The Cambridge Companion to Plato's "Republic,"* ed. G. R. F. Ferrari (Cambridge University Press, 2007), 232–55.

29. Mumford, *Story of Utopias*, 22. I return to Plato's *Republic* in chapter 1.

30. Karl Popper, *The Open Society and Its Enemies, Vol. 1: The Spell of Plato* (Routledge, [1945] 2011), 149.

31. Popper, *The Open Society and Its Enemies*, 1:184–89.

32. Plato, *Republic*, books 6–10, trans. Chris Emlyn-Jones and William Preddy (Harvard University Press, 2013), 6.527c2.

33. Plato, *Republic*, 2.369a-e, in Plato, *Republic*, books 1–5, trans. Chris Emlyn-Jones and William Preddy (Cambridge, MA: Harvard University Press, 2013), 5.472d; 6.502b; 7.541b.

34. For a study of Plato's *Republic* in particular, see Gerard Boter, *The Textual Tradition of Plato's "Republic"* (Brill, 1989).

35. *Three Early Modern Eutopias: Thomas More, "Utopia"; Francis Bacon, "Atlantis"; Henry Neville, "Isle of Pines,"* ed. Susan Bruce (Oxford University Press, 2008), 128 (from *The English Translation Thereof* by Raphe Robynson, 2nd ed., 1556).

36. Sarah Hogan, *Other Englands: Utopia, Capital, and Empire in an Age of Transition* (Stanford University Press, 2018), 30.

37. Thomas Smith and son referred to their plan for Ireland as *Eutopia* in 1572 (as discussed in Hogan, *Other Englands*, 97).

38. Melissa Lane briefly sketches the vicissitudes of Plato's reception as a political theorist, summing up the range as "the first totalitarian, the first communist, the first idealist?" See Melissa Lane, *Plato's Progeny: How Plato and Socrates Still Captivate the Modern Mind* (London: Duckworth, 2001), 97–134, 97.

39. Fredric Jameson, "Varieties of the Utopian," in *Archaeologies of the Future: The Desire Called Utopia and Other Science Fictions* (Verso, 2007), 1–9.

40. Howard P. Segal, *Technological Utopianism in American Culture* (University of Chicago Press, 1985), 21.

41. William E. Akin, *Technocracy and the American Dream* (University of California Press, 1977). The technocrats have been part of the scene in 2020s because Elon Musk is ubiquitous, and his grandfather was Joshua N. Haldeman, a Canadian technocrat; see Jonathan Taplin, *The End of Reality: How Four Billionaires Are Selling a Fantasy Future of the Metaverse, Mars, and Crypto* (Public Affairs, 2023), 1 (and all of part 1). For an exploration of the technocratic hue of Musk destroying the US government's administrative apparatus in untold amounts, see Jill Lepore, "The Failed Ideas That Drive Elon Musk," *New York Times*, April 4, 2025, https://www.nytimes.com/2025/04/04/opinion/elon-musk-doge-technocracy.html.

42. Alvin M. Weinberg, "Can Technology Replace Social Engineering?," *Bulletin of the Atomic Scientists* 22, no. 10 (1966): 4–8, 5. The reference to the "affluent society" likely alludes to economist John Kenneth Galbraith, *The Affluent Society* (Mentor, 1958). The *OED* entry for "social engineer" dates the term to 1842 and defines it as "a person who uses centralized planning in an attempt to manage social change and regulate the future development and behaviour of a society."

43. Howard P. Segal, "Practical Utopias: America as Techno-Fix Nation," *Utopian Studies* 28, no. 2 (2017): 231–46.

44. Evgeny Morozov, *To Save Everything, Click Here: The Folly of Technological Solutionism* (PublicAffairs, 2014), 6. Morozov criticizes notions not of automated Athens, as I do, but of "silicon Eden" (xii).

45. Meredith Broussard, *Artificial Unintelligence: How Computers Misunderstand the World* (MIT Press, 2019), 7–8, both quotes from 8.

46. Emily Chang, *Brotopia: Breaking Up the Boy's Club of Silicon Valley* (Penguin, 2019).

47. Adam Becker, *More Everything Forever: AI Overlords, Space Empires, and Silicon Valley's Crusade to Control the Fate of Humanity* (Basic Books, 2025), 29, italics in original.

48. Becker, *More Everything Forever*, 249.

49. Becker, to be fair, does consider science fiction from the 1940s on, but he does not look at actual public discourse from decades earlier than the 1990s. For treatments of tech from the mid 1950s to the 1970s, see Jill Lepore, *If Then: How the Simulmatics Corporation Invented the Future* (Liverlight, 2020); Matt Tierney, *Dismantlings: Words Against Machines in the American Long Seventies* (Cornell University Press, 2019); Caroline Bassett, *Anti-Computing: Dissent and the Machine* (Manchester University Press, 2021); and Jason Resnikoff, *Labor's End: How the Promise of Automation Degraded Work* (University of Illinois Press, 2021).

50. Thucydides, *History of the Peloponnesian War*, vol 1, trans. C. F. Smith (Harvard University Press, 1919), 2.41.1.

51. Plato, *Gorgias, Menexenus, Protagoras*, trans. Malcolm Schofield (Cambridge University Press, 2009). The classic work on the Athenian funeral oration is Nicole Loraux, *The Invention of Athens: The Funeral Oration in the Classical City*, trans. Alan Sheridan (Zone, [1991] 2006). For a study of *Menexenus* as parody, see Robert Hariman, "Political Parody and Public Culture," *Quarterly Journal of Speech* 94, no. 3 (2008): 247–72.

52. Johanna Hanink and Demetra Kasimis, "Introduction: In Terms of Athens," *Ramus* 50, nos. 1–2 (2021): 2–3. In *The Classical Debt: Greek Antiquity in an Era of Austerity* (Harvard University Press, 2017), Hanink examines how the reputation ancient Athenians fashioned for themselves has been mobilized since the eighteenth century for or against modern Greece.

53. John Ma, *Polis: A New History of the Ancient Greek City-State from the Early Iron Age to the End of Antiquity* (Princeton University Press, 2024), 451.

54. These formulations are not, I think, what sociologist Zygmunt Bauman calls *retrotopias*, "visions located in the lost/stolen/abandoned but undead past"—see *Retrotopia* (Polity, 2017), 5)—or what tech papa Kevin Kelly calls *protopias*, not just a vision of where we might arrive with steady technological progress but an appreciation for our current position, a recognition "that things are better today than they were yesterday, although only a little better"; see Kevin Kelly, *The Inevitable: Understanding the 12 Technological Forces That Will Shape Our Future* (Penguin, 2017), 13–14. The latter view has a lot in common with J. Bradford DeLong, *Slouching Toward Utopia: An Economic History of the Twentieth Century* (Basic Books, 2022).

55. For a critical assessment of "black classics," see Dan-El Padilla Peralta, *Classicism and Other Phobias* (Princeton University Press, 2025). For labor organizing, see Stephen M. Ward, ed., *Pages from a Black Radical's Notebook: A James Boggs Reader* (Wayne State University Press, 2011); Tom Kahn, *The Economics of Equality* (League for Industrial Democracy, 1964); and Jason Resnikoff, "The Myth of Black Obsolescence," *International Labor and Working-Class History* 102 (2023): 124–45. For utopian imaginings, see Alex Zamalin, *Black Utopia: The History of an Idea from Black Nationalism to Afrofuturism* (Columbia University Press, 2019); and Aaron Robertson, *The Black Utopians: Searching for Paradise and the Promised Land in America* (Farrar, Straus & Giroux, 2024).

56. One notable exception comes from 1948, the same year Wiener's *Cybernetics* was published, in a speech W. E. B. Du Bois delivered at the California Labor School; see Michele Kennerly, "The Place of Ancient Greece in W. E. B. Du Bois's 'The Workers' (1948)," forthcoming.

Chapter One

An earlier version of this chapter was published as Michele Kennerly, "Cybernetics in the Republic," *History of the Human Sciences* 36, no. 1 (2023): 80–102.

1. Ronald R. Kline, *The Cybernetics Moment; or Why We Call Our Age the Information Age* (Johns Hopkins University Press, 2015), documents the rise and fall of "cybernetics." Stefanos Geroulanos and Leif Weatherby, "Cybernetics and the Human Sciences," *History of the Human Sciences* 33, no. 1 (2020): 3–11, argue for the importance of the study of cybernetics today precisely because of how consequential it was for the twentieth century.

2. Owing to "cyberspace" splashing out of William Gibson's 1984 science-fiction novel *Neuromancer*, "cyber-" was so common by 1996 that critics were calling for a moratorium; see, for example, David Wallis, "After Cyberoverkill Comes Cyberburnout," *New York Times*, August 4,

1996, Section 1, 43. These days, we have "cybersecurity," "cybertruck" (that regrettable-looking electric vehicle), "cyberpunk," and the odd throwback academic term such as "cyberformalism." See Daniel Shore, *Cyberformalism: Histories of Linguistic Forms in the Digital Archive*(Johns Hopkins University Press, 2018). "Cyborg" (from "cybernetic organism") never went away.

3. Wiener, *Cybernetics*, 24; Norbert Wiener, *I Am a Mathematician*, in *A Life in Cybernetics* [*Ex Prodigy: My Childhood and Youth* and *I Am a Mathematician: The Later Life of a Prodigy*] (MIT Press, [1956] 2017), 454. See also Christopher Johnson, "'French' Cybernetics," *French Studies* 69, no. 1 (2014): 60–61; and Bernard Dionysius Geoghegan, "Textocracy, or, the Cybernetic Logic of French Theory," *History of the Human Sciences* 33, no. 1 (2020): 53–54.

4. Wiener, *I Am a Mathematician*, 454.

5. Wiener, 419–20. For a study of one of those groups, which came together for the Macy Foundation conferences, see Steve Joshua Heims, *The Cybernetics Group* (MIT Press, 1991).

6. For a study of the "cybernetic rhetoric" of Rosenblueth, see José G. Izaguirre III, "Reckoning with Tlateloloco: Arturo Rosenblueth and a Cybernetic Rhetoric," *Rhetoric & Public Affairs* 25, no. 2 (2022): 57–90.

7. Wiener, *Cybernetics*, 11–12. Perhaps it was the typesetter who inserted a *chi* for a *kappa*.

8. Wiener, 27.

9. Wiener, 27.

10. I take a much longer look at this in chapter 5. For the more recent history, see Ron Eglash, "Broken Metaphor: The Master-Slave Analogy in Technical Literature," *Technology and Culture* 48, no. 2 (2007): 360–69. For extensive critical analysis on machines/robots and subordination, see Neda Atanasoski and Kalindi Vora, *Surrogate Humanity: Race, Robots, and the Politics of Technological Futures* (Duke University Press, 2019); Ruha Benjamin, *Race After Technology: Abolitionist Tools for the New Jim Code* (Polity, 2019), 49–76; Louis Chude-Sokei, *The Sound of Culture: Diaspora and Black Technopoetics* (Wesleyan University Press, 2016), 78–127; and Louis Chude-Sokei, "Race and Robotics," in *Cyborg Futures: Cross-Disciplinary Perspectives on Artificial Intelligence and Robotics*, ed. Teresa Heffernan (Palgrave Macmillan, 2019), 159–71 (which includes analysis of Wiener's and Samuel Butler's use of the machine-slave metaphor); Markus Krajewski, *The Server: A Media History from the Present to the Baroque*, trans. Ilinca Iurascu (Yale University Press, [2011] 2018); and Jennifer Rhee, *The Robotic Imaginary: The Human and The Price of Dehumanized Labor* (University of Minnesota Press, 2018).

11. Samuel Butler, *Erewhon Erewhon and Erewhon Revisited* (Dover, [1872] 2015), 138–60. "Erewhon" is (nearly) "nowhere" backward and thus a utopia pun.

12. Wiener, *Cybernetics*, 27; Wiener, *The Human Use of Human Beings*, rev. ed. (De Capo, 1954), 182–83; Norbert Wiener, "Some Moral and Technical Consequences of Automation," *Science* 131, 3410 (1960): 1355, 1357.

13. Karel Čapek, *RUR*, trans. Paul Selver and Nigel Playfair (Dover, 2001). During a congressional hearing in 1964 to determine whether a National Commission on Automation and Technological Progress ought to be established, secretary of labor under President Johnson W. Willard Wirtz urged that this play ought to be read by anyone who wondered whether "the soul of man will be destroyed by automation." See National Commission on Technology, Automation, and Economic Progress, "Hearings Before the Select Subcommittee on Labor of the Committee on Education and Labor, House of Representatives," 88th Cong., 2nd sess., on H.R. 10310 and Related Bills, April 14, 15, and 27, 1964 (Government Printing Office, 1964), 23.

14. Čapek, *RUR*, 15.

15. Norbert Wiener, *God and Golem, Inc.: A Comment on Certain Points Where Cybernetics Impinges on Religion* (MIT Press, 1964), 55; Norbert Wiener, "Prologue: *Rossum's Universal Robots* by Karel Çapek [*sic*], presented by NW for dramatic performance," cuid16534, Box 29B, Folder 657, Norbert Wiener Papers, MC-0022, Massachusetts Institute of Technology Libraries, Department of Distinctive Collections. Wiener's introduction of the play includes a take on Plato's "philosopher king" imaginary from the *Republic*: the term "poet engineer."

16. Wiener, *Cybernetics*, 27.

17. Norbert Wiener, "Some Moral and Technical Consequences of Automation," *Science* 131, no. 3410 (1960): 1357.

18. A. L. Samuel, "Some Moral and Technical Consequences of Automation—A Refutation," *Science* 132, 3429 (1960): 741. For the current state of the debate, see David J. Gunkle, *Person, Thing, Robot: A Moral and Legal Ontology for the Twenty-First Century and Beyond* (MIT Press, 2023).

19. Wiener, *Cybernetics*, 27.

20. Wiener, 27–28.

21. Wiener, 28.

22. Wiener, *Cybernetics*, 28; Wiener, *I Am a Mathematician*, 450–51. One of Wiener's labor letters, to Walter Reuther, then president of the Union of Automobile Workers, can be found here: Libcom.org, http://libcom.org/history/father-cybernetics-norbert-wieners-letter-uaw-president-walter-reuther. For a study of Reuther's tactics regarding automation when he led the UAW, see David Steigerwald, "Walter Reuther, the UAW, and the Dilemmas of Automation," *Labor History* 51, no. 3 (August 2010): 429–53.

23. Wiener, *Cybernetics*, 28; see also Wiener, *I Am a Mathematician*, 441–47.

24. Wiener, *Cybernetics*, 28.

25. Norbert Wiener, "A Scientist Rebels," *Atlantic* 179 (1947): 46; Wiener, *I Am a Mathematician*, 438–40.

26. Norbert Wiener, *The* Human *Use of Human Beings: Cybernetics and Society* (Houghton Mifflin, 1950), 9. The first edition of the book places typographic emphasis on the first "human," and I follow suit.

27. Wiener, 206–9.

28. Some touchstones are: Jérôme Segal, *Le zéro et le un: histoire de la notion scientifique d'information au 20e siècle* (Éditions Syllepse, 2003); David A. Mindell, Jérôme Segal, and Slava Gerovitch, "From Communications Engineering to Communications Science: Cybernetics and Information Theory in the United States, France, and the Soviet Union," in *Science and Ideology: A Comparative History*, ed. Mark Walker (Routledge, 2003), 66–96; Céline Lafontaine, *L'empire cybernétique: des machines à penser à la pensée machine. Essai* (Éditions du Seuil, 2004); Mathieu Triclot, *Le moment cybernétique: la constitution de la notion d'information* (Éditions Champ Vallon, 2008); Johnson, "'French' Cybernetics," 2014; Ronan Le Roux, *Une histoire de la cybernétique en France, 1948–1975* (Classiques Garnier, 2018); Bernard Dionysius Geoghegan, "Textocracy, or, The Cybernetic Logic of French Theory," in *Code: From Information Theory to French Theory* (Duke University Press, 2023); and Jacob Krell, "What Is the 'Cybernetic' in the 'History of Cybernetics'? A French Case, 1968 to the Present," *History of the Human Sciences* 33, no. 1 (2020): 188–211.

29. In their comparative study of the uptake of cybernetics, Mindell et al. mention only the French writers' insistence on Ampère's "priority," but these writers are equally insistent that Plato be acknowledged ("From Communications Engineering to Communications Science," 89).

30. Pierre de Latil, *La pensée artificielle: Introduction à la cybernétique* (Gallimard, 1953). Four years later, it was translated into English as Pierre de Latil, *Thinking by Machine: A Study of Cybernetics*, trans. Y. M. Golla (Houghton Mifflin, 1957).

31. Latil, *La pensée artificielle*. The epigraph is from Plato, *Gorgias*—see Plato, *Lysis; Symposium; Gorgias*, trans. W. R. M. Lamb (Harvard University Press, 2001), 511d—and the translation from the French is mine. All other translations throughout are mine.

32. French mathematician Georges-Théodule Guilbaud shares an amusing anecdote about classicists: "When someone eventually turned up the new term in Plato, some of the experts rose in horror, declaring that *kybernētikē* should on no account be translated 'cybernetics.'" Georges-Théodule Guilbaud, *What Is Cybernetics?*, trans. Valerie MacKay (Grove, 1960), 3).

33. Latil, *La pensée artificielle*, 13.

34. Latil, 23.

35. Ampère, *Essai sur la philosophie des sciences*, 143.

36. Ampère, 143.

37. "Although James Watt had patented the centrifugal governor in 1784, Ampère showed no awareness of the existence of regulatory processes outside politics, and of the feedback of information as a key element in regulation. In his time, even the concept of energy had not taken hold, let alone information." Pesi Rostum Masani, *Norbert Wiener, 1894–1964* (Birkhäuser Verlag, 1990), 252.

38. Georges-Théodule Guilbaud, *La cybernétique* (Presses Universitaires de France, 1954). The quotations that follow come from the translation (Guilbaud, *What Is Cybernetics?*).

39. Guilbaud, *What Is Cybernetics?*, 1.

40. Guilbaud, 1.

41. Guilbaud, 2. Some more recent commentators still attribute Wiener's lack of attention to Plato as a problem of knowledge; see, for example, Masani, *Norbert Wiener*: "What Wiener never found out, however, was that the term κυβερνητική, the art of steersmanship, occurs in 'Gorgias,' a dialogue of Plato, in a passage on the arts of navigation and rhetoric" (252).

42. Wiener, *Human Use of Human Beings*, rev. ed., 15. The Polish thinker was the philosopher Bronisław Trentowski, who used *cybernetyki* in 1843 in the sense of "the art of governing a nation"; see Bronisław Trentowski, *Stosunek filozofii do cybernetyki, czyli sztuki rządzenia narodem* (Nakładem Ksiegarni J. K. Żupańskiego, 1843).

43. Wiener, *Human Use of Human Beings*, rev. ed., 95.

44. Plato, *Republic*, 514a–20a.

45. Wiener, *I Am a Mathematician*, 458. The word "angel" never takes off in the messenger systems of the analog and digital ages, but "demon" does; see, for example, Markus Krajewski, *The Server: A Media History from the Present to the Baroque*, trans. Ilinca Iurascu (Yale University Press, [2011] 2018), 169–213; and Simone Natale, *Deceitful Media: Artificial Intelligence and Social Life After the Turing Test* (Oxford University Press, 2021), 68–86. Rafael Capurro, though, has been trying with the angelic vocabulary since the 1970s; see Rafael Capurro and John Holgate, *Von Boten und Botschaften—Die Angeletik als Weg zur Phänomenologie der Kommunikation* (Wilhelm Fink Verlag, 2011).

46. Wiener, *Ex-Prodigy*, 82; Wiener, *I Am a Mathematician*, 234.

47. Wiener, *Ex-Prodigy*, 82.

48. Wiener, 117.

49. Wiener, 117–18.

50. Norbert Wiener, *Ex-Prodigy* (revision), chapters 1–12, 1953, Box 30B, Folder 718, Norbert

Wiener Papers, MC-0022, Massachusetts Institute of Technology Libraries, Department of Distinctive Collections; see also Norbert Wiener, *The Bent Twig* (*Ex-Prodigy*), original manuscript, chapters 1–7, 1953, cuid16569, Box 29C, Folder 693, Norbert Wiener Papers, MC-0022, Massachusetts Institute of Technology Libraries, Department of Distinctive Collections.

51. Wiener, *Ex-Prodigy*, 129.

52. Wiener, 134.

53. Norbert Wiener, "Philosophy Notebooks, 1911–1912," cuid16363, Box 27A, Folder 444, DigitalStorage: 2020_009RR_001, Norbert Wiener Papers, MC-0022, Massachusetts Institute of Technology Libraries, Department of Distinctive Collections, https://archivesspace.mit.edu/repositories/2/archival_objects/151322, 19.

54. Wiener, *Ex-Prodigy*, 133.

55. Plato, *Republic*, book 1:332e, 333c, 341c–d, 342d–e, 346a–b; book 3:389b–d; book 6:488a7–89a6, in Plato, *Republic*, trans. Chris Emlyn-Jones and William Preddy (Harvard University Press, 2013). For an analysis of the "ship of state" *eikōn* in book 6, see David Keyt, "Plato and the Ship of State," in *The Blackwell Guide to Plato's "Republic,"* ed. Gerasimos Santas (Wiley, 2006), 189–213. "Paradigm of a good polis" comes in book 5, 472d.

56. Plato, *Republic*, 488a.

57. "Invention" is an exciting word for rhetoricians, referring as it does to the first stage of the rhetorical process, coming upon and coming up with something to say (in Latin, *inventio*). For Wiener, its foundation is in thinking productive of the "new and as yet nonexisting" (*Invention*, 3).

58. Wiener, 58, italics mine.

59. Wiener, 56. The line is Plato, *Republic*, 5.473d.

60. Wiener, 56.

61. Wiener, 57.

62. Aristotle, *Politics*, 3.1278a.7–8.

63. Wiener, *Cybernetics*, 39. Incidentally, Plato's Socrates mentions the moving statues of Daedalus at *Euthyphro* 11c-2 and *Meno* 97dff. See Plato, *Euthyphro; Apology; Crito; Phaedo*, trans. C. Emlyn-Jones and W. Preddy (Harvard University Press, 2017); and Plato, *Laches; Protagoras; Meno; Euthydemus*, trans. W. R. M. Lamb (Harvard University Press, 1924). For a study of Daedalus's work as a forerunner of today's "biotechno-wonders," see Adrienne Mayor, *Gods and Robots: Myths, Machines, and Ancient Dreams of Technology* (Princeton University Press, 2018), 61–104, 44.

64. Wiener, *Invention*, 57.

65. N. Katherine Hayles, *How We Became Posthuman: Virtual Bodies in Cybernetics, Literature, and Informatics* (University of Chicago Press, 1999), 87.

66. Ronald E. Day, "The 'Conduit Metaphor' and the Nature and Politics of Information Studies," *Journal of the American Society for Information Science* 51, no. 9 (2000): 811.

67. John Durham Peters and Benjamin Peters, "Norbert Wiener as Pragmatist," *Empedocles* 7, no. 2 (2016): 157–72.

68. Kline, *Cybernetic Moment*, 80; Wiener, *The* Human *Use of Human Beings*, 2. See also Wiener, *I Am a Mathematician*: "The sincere scientist must back his bets and guesses, even when he is a Cassandra and no one believes him. I had behind me many years of lonely work in science where I had finally proved to be in the right" (446).

69. Wiener, *The* Human *Use of Human Beings*, 15.

70. Melissa Lane, *Plato's Progeny: How Plato and Socrates Still Cultivate the Modern Mind* (Duckworth, 2001), 118. Two recent books that take on Plato and his reputations are James L.

Kastely, *The Rhetoric of Plato's "Republic": Democracy and the Philosophical Problem of Persuasion* (University of Chicago Press, 2015); and Carol Atack, *Plato: A Civic Life* (Reaktion, 2024).

71. Karl Popper, *The Open Society and Its Enemies, Vol. 1: The Spell of Plato* (Routledge, [1945] 2011).

72. Wiener, *The* Human *Use of Human Beings*, 15.

73. Wiener, *The Human Use of Human Beings*, rev. ed., 50.

74. Wiener, 50.

75. Wiener, 50.

76. Wiener, 50.

77. Wiener, 51.

78. Wiener, *The* Human *Use of Human Beings*, 2.

79. Plato, *Statesman*, 266e, in Plato, *Statesman; Philebus; Ion*, trans. H. N. Fowler and W. R. M. Lamb (Harvard University Press, 1925).

80. Wiener, *The* Human *Use of Human Beings*, 2.

81. Wiener does not engage by name with Aristotle, his *Politics*, or his politics. Isocrates is never mentioned.

82. Wiener, *The Human Use of Human Beings*, rev. ed., 52.

83. Wiener, 181.

84. Giorgio (George) de Santillana, "Life of Norbertos" and "Life of Wieneros," n.d., cuid16754, Box 33C, Folder 950, Norbert Wiener Papers, MC-0022, Massachusetts Institute of Technology Libraries, Department of Distinctive Collections, 1.

85. De Santillana, "Life of Norbertos," 2.

86. Ronald R. Kline, *The Cybernetics Moment, Or Why We Call Our Age the Information Age* (Johns Hopkins University Press, 2015).

87. Donald Campbell and Norbert Wiener, "Automatization (Automatic Factories: Fact and Fiction)," 1954, cuid16596, Box 30C, Folder 746, Norbert Wiener Papers, MC-0022, Massachusetts Institute of Technology Libraries, Department of Distinctive Collections. This piece was published, with a softened version of that line, as Norbert Wiener and Donald Campbell, "'Automatization': Norbert Wiener's Concept of Fully Mechanized Industry," *St. Louis Post-Dispatch*, December 5, 1954, 1. Wiener had no beef with "automatic," calling his time "the new automatic age" in *The Human Use of Human Beings* (rev. ed., 153). A book from 1963 demonstrates lingering confusion over what "automation" means: "We have had the words *automatic, automaton* and even *automatism* and *automatization* for a long time, but the word *automation* has only recently crept into our dictionaries." Pauline Arnold and Percival White, *The Automatic Age* (Holiday House, 1963), 13.

88. "It may very well be a good thing for humanity to have the machine remove from it the need of menial and disagreeable tasks, or it may not. I do not know" (Wiener, *Cybernetics*, 27).

89. Wiener, *The Human Use of Human Beings*, rev. ed., 161.

90. Wiener, 162.

91. Norbert Wiener, "Untitled Article Regarding Automatic Factories," ca. 1954, cuid16595, Box 30C, Folder 745, Norbert Wiener Papers, MC-0022, Massachusetts Institute of Technology Libraries, Department of Distinctive Collections, 5. (In this paper, Wiener wanders into ableism—a position I don't see espoused in any of his other work, and it may speak to an emerging eugenicist discourse of human optimization in the cybernetic age.)

92. Juvenal, *Satires* 10.77–81, in Juvenal and Persius, trans. G. G. Ramsey (William Heineman, 1918), n.p.

93. "Automation and Technological Change," Hearings Before the Subcommittee on Economic Stabilization of the Joint Committee on the Economic Report Congress of the United States, 84th Cong., 1st sess., October 14, 15, 17, 18, 24, 25, 26, 27, and 28, 1955, printed for the use of the Joint Committee on the Economic Report (Government Printing Office, 1955). The year 1955 also saw the publication of Warner Bloomberg Jr., *The Age of Automation: Its Effects on Human Welfare* (League for Industrial Democracy, 1955), a forty-page pamphlet brimming with forecasts.

94. John Diebold, *Automation: The Advent of the Automatic Factory* (D. Van Nostrand, 1952). In the book, Diebold quotes from Wiener's *The* Human *Use of Human Beings* several times, including the oar quote (163).

95. Diebold, *Automation*, 166. The footnote at the end of this sentence is to Josef Pieper, *Muße und Kult* (Kösel-Verlag, 1948), translated into English as *Leisure: The Basis of Culture*, a very antiquity-oriented book.

96. John Diebold (testimony), "Automation and Technological Change," 27.

97. Diebold, "Automation and Technological Change," 14.

98. Consider, for example, "Economic Possibilities for Our Grandchildren," a speech delivered in 1930 by British economist John Maynard Keynes that popularized the term "technological unemployment." He passes over the matter of involuntary under- or unemployment; instead, he wonders and worries about how "man [*sic*]" will "use his freedom from pressing economic cares" and "occupy his leisure" once workers work fewer hours per day for better pay. "I think with dread," he writes, "of the readjustment of the habits and instincts of the ordinary man, bred into him for countless generations, which he may be asked to discard within a few decades. . . . To use the language of to-day must we not expect a general 'nervous breakdown'? . . . There is no country and no people, I think, who can look forward to the age of leisure and abundance without a dread. For we have been trained too long to strive and not to enjoy." John Maynard Keynes, "Economic Possibilities for our Grandchildren," in *Essays in Persuasion* (W. W. Norton, 2011), ebook.

99. Walter P. Reuther (testimony), "Automation and Technological Change," 120.

Chapter Two

1. Anthropologist Margaret Mead contributed a piece, the only one written by a woman. For a study of the work of Mead and George Bateson, including their contributions to the Macy conferences, see Bernard Dionysius Geoghegan, *Code: From Information Theory to French Theory* (Duke University Press, 2023), chapter 2, For a look at Mead's own, chemically oriented approach to arriving at utopia, see Benjamin Breen, *Tripping on Utopia: Margaret Mead, the Cold War, and the Troubled Birth of Psychedelic Science* (Grand Central, 2024).)

2. Paul F. Douglass, "Foreword," *Annals of the American Academy of Political and Social Science* 313 (September 1957): ix.

3. Williard C. Sutherland, "A Philosophy of Leisure," *Annals of the American Academy of Political and Social Science* 313 (September 1957): 3; Thomas Woody, "Leisure in the Light of History," *Annals of the American Academy of Political and Social Science* 313 (September 1957): 5. This etymology continues to excite people who study work and leisure; see, for example, Sean Carroll's Mindscape podcast conversation with Astra Taylor, "Astra Taylor on the Promise and Challenge of Democracy," Preposterous Universe, July 29, 2019, https://www.preposterousuniverse.com/podcast/2019/07/29/57-astra-taylor-on-the-promise-and-challenge-of-democracy/.

Taylor: "So, for the Ancient Greeks, there was a contempt of labor. They associated leisure with democracy, with that freedom, that space to govern. In fact, I just learned that the roots of the word 'school' actually also had to do with free time. They needed that time to engage in the learning, to engage in the more elevated modes of life, which included being able to go to the assembly and stuff like that."

4. Charlesworth, "Bold Program for Recreation," 142.

5. Charlesworth, 143.

6. Charlesworth, 144.

7. Hannah Arendt, *The Human Condition*, 2nd ed., ed. Margaret Canovan (University of Chicago Press, 1998), 4. For an overview of Arendt's writing on automation during the 1950s (which, but for the very first sentence of *The Human Condition*, does not mention ancient Athens), see Brian Simbirski, "Cybernetic Muse: Hannah Arendt on Automation, 1951–1958," *Journal of the History of Ideas* 77, no. 4 (2016): 589–613. A chapter in Caroline Bassett, *Anti-Computing: Dissent and the Machine* (Manchester University Press, 2021), focuses on the Athens-filled talk Arendt gave at the first Conference on the Cybercultural Revolution, whose themes were cybernation and automation, and that was organized by Alice Mary Hilton in 1964. Since Hilton is the focus of my next chapter, I engage Bassett's work there.

8. Arendt, *Human Condition*, 4.

9. Arendt, 5.

10. Arendt, 5.

11. Arendt, 5. For a study of Arendt's take on thinking, see Benjamin Aldes Wurgaft, *Thinking in Public: Strauss, Levinas, Arendt* (University of Pennsylvania Press, 2016).

12. Arendt, 5, 3. It is noteworthy that she joins Reuther (in his congressional testimony) in showing a suspicious regard for "know-how." Wiener, too, had marked it as problematic.

13. Arendt's own translation of *The Human Condition* into German in 1960 bears the title *Vita activa: oder, vom tätigen Leben* (W. Kohlhammer, 1960): "Vita activa: or from the active life." Crucially, Arendt believes that thinking is a core human activity, but she excludes it, with some saltiness: "'What we are doing' is indeed the central theme of this book. It deals only with the most elementary articulations of the human condition, with those activities that traditionally, as well as according to current opinion, are within the range of every human being. For this and other reasons, the highest and perhaps purest activity of which men are capable, the activity of thinking, is left out of these present considerations" (5).

14. For exceptions, see, again, Simbirski, "Cybernetic Muse"; and Bassett, *Anti-Computing*. I address its Greekness later in this chapter. "Most Greek" appears, for example, in Bonnie Honig, "What Kind of Thing Is Land? Hannah Arendt's Object Relations, or: The Jewish Unconscious of Arendt's Most 'Greek' Text," *Political Theory* 44, no. 3 (2016): 307–36. "Her most Hellenic work" appears in J. Peter Euben, "Arendt's Hellenism," in *Cambridge Companion to Hannah Arendt*, ed. Dana R. Villa (Cambridge University Press, 2000), 162. Arendt's tripartite activity structure is sometimes read back onto ancient Greece. For instance, at two key points in his massive history of the polis, classicist John Ma engages Arendt's division; regrettably, he seems accidentally to exclude "action" and treat "work" the way Arendt, in fact, treats action. John Ma, *Polis: A New History of the Ancient City-State from the Early Iron Age to the End of Antiquity* (Princeton University Press, 2024), 450–51, 554.

15. Arendt, *Human Condition*, 93. She opens the chapter by stating that Marx "will be criticized," even though criticizing Marx puts her in company she says she does not want to keep (79).

16. Arendt, 119–21.

17. Karl Marx, *Grundrisse: Foundations of the Critique of Political Economy (Rough Draft)*, trans. Martin Nicolaus (Penguin, 1993), 84. See Jürgen Habermas, *The Structural Transformation of the Public Sphere: An Inquiry into a Category of Bourgeois Society*, trans. Thomas Burger ([1962] MIT Press, 1991).

18. Marx, *Capital: A Critique of Political Economy, Volume 1*, trans. Ben Fowkes (Penguin, 1976), 283. Arendt very rarely cites her Marx.

19. Marx, *Capital*, 1:270.

20. Marx, 1:290 ("metabolic interaction"), 198 ("social metabolism").

21. Marx, 1:290.

22. Hannah Arendt, "From Hegel to Marx," in *The Promise of Politics*, ed. Jerome Kohn (Schocken, 2005), 80.

23. Arendt, *Human Condition*, 5.

24. Marx, *Capital*, 1:1033, 1034.

25. Arendt, *Human Condition*, 5.

26. Arendt, 136n1.

27. Aristotle, *Politics*, books 3 and 4, trans. Richard Robinson (Clarendon, [1962] 1995), 1278a2–12; on the works of *banausoi* making a *polis* habitable, see 1290b37. Robinson's commentary on this chapter subtly inveighs against the egalitarianism of his own time: "This chapter exhibits Aristotle's feeling that it is an essential part of human goodness to live the life of leisure. He infers that workmen and labourers cannot be good men. He does not feel any reluctance or shame or sorrow in accepting this conclusion. We, on the contrary, are liable to feel so intensely ashamed as to pretend we do not believe it if we do. Perhaps, if it were not for this intense shame, we should think that it is almost impossible to be a high type of man while passing one's working life on an assembly line" (17). At 1328b32–43, Aristotle writes: "The citizens must not live the life of a vulgar craftsman or a commercial life. For such a life is ignoble and contrary to virtue. Nor should those who are to be citizens be farmers. For leisure is needed, both for the development of virtue and for political actions." Aristotle, *Politics*, books 7 and 8, trans. Richard Kraut (Clarendon, 1997). It has been argued recently that Aristotle's views on making (*poesis*) in his other works do not seem to support the exclusion of *banausoi* from political virtue and political life, thereby pointing to inconsistencies in Aristotle's system of thought; see Cary J. Nederman, "Men at Work: *Poesis*, Politics, and Labor in Aristotle and Some Aristotelians," *Analyse & Kritik* 30, no. 1 (2008): 17–31. On the topic of Aristotle's views on fabricators of things, Arendt cites Aristotle, *Politics*, 1258b35ff, which is not as clear on Aristotle's exclusion of *banausoi* as the two places I have cited; see Arendt, *Human Condition*, 82n7.

28. Arendt, 143.

29. Arendt, 148. (See chapter 4 in this volume for more on the "extension" thesis of tools and media.) She cites Diebold on 149, 151, and 152, too. His 1952 book, *Automation*, is the only work strictly about automation that she cites. On the criticism of terms coming out of management as industry adopts automation, she cites Daniel Bell, *Work and Its Discontents: The Cult of Efficiency in America* (Beacon, 1956), which does touch on automation in places, and R. P. Genelli, "Facteur humain ou facteur social du travail," *Revue française du travail* 7, nos. 1–3 (1952), at 149n12. She also cites Charles R. Walker and Robert H. Guest, *The Man on the Assembly Line* (Harvard University Press, 1952), a study of nearly two hundred auto assembly line workers detailing worker dissatisfaction with laboring on the line.

30. Arendt, 9; see also 147.

31. Arendt, 147; see also 145.

32. Arendt, 145.

33. Arendt, 151.

34. Arendt did not write about environmental issues as such, so this is not an environment-based critique.

35. Arendt spends some quality time with Plato and his issues with democracy and action in Hannah Arendt, "Socrates," in *The Promise of Politics*, ed. Jerome Kohn (Schocken), 5–39.

36. Arendt, *Human Condition*, 197. I quote the "everybody," because, of course, not everybody was permitted to speak and act in public in ancient democratic Athens. Arendt does name some exclusions, but she never names women or citizens successfully prosecuted for doing sex work.

37. Arendt, 197, 205.

38. Arendt, 179. The polis is also about hearing and being heard, and rhetoric was the teachable, learnable system for it; Arendt mentions rhetoric directly on p. 26, the only explicit mention in *The Human Condition*.

39. Arendt, 188.

40. Arendt, 188–89.

41. Arendt, 189.

42. Arendt, 28.

43. Hanna Fenichel Pitkin, *The Attack of the Blob: Hannah Arendt's Concept of the Social* (University of Chicago Press, 1998), 16. When Jürgen Habermas writes a history and theory of the bourgeois public sphere in 1962, he cites Arendt (*Structural Transformation of the Public Sphere*, 19), and her thought infuses especially the early chapters of the book.

44. Arendt, *Human Condition*, 188–89.

45. Arendt, 175.

46. Arendt, 194.

47. Arendt, 59 (loneliness), 134 (demand for happiness that makes people obsess over unhappiness).

48. Arendt, 188–89.

49. Arendt, 131.

50. Arendt, 131n82.

51. Arendt, 133.

52. She does not explain this point about technology. I take up the topic of Marx and technology in chapter 5.

53. Arendt, 327. These lectures were given as the Christian Gauss Seminar in Criticism. Samantha Rose Hill points out that Arendt was delivering them during the McCarthy trials. Samantha Rose Hill, *Hannah Arendt* (Reaktion, 2021), 133).

54. Arendt planned to write a book about Marx and to title it "Karl Marx and the Tradition of Political Thought." Efforts have been made to piece it together; see Hannah Arendt, *The Modern Challenge to Tradition: Fragmente eines Buchs*, ed. Barbara Hahn and James McFarland, with Ingo Kielich and Ingeborg Nordmann (Wallstein Verlag, 2018).

55. Hannah Arendt, "Karl Marx and the Tradition of Western Political Thought," in *Thinking Without a Banister: Essays in Understanding, 1953–1975*, ed. Jerome Kohn (Schocken, 2018), 6. Again, Arendt seldom cites Marx, which makes it difficult to tell whether she is quoting, paraphrasing, or extrapolating.

56. For a study of how what Marx writes about Democritus and Epicurus presages his political philosophy, see John Stanley, "The Marxism of Marx's Doctoral Dissertation," *Journal of the History of Philosophy* 33, no. 1 (1995): 133–58.

57. Bruno Kaiser, *Ex Libris Karl Marx und Friedrich Engels: Schicksal und Verzeichnis Einer Bibliothek* (Dietz Verlag, 1967), 221–22, lists the titles. For a meta-analysis of Marx's annotations as a product of his classically based education, see William E. Engel, "Marx's Scholia: Annotations Involving Classical and Renaissance Texts in *Capital*," *Connotations* 29 (2020): 189–219. For Marx and antiquity, see, for example, Rolf t, *Marx und die Antike* (Verlagsansalt Benziger, 1956); George E. McCarthy, *Marx and the Ancients: Classical Ethics, Social Justice, and Nineteenth-Century Political Economy* (Rowman & Littlefield, 1990); and George E. McCarthy, ed., *Marx and Aristotle: Nineteenth-Century German Social Theory and Classical Antiquity* (Rowman & Littlefield, 1992). For a reevaluation of the relationship between Aristotle's and Marx's views of political economy, see Claudio Katz, "The Socialist Polis: Antiquity and Socialism in Marx's Thought," *Review of Politics* 56, no. 2 (1994): 237–60.

58. Arendt, "Karl Marx," 20.

59. Arendt, 20.

60. Arendt, 16, italics in original.

61. Arendt, 38. She quotes a longer version of that line on p. 22 and does not provide a citation either time.

62. Karl Marx, *Capital: A Critique of Political Economy, Vol. 3*, trans. David Fernbach (Penguin, [1981] 1991), 958–59.

63. Arendt, "Karl Marx," 21. She is still not quoting her Marx; the painting quote comes from the section "Organization of Labor" in chapter 3, volume 1, of Karl Marx and Friedrich Engels, *The German Ideology*, https://www.marxists.org/archive/marx/works/1845/german-ideology/ch03l.htm.

64. Arendt, 21.

65. Arendt, 12.

66. Arendt, 22.

67. In her essay "What Is Freedom?," Arendt, attempting to separate freedom and free will, writes, "Let us therefore go back once more to antiquity, i.e., to its political and pre-philosophical traditions, certainly not for the sake of erudition and not even because of the continuity of our tradition, but merely because a freedom experienced in the process of acting and nothing else—though, of course, mankind never lost this experience altogether—has never again been articulated with the same classical clarity." Hannah Arendt, "What Is Freedom?," in *Between Past and Future: Six Exercises in Political Thought* (Viking, 1961), 165.

68. Margaret Canovan, *The Political Thought of Hannah Arendt* (J. M. Dent, 1974), 4. For sensitive engagement of Arendt's relationship with Heidegger, see Hill, *Hannah Arendt*, chapter 2. For brief engagement, see Miriam Leonard, "Hannah Arendt and the Ancients: Preface," *Classical Philology* 113 (2018): 1; and Miriam Leonard, "Arendt's Revolutionary Antiquity," *Classical Philology* 113 (2018): 65.

69. Canovan, *Political Thought of Hannah Arendt*, 10.

70. Canovan, 62.

71. Canovan, 79.

72. Blair Campbell, "Paradigms Lost: Classical Athenian Politics in Modern Myth," *History of Political Thought* 10, no. 2 (1989): 190.

73. Campbell, "Paradigms Lost," 189.

74. The kind of declaration Campbell means is one like this: "If, then, we understand the political in the sense of the *polis*, its end or *raison d'être* would be to establish and keep in existence a space where freedom as virtuosity can appear." Arendt, "What Is Freedom?," 154.

75. Not available to Campbell is Matthew Leigh, *From* Polypragmon *to* Curiosus*: Ancient Concepts of Curious and Meddlesome* (Oxford University Press, 2013). For Aristophanes, see any translation of *Lysistrata* or *Thesmophoriazusae*.

76. Canovan, *Political Thought of Hannah Arendt*; Margaret Canovan, "Introduction," in *Human Condition*, viii.

77. J. Peter Euben, "Arendt's Hellenism," in *Cambridge Companion to Hannah Arendt*, ed. Dana R. Villa (Cambridge University Press, 2000), 163, 152. For an example of his own combinational experiments, see J. Peter Euben, *Platonic Noise* (Princeton University Press, 2003), whose third chapter is a minor revision of the Arendt chapter from the *Cambridge Companion*.

78. Leonard, "Arendt's Revolutionary Antiquity," 55.

79. Leonard, "Hannah Arendt and the Ancients," 2. One flat-out factually incorrect claim in *The Human Condition* serves as representative: "The incapacity of the *animal laborans* for distinction and hence for action and speech seems to be confirmed by the striking absence of serious slave rebellions in ancient and modern times" (215). This nontrivial error comports with Arendt's infamous exclusion of the Haitian revolution in her study *On Revolution* (Penguin, [1963] 2006). For attention to anti-blackness in Arendt's ancient-Athens-based ideas about action, publicness, and humanness in *The Human Condition* and *On Violence*, see Harriet Fertik, "Antiquity, Tradition, and Anti-Blackness in Hannah Arendt's Public Sphere," *TAPA* 154, no. 1 (2024): 271–94. For a more thorough analysis of Arendt and anti-blackness, see Kathryn T. Gines, *Hannah Arendt and the Negro Question* (Indiana University Press, 2014).

80. David Marshall, "The Polis and Its Analogues in the Thought of Hannah Arendt," *Modern Intellectual History* 7, no. 1 (2010): 131, italics in original. See also David Arndt, *Arendt on the Political* (Cambridge University Press, 2019), chapter 3.

81. Pitkin, *Attack of the Blob*, 148, 174–75.

82. I take up Arendt's mention of Aristotle in particular in chapter 5.

83. Arendt, *Human Condition*, 5.

84. Arendt, 322.

85. Arendt, 322.

86. Arendt, 323–24.

Chapter Three

1. She edited the 1971 proceedings from the conference "International Pollution Control," which took place at the University of Trondheim during her presidential tenure; Alice Mary Hilton, ed., *Against Pollution and Hunger: Notes Toward a New World* (John Wiley & Sons, 1974). For more on the SSRS, see Kelly Moore, *Disrupting Science: Social Movements, American Scientists, and the Politics of the Military, 1945–1975* (Princeton University Press, 2008), chapter 3.

2. Though Hilton often provides a biography with her publications, this one is the result of additional sleuthing and exchanging emails with Barbara Hayward, one of Hilton's daughters.

3. Alice Mary Hilton, *Logic, Computing Machines, and Automation* (Spartan, 1963), xv.

4. Hilton, *Logic, Computing Machines, and Automation*, xv, italics in original. Ever the finicky philologist's son, Wiener did not like the construction of *this* word, either: "These portmanteau words rub me the wrong way and they sound to me like a streetcar making a turn on rusty nails." He did, however, write to Hilton to express his support for her book project on cyberculture. In her reply, she thanked him for his support and for his criticism about jargony portmanteaus, telling him that she is "giving this problem a great deal of thought, but I cannot

yet see a way out of my dilemma." Letter from Norbert Wiener to Alice Mary Hilton, March 8, 1963, private papers of Alice Mary Hilton; letter from Alice Mary Hilton to Norbert Wiener, March 20, 1963, private papers of Alice Mary Hilton. Thanks to Barbara Hayward for sharing this correspondence with me.

5. Hilton, *Logic, Computing Machines, and Automation*, 3. On this same page, she provides the etymology of "cybernetics" and immediately connects the word to Plato.

6. I discuss this notion of "extension" in chapter 4.

7. Hilton, *Logic, Computing Machines, and Automation*, xv–xvi.

8. Thomas Rid calls Wiener the leader of "the prophets of doom" and Hilton the leader of "the dreamers" (*Rise of the Machines*, 109), an assessment that holds except that Hilton was a deep admirer of Wiener's work and leans toward dreaming largely because she felt that was where that vision was most needed, given the obvious risks of either nothing really changing or humanity destroying itself with weapons tech.

9. Hilton, *Logic, Computing Machines, and Automation*, xvi. Matt Tierney points out that the *Oxford English Dictionary* entry for "cyberculture" cites this line, thus making Hilton out to be a sort of retrotopian futurist. Matt Tierney, *Dismantlings: Words Against Machines in the American Long Seventies* (Cornell University Press, 2019), 82.

10. Alice Mary Hilton, "Cyberculture—The Age of Abundance and Leisure," *Michigan Quarterly Review* 3, no. 4 (1964): 222; Alice Mary Hilton, "The Bases of Cyberculture: Scientific, Technical, Philosophical, Socio-economic, Political," in *The Evolving Society: The Proceedings of the First Annual Conference on the Cybercultural Revolution*, ed. Alice Mary Hilton (Institute for Cybercultural Research, 1966), 20. Schlaraffenland is sometimes rendered into English as the Land of Cockaygne, which is the name that J. C. Davis gives to a type of early modern English utopia characterized by "satisfactions enough to satiate the grossest appetite." J. C. Davis, *Utopia and the Ideal Society: A Study of English Utopian Writing, 1516–1700* (Cambridge University Press, 1981), 21.

11. Alice Mary Hilton, "Dr. Alice Mary Hilton in Conversation with Studs Terkel," WFMT Radio Network (Chicago), 1967, https://studsterkel.wfmt.com/programs/dr-alice-mary-hilton-conversation-studs-terkel. (He also had her on the show in 1965.)

12. Hilton, *Logic, Computing Machines, and Automation*, 300.

13. "Dr. Norbert Wiener Dead at 69; Known as Father of Automation," *New York Times*, March 19, 1964, https://www.nytimes.com/1964/03/19/archives/dr-norbert-wiener-dead-at-69-known-as-father-of-automation.html.

14. I have not been able to determine whether Wiener had agreed to appear or to speak at the conference, but papers preserved by Barbara Hayward show that he had agreed to serve on the editorial board of the Age of Cyberculture book series that Hilton was planning to launch (as reported by Rid, *Rise of the Machines*, 103).

15. Hilton, *Evolving Society*, n. p.

16. I do not know how Hilton felt about this fact, but she and Frances W. Herring, a peace activist and professor of government at Berkeley, were the only women members. When I asked Hilton's daughter Barbara about it, she said: "AMH did not like labeling or 'pigeonholing' herself or others, thus my sister and I do not think she thought of herself as an activist. Nor a feminist. If anything, AMH thought of herself as an independent thinker: a maverick!" (personal email correspondence, July 13, 2023). I will return to several other members later.

17. "The Triple Revolution: An Appraisal of the Major US Crises and Proposals for Action," *International Socialist Review* 25, no. 3 (1964): 85. Engineer and physicist Dennis Gabor (inventor

of the hologram) also envisioned a big triple, which he called "the Trilemma": "Our civilization faces three great dangers. The first is destruction by nuclear war, the second is overpopulation, and the third is the Age of Leisure." Dennis Gabor, *Inventing the Future* (Knopf, 1964), 3).

18. "Triple Revolution," 85.

19. "Triple Revolution," 85.

20. "Triple Revolution," 86.

21. "Triple Revolution," 86.

22. "Triple Revolution," 87.

23. "Triple Revolution," 87.

24. "Triple Revolution," 89.

25. "Triple Revolution," 89.

26. "Triple Revolution," 89.

27. National Commission on Technology, Automation, and Economic Progress, Hearings Before the Select Subcommittee on Labor of the Committee on Education and Labor, House of Representatives, 88th Cong., 2nd sess., on H.R. 10310 and Related Bills, to Establish a National Commission on Automation and technological Progress, Washington, DC, April 14, 15, and 27, 1964 (Government Printing Office, 1964), 126.

28. National Commission on Technology, Automation, and Economic Progress, 125–35.

29. Lyndon B. Johnson, "Remarks upon Signing Bill Creating the National Commission on Technology, Automation, and Economic Progress," American Presidency Project, accessed November 12, 2025, https://www.presidency.ucsb.edu/node/241917.

30. Alice Mary Hilton, "An Ethos for the Age of Cyberculture," in *AFIPS Conference Proceedings, Vol. 25: 1964 Spring Joint Computer Conference* (Spartan, 1964), 142. The Protestant ethic, first named in the early twentieth century by Max Weber in *The Protestant Ethic and the "Spirit" of Capitalism*, translated by Peter Baehr and Gordon C. Wells (Penguin, 2002), is better known today as the Protestant work ethic.

31. Hilton, "Ethos for the Age of Cyberculture," 142, 144.

32. Hilton, *Logic, Computing Machines, and Automation*, xvi.

33. Hilton, "Ethos for the Age of Cyberculture," 142, 144.

34. Hilton, 145.

35. Hilton, 145.

36. Hilton, 146.

37. Hilton, 146.

38. Hilton, 162.

39. Hilton, 148.

40. Alice Mary Hilton, "Cyberculture in the Transition from a War to a Peacetime Economy," *Fellowship* (May 1964): 7.

41. Hilton, "Ethos for the Age of Cyberculture," 152. The full line from Plato's *Apology* of Socrates is: "The unexamined life is not worth living for a human." In Plato, *Euthyphro; Apology; Crito; Phaedo*, trans. C. Emlyn-Jones and W. Preddy (Harvard University Press, 2017)), 38a5–6.

42. All quotations come from Hannah Arendt, Hannah Arendt Papers: Correspondence, 1938 to 1976; Organizations, 1943 to 1976; Conference on Cybernetics, New York, NY, 1964–66, Manuscript/Mixed Material, Library of Congress, https://www.loc.gov/item/mss1105600339/.

43. Donald N. Michael, *Cybernation: The Silent Conquest* (Center for the Study of Democratic Institutions, 1962). According to Nils Petter Gleditsch, Norwegian sociologist and research professor at the Peace Research Institute in Oslo (PRIO), the Peace Research Institute

in Washington, DC, became "the better known and more enduring" Institute for Policy Studies (personal email correspondence, May 4, 2023). Thanks to my Penn State colleague Cyanne Loyle, a fellow at PRIO, for pointing me toward Gleditsch. Note the (likely not intentional) titular similarity of Michael's book to Michael Angelo Garvey, *The Silent Revolution; or, the Future Effects of Steam and Electricity upon the Conditions of Mankind* (William & Friederich G. Cash, 1852).

44. Michael, *Cybernation*, 5.

45. Michael, 5.

46. Michael, 9, 10.

47. Michael, 45.

48. Michael, 46.

49. All quotations come from: letters from Alice Mary Hilton to Hannah Arendt, March–May 1964, Hannah Arendt Papers: Correspondence, 1938–76; Organizations, 1943–76; Conference on Cybernetics, New York, NY, 1964–66, https://www.loc.gov/resource/mss11056dig.021940/?st=pdf&pdfPage=4.

50. Donald N. Michael, "Free Time—The New Imperative in Our Society," in *Automation, Education, and Human Values*, ed. William W. Brickman and Stanley Lehrer (School & Society, 1966), 300. This piece was delivered at one of Maxwell Goldberg's conferences. In the late 1980s, Michael reflected on speculating about the future, including his own speculations; Donald N. Michael, "On Thinking About the Future," *Journal of Humanistic Psychology* 20, no. 1 (1989): 37–53.

51. Stephen M. Ward, ed., *Pages from a Black Radical's Notebook: A James Boggs Reader* (Wayne State University Press, 2011).

52. One of her letters to him was preserved with his papers. Alice Mary Hilton, Correspondence, 1963, Box 1, Folder 17, James and Grace Lee Boggs Papers, UP001342, Walter P. Reuther Library.

53. Betty Friedan, *The Feminine Mystique* (W. W. Norton, 1963). For a study of the gendered entailments of automation hitting the domestic space, see Jason Resnikoff, *Labor's End: How the Promise of Automation Degraded Work* (University of Illinois Press, 2021), chapter 6. Looking into the later 1960s, Scott Selisker observes, "'Automation' is arguably the central term for both Solanas's 'SCUM Manifesto' from 1967 and Shulamith Firestone's book-length work *The Dialectic of Sex*." Scott Selisker, *Human Programming: Brainwashing, Automatons, and American Unfreedom* (University of Minnesota Press, 2016), 107.

54. "The Negro Movement: Where Shall It Go Now?," *Dissent* (1964): 279–95.

55. Tom Kahn, *The Economics of Equality* (League for Industrial Democracy, 1964).

56. Alice Mary Hilton, "Basic Assumptions," in *The Evolving Society: The Proceedings of the First Annual Conference on the Cybercultural Revolution*, ed. Alice Mary Hilton (Institute for Cybercultural Research, 1966), 2.

57. Hilton, "Bases of Cyberculture," 8.

58. Hilton, 8.

59. Hilton, "Basic Assumptions," 6. She repeats "the Good Life" in Hilton, "Bases of Cyberculture," 16 and 18. I devote chapters 5 and 6 to this Aristotle line.

60. Hilton, "Basic Assumptions," 6.

61. Hilton, "Bases of Cyberculture," 17.

62. Hilton, 19, italics in original.

63. Hilton, 19, italics in original.

64. Herbert Layton Hayward, "Panel Discussion," in *The Evolving Society: The Proceedings of the First Annual Conference on the Cybercultural Revolution*, ed. Alice Mary Hilton (Institute for Cybercultural Research, 1966), 63–64. Hilton's daughter Barbara receives her mother's praise in the volume's forward for managing "the enormous number of abstracts, biographies, papers, etc. for participants, press, and audience" (xiv).

65. Ted F. Silvey, "Production Control," in *The Evolving Society: The Proceedings of the First Annual Conference on the Cybercultural Revolution*, ed. Alice Mary Hilton (Institute for Cybercultural Research, 1966), 127.

66. Hayward, "Panel Discussion," 63–64.

67. Silvey, "Production Control," 128.

68. Alice Mary Hilton, "The Evolving Society," in *The Evolving Society: The Proceedings of the First Annual Conference on the Cybercultural Revolution*, ed. Alice Mary Hilton (Institute for Cybercultural Research, 1966), 148–49. This panel introduction features a sketch of Bertrand Russell smiling benevolently in front of Leonardo da Vinci's *Vitruvian Man.*

69. Hannah Arendt, "On the Human Condition," in *The Evolving Society: The Proceedings of the First Annual Conference on the Cybercultural Revolution*, ed. Alice Mary Hilton (Institute for Cybercultural Research, 1966), 217.

70. Arendt, "On the Human Condition," 219. For a closer look of Arendt's talk, see Caroline Bassett, *Anti-Computing: Dissent and the Machine* (Manchester University Press, 2021), 105–39.

71. Alice Mary Hilton, "Panel Discussion," in *The Evolving Society: The Proceedings of the First Annual Conference on the Cybercultural Revolution*, ed. Alice Mary Hilton (Institute for Cybercultural Research, 1966), 234.

72. Grace Lee Boggs, "Panel Discussion," in *The Evolving Society: The Proceedings of the First Annual Conference on the Cybercultural Revolution*, ed. Alice Mary Hilton (Institute for Cybercultural Research, 1966), 234.

73. James Houghton, "Panel Discussion," in *The Evolving Society: The Proceedings of the First Annual Conference on the Cybercultural Revolution*, ed. Alice Mary Hilton (Institute for Cybercultural Research, 1966), 237.

74. Hilton, "Panel Discussion," 238.

75. Hilton speaks about this magazine in her 1965 interview with Studs Terkel. Alice Mary Hilton, "Cybernetics and the Future," WFMT Radio Network (Chicago), July 12, 1965, https://studsterkel.wfmt.com/programs/discussing-cybernetics-and-future-and-interviewing-dr-alice-mary-hilton-part-1. Quote from Norbert Wiener, *The Human Use of Human Beings*, rev. ed., 186.

76. Maxwell H. Goldberg, who participated in the first conference, participated in the second one, too, and published a revised version of his talk, about the importance on lifelong general education to seeing people through the age of automation, as an article. Maxwell H. Goldberg, "Continuous Education As a Way of Life," *Adult Education* (1965): 3–10. He summarizes some of the other papers given, too. In 1965, Hilton gave at least one other talk that amplifies upon her usual themes: Alice Mary Hilton, "Individual Responsibility in a Cybercultural Society," *Quest* 5, no. 1 (1965): 37–47.

77. Alice Mary Hilton, "Homo Faber, Homo Sapiens, Homo Poeta," *American Journal of Psychotherapy* 20, no. 4 (1966): 629.

78. Hilton, "Homo Faber, Homo Sapiens, Homo Poeta," 630.

79. Hilton, 634, 633.

80. Hilton, 634.

81. Hilton, 630.

82. Hilton, 629.

83. Hilton, 629.

84. Hilton, 632.

85. Hilton, 631.

86. Hilton, 634.

87. Alice Mary Hilton, "Cybernetics: Its Impact on the Processes of Learning, Politics, and Production," in *Progress of Cybernetics*, vol. 3, ed. J. Rose (Gordon & Breach Science Publishers, 1970), 1295.

88. All quotations come from: letters from Alice Mary Hilton to Hannah Arendt, March–May 1964; Hannah Arendt Papers: Correspondence, 1938–76; Organizations, 1943–76; Conference on Cybernetics, New York, NY, 1964–66, https://www.loc.gov/resource/mss11056dig.021940/?st=pdf&pdfPage=4.

89. Probably the most interesting appearance of cybernetics in the 1970s is in Chile. Its democratically elected socialist president Salvador Allende hired the British consultant Stafford Beer, who had pulled cybernetic ideas into management in several industries, to apply cybernetic thinking to Chile's national systems, including its economy. Allende died by suicide on September 11, 1973, during the US-backed military coup, before the cybernetic experiment went into operation. For a telling, see Eden Medina, *Cybernetic Revolutionaries: Technology and Politics in Allende's Chile* (Cambridge, MA: MIT Press, 2014 [2011]).

Chapter Four

1. Hesiod, *Works and Days*, line 114, in Hesiod, *Theogony, Works and Days, Testimonia*, trans. Glenn W. Most (Harvard University Press, 2018). Hesiod's *Works and Days* is one source of the Pandora tale, so often a fixture of techno-cautious writing (lines 53–105). His *Theogony* is the other source (lines 507–616). For a study of Pandora in tech contexts from Hesiod on, see, for example, Mayor, *Gods and Robots*, chapter 8; and Jennifer Buchan, "Rhetoric, Gender, and Myth in the Age of the Technoapocalypse" (master's thesis, Pennsylvania State University, 2021).

2. Davide Napoli, "The Shape of Early Greek Utopia," *Classical Quarterly* 71, no. 2 (2021): 469.

3. Hesiod, *Works and Days*, line 311. Hesiod uses ἔργον and its alpha-privative adjectival form, ἀεργὸς, which I try to capture here.

4. Emerson, "Works and Days," 131. It is important to note that Hesiod does not refer to each item in his metallic sequence as an age but as a race (*genós*). He also does not refer to it as a place.

5. These were mentioned in the introduction. Carlyle and Emerson were correspondents.

6. Emerson, "Works and Days," 131. Hand as "instrument of instruments" comes from book 4 of Aristotle, *Parts of Animals*, trans. A. L. Peck (Harvard University Press, 1961), 4.10.687a21. "The human is the measure" maxim is commonly attributed to the fifth-century BCE sophist Protagoras.

7. Emerson, "Works and Days," 131.

8. Emerson, 137–38.

9. Emerson, 140.

10. Hesiod, *Works and Days*, lines 11–24.

11. Emerson, "Works and Days," 150–51.

12. Marshall McLuhan, *The Gutenberg Galaxy: The Making of Typographic Man* (University of Toronto Press, 1962), 5.

13. Edward T. Hall, *The Silent Language* (Doubleday, 1959), 79.

14. Lewis Mumford, *Technics and Civilization* (University of Chicago Press, [1934] 2010), 321. Mumford's book is listed in "Further Readings for Media Study," in Marshall McLuhan, *Understanding Media: The Extensions of Man*, 2nd ed. (Signet, 1964), 317.

15. McLuhan, *Understanding Media*, 2nd ed., 23. All quotations from *Understanding Media* are from this version.

16. McLuhan, 19.

17. McLuhan, 23. In his introduction to the second edition, McLuhan refers readers who want to understand more clearly what he means by "the medium is the message" to Eric A. Havelock, *Preface to Plato* (Cambridge, MA: Harvard University Press, 1963), which undertakes to describe Plato's response to the dimming of poetic orality and the dawning of rhetoric and writing. Havelock is one source of McLuhan's interest in "the tribal."

18. McLuhan, 20, italics in original. The full quote is: "Electric speed in bringing all social and political functions together in a sudden implosion has heightened human awareness of responsibility to an intense degree. It is this implosive factor that alters the position of the Negro, the teen-ager, and some other groups. They can no longer be *contained*, in the political sense of limited association. They are now *involved* in our lives, as we in theirs, thanks to electric media." For critical attention to race in McLuhan, including that line, see Michael Litwack, "Extensions After Man: Race, Counter/insurgency and the Futures of Media Theory," *Media, Culture & Society* 43, no. 7 (2021): 1350–63; and Armond R. Towns, *On Black Media Philosophy* (University of California Press, 2022), 1–17.

19. Mumford understands the rise of mechanization from the other direction: It was able to take hold because of certain preexisting cultural conditions—most famously, the regimentation secured by the clock. McLuhan is sometimes called a technological determinist because a medium seems to arrive and steer culture. For the debate on technological determinism, see, for example, Merritt Roe Smith, "Technological Determinism in American Culture," in *Does Technology Drive History? The Dilemma of Technological Determinism*, ed. Merritt Roe Smith and Leo Marx (MIT Press, 1994), 1–35; Langdon Winner, *The Whale and the Reactor: A Search for Limits in an Age of High Technology*, 2nd ed. (University of Chicago Press, [1986] 2020), 3–18; and John Durham Peters, "'You Mean My Whole Fallacy Is Wrong': On Technological Determinism," *Representations* 140 (2017): 10–26.

20. See, for example, McLuhan, *Understanding Media*, 48.

21. McLuhan, 129.

22. McLuhan, 129.

23. McLuhan, 148. All quotes in this paragraph are from this page.

24. McLuhan, 301.

25. McLuhan, 301.

26. McLuhan, 301.

27. McLuhan, 310, 304, 23.

28. McLuhan, 310.

29. Marshall McLuhan, *The Classical Trivium: The Place of Thomas Nashe in the Learning of His Time*, ed. W. Terrence Gordan (Gingko, 2006). It is detectable, too, in McLuhan's early modern references (e.g., Shakespeare, Marvell, and Milton) throughout *Understanding Media*.

30. McLuhan, *Understanding Media*, 310, 301. This second line is very similar to a line in the concluding pages of Michael, *Cybernation*, 44 (italics mine), from 1962: "Our schools will probably be turning out a larger proportion of the population better educated than they are today, but most of *our citizens will be unable to understand the cybernated world in which they live.*"

31. McLuhan, 311.

32. McLuhan, 310. See R. Buckminster Fuller, "Education Automation: Freeing the Scholar to Return to His Studies," in *Education Automation: Comprehensive Learning for Emergent Humanity*, ed. Jaime Snyder (Lars Müller, 2010), 31–108, especially 68–69. The work is listed at the end of *Understanding Media* in a section titled "Further Readings for Media Study," 316.

33. Robert M. Hutchins, *The University of Utopia*, 2nd ed. (University of Chicago Press, [1953] 1964), vii.

34. Hutchins, *University of Utopia*, 8.

35. Hutchins, 33.

36. Hutchins, 46.

37. Hutchins is perhaps best known for coestablishing the "great books" curriculum at the University of Chicago with Mortimer Adler.

38. Hutchins, *Great Conversation*, 43.

39. Hutchins, 23.

40. Hutchins, 23. Hutchins seems unaware of what "robot" literally means.

41. Maxwell H. Goldberg, "The Displacement of Human Labor: Historic Trends," in *The Evolving Society: The Proceedings of the First Annual Conference on the Cybercultural Revolution*, ed. Alice Mary Hilton (Institute for Cybercultural Research, 1966), 153–58. His piece appeared in the same segment of the conference and proceedings as the papers by Seligman, Boggs, Michael, and Arendt. Hilton published her piece for Goldberg's conference as Alice Mary Hilton, "Cyberculture—The Age of Abundance and Leisure," *Michigan Quarterly Review* 3, no. 4 (1964): 217–29.

42. Robert T. Oliver, "Education in the Year 2000 A.D.," *Michigan Quarterly Review* 3, no. 4 (1964): both quotes from 236. On the previous page, Oliver valorizes one of the best-known educators of orators, writing that "it is predictable that Speech will be the heart of the liberalizing curriculum, just as it was in the time of Quintilian in ancient Rome" (235).

43. Maxwell H. Goldberg, ". . . And See it Whole," in *Automation, Education, and Human Values*, ed. William B. Brickman and Stanley Lehrer (School & Society, 1966), 350 (all quotes in this paragraph are from this page). Again, anthropologist Margaret Mead is the only woman whose work is featured (though, as I mentioned, Alice Mary Hilton presented at the event itself).

44. Roy C. Buck, "Education, Technological Change, and the New Society," in *Automation, Education, and Human Values*, ed. William B. Brickman and Stanley Lehrer (School & Society, 1966), 200. All Buck quotes are from this page unless otherwise noted.

45. Buck, "Education, Technological Chance, and the New Society," 200–201, brackets mine.

46. Maxwell H. Goldberg and Patricia Kochanek, eds., *Technical Change and Human Dignity: A Study in Human Values. Text with Questions and Readings from the CCLE-IBM Humanities Project on Technological Change* (Center for Continuing Education at Penn State University, 1966), R12–36, 161, underlining and parentheses in original.

47. Buck, "Education, Technological Chance, and the New Society," 212.

48. Hyman G. Rickover, *American Education—A National Failure: The Problem of Our Schools and What We Can Learn from England* (E. P. Dutton, 1963), 26.

49. It went on to be published as Charles R. Dechert, "Cybernetics and the Human Person," *International Philosophical Quarterly* 5, no. 1 (1965): 5–36.

50. Marshall McLuhan, "Cybernation and Culture," in *The Social Impact of Cybernetics*, ed. Charles R. Dechert (Simon & Schuster, 1966), 95–108.

51. Hyman G. Rickover, "A Humanistic Technology," in *The Social Impact of Cybernetics*, ed. Charles R. Dechert, (Simon & Schuster, 1966), 110. John Diebold also presented at the event and has a piece in the volume.

52. Warner G. Rice, "Humanities in the Sixties," in *Automation, Education, and Human Values*, ed. Brickman and Lehrer, 87–98, 92.

53. Rice, "Humanities in the Sixties," 97.

54. Rickover, "Humanistic Technology," 126–27.

55. For a more recent take on what education should look like in our technological times, see Frank Pasquale, *New Laws of Robotics: Defending Human Expertise in the Age of AI* (Belknap Press of Harvard University Press, 2020), especially 178 and 224, where he advocates for rhetorical training—rhetoric, of course, being one of the seven original liberal arts.

56. McLuhan, *Understanding Media*, 310.

57. "About the Reith Lectures," BBC, accessed June 23, 2024, https://www.bbc.co.uk/programmes/articles/4ZTNLKgrG2mSzfgC1ZYlNmV/about-the-reith-lectures#:~:text=The%20aim%20is%20to%20advance,significant%20issues%20of%20contemporary%20interest.

58. "Reith Lectures Will Be on Automation: Sir Leon Bagrit," *London Times*, May 22, 1964, 8.

59. Leon Bagrit, *The Age of Automation: The BBC Reith Lectures 1964* (Mentor, 1965), 35. Bagrit does not mention McLuhan's convergent extension thesis (or Emerson's far earlier one).

60. Bagrit, *Age of Automation*, 39.

61. Bagrit, 39–40, italics in original.

62. Bagrit, 38.

63. Bagrit, 44.

64. Bagrit, 45.

65. Bagrit, 45.

66. Bagrit, 44.

67. Bagrit, 65, 68.

68. Bagrit, 71–73.

69. Bagrit, 75.

70. Bagrit, 77.

71. Bagrit, 77.

72. Bagrit, chapter 4.

73. Bagrit, 99.

74. Bagrit, 105.

75. Donald N. Michael, "Reviewed Work(s): *The Age of Automation* by Leon Bagrit," *Technology and Culture* 7, no. 2 (1966): 260, italics in original.

76. Ben B. Seligman, "The Social Costs of Automation," in *The Evolving Society*, ed. Alice Mary Hilton, 159–66.

77. See Donald R. Stabile, "Automation, Workers, and Union Decline: Ben Seligman's Contribution to the Institutional Economics of Labor," *Labor History* 49, no. 2 (2008): 275–95, especially 284–90. See also his *New York Times* obituary: "Prof. Ben Seligman of Massachusetts U," *New York Times*, October 25, 1970, 92.

78. Ben B. Seligman, *Most Notorious Victory: Man in an Age of Automation* (Free Press, 1966), 4–5, 10.

79. Seligman, *Most Notorious Victory*, 195.

80. Seligman, 163. The quotes from Wiener on 163–64 are from *Cybernetics*, 2nd ed. (MIT Press, 1961), 27–28.

81. Seligman, 396.

82. Seligman, 395–96.

83. Seligman, 366.

84. Seligman, 366.

85. Seligman, 372.

86. Seligman, 377.

87. Seligman, 383.

88. Seligman, 197, 201, 202, 203, 208, 214, 247, 289, 292, 294, 329, 336.

89. Jerry Prout, *Chasing Automation: The Politics of Technology and Jobs from the Roaring Twenties to the Great Society* (Cornell University Press, 2022).

90. Seligman, *Most Notorious Victory*, 297.

91. Seligman, 293.

92. Seligman, 402.

93. As described by Jill Lepore, *If Then: How the Simulmatics Corporation Invented the Future* (Liveright, 2020), 196–98.

94. Robert Boguslaw, *The New Utopians: A Study of System Design and Social Change* (Prentice-Hall, 1965), 1. Boguslaw engages Plato's *Republic* again in 6–7.

95. Boguslaw, *New Utopians*, 5.

96. Boguslaw, 2.

97. Boguslaw, 27–28.

98. Boguslaw, 26.

99. Boguslaw, 204.

Chapter Five

1. In his preface to the first edition of the first volume of *Capital*, Marx calls England the "locus classicus" for those studying "the capitalist mode of production" but recommends that Germans not shrug as though Germany was not implicated in capitalism; see Karl Marx, *Capital: A Critique of Political Economy*, vol. 1, trans. Ben Fowkes (Penguin, 1990), 90.

2. "In the factory we have a lifeless mechanism which is independent of the workers who are incorporated into it as its living appendages" (Marx, *Capital* 1:548). Marx also somatizes machines, calling them the "bones and muscles of production" (286).

3. Unlike the so-called utopian socialists, Marx is light on specifics as to what the communist future would look like. The best we get comes from his work with Engels: "Therefore as soon as the division of labour starts to develop, each man has a particular, exclusive area of activity that constrains him, that he cannot get out of; he is a hunter, fisherman or herdsman or critical critic & must remain as such unless he wants to lose the means to live—whereas in communist society, where each man does not have an exclusive area of activity, but can rather develop himself in any branch he likes, society regulates the general production & thus makes it possible for me to do one thing today and another tomorrow, in the morning to hunt, in the afternoon to fish, in the evening to herd livestock and to criticize after dinner, just as I have a mind, without ever becomes hunter[,] fisherman, herdsman or critic"; see Terrell Carver and Daniel Blank, ed., *Marx and Engels's "The German Ideology" Manuscripts: Presentation and Analysis of the "Feuerbach Chapter"* (Palgrave Macmillan, 2014), 89–91.

4. Marx, *Capital*, 1:532, 1:532n73. The German that Marx uses for Aristotle is from F. Biese, *Die Philosophie des Aristoteles*, vol. 2 (Reimer, 1842), 408. The English translation used in this edition is Aristotle, *Politics*, trans. Ernest Barker (Oxford, 1946), 10. Marx gets the Antipater poem from *Gedichte aus dem Griechischen, Übersetzt von Christian Graf zu Stolberg* (Carl Ernst Bohn, 1782).

5. Walter Buckingham, *Automation: Its Impact on Business and People* (Harper & Brothers, 1961). Positioned very closely to the title and not set off by quotation marks, the epigraph gets picked up these days by title-scraping algorithms and jammed into the title position.

6. There is debate about whether it is accurate to say that enslavement *enabled* democracy. One idea is that maybe it did not from the very start of Athenian democracy, but it did once it was established, the notion being that Athenian elites turned to enslaving only after the poor were enfranchised.

7. Aristotle, *Politics*, 1253b5. The ancient Greek is from Aristotle, *Politics*, trans. H. Rackham (Harvard University Press, 1944). When I cite from this edition, I provide Bekker numbers only.

8. Aristotle, *Politics*, 1254a18–17 ("advantageous and just"); 1253b21–23, 1255a8–11 (evidence of debate about slavery among Aristotle's contemporaries). Aristotle is clear that he means non-Greek people (i.e., those who live in other areas of Europe and in Asia), though he adds that even among them there can be individuals who do not seem to have servile souls. Greeks did sometimes enslave other Greeks.

9. Peter Garnsey, *Ideas of Slavery from Aristotle to Augustine* (Cambridge University Press, 1996), 6.

10. Aristotle, *Politics*, 1253b23–33.

11. For close attention to the qualifiers *ti* and *hōsper*, see Emily Greenwood, "Reconstructing Classical Philology: Reading Aristotle *Politics* 1.4 After Toni Morrison," *American Journal of Philology* 143, no. 2 (2022): 335–37. Aristotle reiterates that classificatory attitude about slaves in his works on ethics. Aristotle, *Nicomachean Ethics*, trans. H. Rackham (Harvard University Press, 1926), 1161b4–5; Aristotle, *Eudemian Ethics*, trans. H. Rackham (Harvard University Press, 1935), 1241b23–24. His argument about natural slaves appears in no other works.

12. Aristotle, *Politics*, 1253b33–54a1.

13. See Plato, *Meno* 97e–98a and *Euthyphro* 11c, 15b. Palaephatus, *On Unbelievable Tales*, trans. Jacob Stern (Wauconda, Illinois: Bolchazy-Carducci, 1996), explains what was *really* going on: "The truth is this. Sculptors of Daedalus' day made statues with their feet fused together and their hands at their sides. Daedalus was the first to make one foot striding forward. And so people said: 'Daedalus made his statue walking, not standing.' Even today we say: 'fighting men were depicted,' or 'running horses,' or 'a ship tossing in a storm.' So with Daedalus, people said that he made walking statues" (52, tale 21). Daedalus was an important figure for Wiener, too; see my discussion in chapter 1.

14. Homeri, *Opera* (Oxford University Press, 1920), 2:18.376. Notably, Aristotle does not mention the seemingly living girls made of gold who bustle about Hephaestus as he tidies up and whom Homer describes as "having a mind in their core, and human speech, and strength," having come to know their "work" by the deathless gods (18.417–20). Jane Draycott argues that the tripods and golden girls are both means of extension and assistive technologies for the famously disabled god; see Jane Draycott, "Automata, Cyborgs, and Hybrids: Bodies and Machines in Antiquity," in *Body and Machine in Classical Antiquity*, ed. Maria Gerolemou and George Kazantzidis (New York: Cambridge University Press, 2023), 48–69.

15. Aristotle, *The Politics*, trans. Thomas Allen Sinclair (Penguin, [1962] 1980), 34–35.

16. Classicist Page duBois believes that scholars spend an undue amount of effort trying to understand and rationalize Aristotle's claim about natural slaves, perhaps out of a sensitivity to the justifications of enslavement, underwritten by Aristotle, in its nineteenth-century racialized form. She urges interpreters not to forget the social position Aristotle and his students occupied, which was that of the ultimate subordinator: "The crucial understanding to be communicated to Aristotle's listeners and readers concerns not 'natural slavery,' the natural slavishness of some human beings, but rather the primacy of the master, and the absolute naturalness of slavery itself." Page duBois, *Slaves and Other Objects* (University of Chicago Press, 2003), 205.

17. Martin Devecka, "Did the Greeks Believe in Their Robots?," *Cambridge Classical Journal* 59 (2013): 55.

18. For his part, Dew professed history and political law at and then presided over William and Mary College in Virginia; see Chad Vanderford, "Proslavery Professors: Classic Natural Right and the Positive Good Argument in Antebellum Virginia," *Civil War History* 55, no. 1 (2009): 5–30. For additional study of the reception of Aristotle by proslavery writers in the nineteenth-century US American context, see Harvey Wish, "Aristotle, Plato, and the Mason Dixon Line," *Journal of the History of Ideas* 10 (1949): 254–66; Edwin A. Miles, "The Old South and the Classical World," *North Carolina Historical Review* 48, no. 3 (1971): 258–75; J. Drew Harrington, "Classical Antiquity and the Pro-Slavery Argument," *Slavery and Abolition* 10, no. 1 (1989): 60–72; Caroline Winterer, *The Culture of Classicism: Ancient Greece and Rome in American Intellectual Life* (Johns Hopkins University Press, 2002), 74–76; Steven Mailloux, "Re-Marking Slave Bodies: Rhetoric as Production and Reception," *Philosophy and Rhetoric* 35, no. 2 (2002): 96–119; S. Sara Monoson, "Navigating Race, Class, Polis, and Empire: The Place of Empirical Analysis in Aristotle's Account of Natural Slavery," in *Reading Ancient Slavery*, ed. Richard Alston, Edith Hall, and Laura Proffitt (Bristol Classical Press, 2011), 133–51; S. Sara Monoson, "Recollecting Aristotle: Pro-Slavery Thought in Antebellum America and the Argument of *Politics*, Book 1," in *Ancient Slavery and Abolition: From Hobbes to Hollywood*, ed. Edith Hall, Richard Alston, and Justine McConnell (Oxford University Press, 2011), 247–78; Margaret Malamud, "The *Auctoritas* of Antiquity: Debating Slavery Through Classical Exempla in the Antebellum USA," in *Ancient Slavery and Abolition*, ed. Hall, Alston, and McConnell, 279–318; Margaret Malamud, *African Americans and the Classics: Antiquity, Abolition, and Activism* (I. B. Tauris, 2019), 105–47; Greenwood, "Reconstructing Classical Philology"; and Christopher S. Parmenter, "'But They Were a Race of Whites': Race and the Making of Ancient Slavery in the Anglophone World, 1785–1980," *TAPA* 154, no. 1 (2024): 295–330. For "an introduction to the study of Greek slavery," see Deborah Kamen, *Greek Slavery* (De Gruyter, 2023), of which chapter 8 contains the most on Aristotle's legacy.

19. Thomas R. Dew, *An Essay on Slavery*, 2nd ed. (J. W. Randolph, [1832] 1849), 13. A note cites *Politics*, book 1, chapter 4 (https://babel.hathitrust.org/cgi/pt?id=osu.32435005077409&view=1up&seq=7&q1=Aristotle).

20. George Frederick Holmes, "Observations on a Passage in the Politics of Aristotle Relative to Slavery," *Southern Literary Messenger* 16 (1850): 193–205. The line is Aristotle, *Politics*, 1255a1–3. Curiously, the epigraph is in Latin. Holmes explains in his first note that he could not access the translation by John Gillies (1797) and so used an edition in ancient Greek instead, but, "for the convenience of the printer, and the majority of readers," he cites "from the Latin interpretation of Dionysius Lambinus" (Holmes, "Observations," 193, note). For attention to these choices of text and translation, see Allison Dziuba and Jerry Won Lee, "Post-Aristotelianism and the Specters of Monolingualism," *Rhetoric Review* 40, no. 3 (2021): 257–269, 262–265.

21. Holmes, "Observations," 202. As he notes on the first page, he is working with "the edition of Aristotle's whole works, edited by Bekker & Brandis, under the auspices of the Berlin Academy" (193, note).

22. George Frederick Holmes, *A Science of Society* (Anderson Brothers, 1884), 25, 158–59.

23. This is according to David Brion Davis, *The Problem of Slavery in Western Culture* (Oxford University Press, [1966]) 1988, 70.

24. See, for example, George E. McCarthy, ed., *Marx and Aristotle: Nineteenth-Century German Social Theory and Classical Antiquity* (Rowman & Littlefield, 1992). As David Harvey notes, in *Capital*, Aristotle "provides a frequent anchor for his arguments" (*Companion to Marx's "Capital,"* 7), and Rolf Sannwald stresses that "Seine lebenslange Auseinandersetzung mit der griechischen Philosophie, vor allem mit Aristoteles, hat sein ganzes Werk, nicht nur sein ökonomisches, entscheidend mitgestaltet" (*Marx und die Antike*, 7).

25. Marx, *Capital* 3:509–510.

26. The translation is my own. The ancient Greek comes from Antipater of Thessalonica, "On a Water-Mill," in *The Greek Anthology*, book 9, trans. W. R. Paton (Harvard University Press, 1917), 9.418. Paton translates *aletrides* in the first line as "women who toil at the mill," but *aletris* typically refers to an enslaved woman who grinds corn, as Marx seems to have recognized.

27. Marx, *Capital*, 1: 532.

28. Marx, 1:533.

29. For views of nineteenth-century black US Americans on the use of "slavery" as an anticapitalist term for all wage workers, see Justin Leroy, "Racial Capitalism and Black Philosophies of History," in *Histories of Racial Capitalism*, ed. Destin Jenkins and Justin Leroy (Columbia University Press, 2021), 169–84.

30. Antipater's poem serves as epigraph to M. J. T. Lewis, *Millstone and Hammer: The Origins of Water Power* (University of Hull Press, 1997), vii, and receives further engagement later in the book (e.g., 66–73). For a study of how ancient *technai* copied and extended natural automatism before Antipater's time, see Maria Gerolemou, *Technical Automation in Classical Antiquity* (Bloomsbury, 2023); her treatment of Aristotle 1.4 appears on 18–19.

31. Langdon Winner, *Autonomous Technology: Technics Out-of-Control as a Theme in Political Thought* (MIT Press, [1977] 1978), 39. Wrestling productively with the question is David Harvey, *A Companion to Marx's "Capital": The Complete Edition* (Verso, 2018), part 4, especially chapter 8.

32. Marx, *Capital*, 1.562–63. This is from chapter 15, where the Aristotle and Antipater quotes also appear.

33. Marx, 1.563.

34. Lafargue undertook his final revisions of his argument in 1883, while incarcerated in the Saint Pélagie prison for his political activities. For publication details, see Judith Adler, "A Black Social Theorist? Reading *The Right to Be Lazy* by *Paul Lafargue*," *Society* 60 (2023): 751. For more on the context of the 1848 debates about the right to work, see Samuel Hayat, "Les controverses autour du travail en 1848," *Raisons politiques* 47 (2012/13): 13–34.

35. Paul Lafargue, *The Right to Be Lazy and Other Essays*, trans. Alex Andriesse (New York Review, 2023), 10. To the best of my knowledge, Norbert Wiener never engages Lafargue; Masani, however, imagines that Wiener would agree with Lafargue that "when Science subdued the forces of nature to the service of man, ought she not to have given leisure to the workers that they might develop themselves physically and intellectually; ought she not to have changed the 'vale of tears' into a dwelling place of peace and joy? I ask you, has not Science failed in

her mission of emancipation?" Pesi Rostum Masani, *Norbert Wiener (1894–1964)* (Birkhäuser Verlag, 1990), 292).

36. Lafargue, *Right to Be Lazy*, 7.

37. Lafargue, 3, 6.

38. Lafargue, 19. On page 23, the translator includes a note to Marx, *Capital*, vol. 1, chapter 15.

39. Lafargue, *Right to Be Lazy*, 36.

40. Lafargue, 39, brackets mine.

41. August Spies, *Auto-Biography; His Speech in Court, and General Notes* (Nina Van Zandt, [1887] 1939), 10.

42. Spies, *Auto-Biography*, 11.

43. Spies, 10, ellipsis in original.

44. Spies, 36–37.

45. "History," Charles H. Kerr Publishing Company, n.d., https://charleshkerr.com/about-1. His translation is now being bound and sold by Columbia University Press in their Eris Gems series for six dollars; before that, it was published as part of Revolutionary Classics series with the press Kerr founded. Paul Lafargue, *The Right to Be Lazy*, trans. Charles H. Kerr (Charles H. Kerr, 1989).

46. Cyrenus Osborne Ward, *The Ancient Lowly: A History of the Ancient Working People from the Earliest Known Period to the Adoption of Christianity by Constantine*, vol. 1, 9th ed. (Charles H. Keer & Company Co-Operative, 1888), 1. The second volume was published in 1900. Ward died shortly after it was published, having been depleted by the work.

47. Stephen Greenberg, "Ward Family Papers, 1870–1953," New York Public Library, Humanities and Social Sciences Library, Manuscripts and Archives Division, compiled by Stephen Greenberg, April 1990, 2–5, 4.

48. Ward, *Ancient Lowly*, 1.33. Not much work has been done on Ward, but the Classics & Class initiative features him in its archive. See "Osborne Ward's Ancient Working People," Classics and Class, https://www.classicsandclass.info/product/166/. Timothy Messer-Kruse, *The Yankee International: Marxism and the American Reform Tradition, 1848–1876* (University of North Carolina Press, 1998), pulls him in at 44, 67, 70, 79, 104, 183, 216, 250, 286.

49. Cyrenus Osborne Ward, *The Ancient Lowly: A History of the Ancient Working People from the Earliest Known Period to the Adoption of Christianity by Constantine, Volume 2—Origins of Socialism* (W. H. Lowdermick, 1900), 94. The footnote here is the entire passage from *Politics* 1.4 in untranslated ancient Greek.

50. Ward, *Ancient Lowly*, 2:143.

51. Lewis Mumford, *Technics & Civilization* (University of Chicago Press, [1934] 2010), 278.

52. Mumford, *Technics & Civilization*, 279. The introduction to this edition was written by Langdon Winner, who engaged Aristotle on automation in his own book, *Autonomous Technology: Technics-out-of-Control as a Theme in Political Thought* (MIT Press, [1977] 1978), 20–21. The translation of Aristotle that Winner uses is Aristotle, *The Politics of Aristotle*, trans. Ernest Barker (Oxford University Press, 1946), which he does cite.

53. Mumford, 280.

54. Mumford, 281.

55. Arendt, *Human Condition*, 122 (see also 4 and 119n69). Arendt does not cite it, but the translation here is from Aristotle, *Politics*, trans. Benjamin Jowett (Random House, 1943).

56. Alice Mary Hilton, "Basic Assumptions," in *The Evolving Society: The Proceedings of the First Annual Conference on the Cybercultural Revolution*, ed. Alice Mary Hilton (Institute for Cybercultural Research, 1966), 6.

57. "Automation and Technological Change," Hearings Before the Subcommittee on Economic Stabilization of the Joint Committee on the Economic Report, Congress of the United States, 84th Cong., 1st sess.. October 14, 15, 17, 18, 24, 25, 26, 27, and 28, 1955. Buckingham's statement is on 29–37, followed by a discussion between Diebold and Buckingham based on questions from the committee members on 37–51.

58. Walter Buckingham, "The *Human Side* of Automation," *Business Horizons* 3, no. 1 (1960): 19. The Diebold pamphlet is John Diebold, *Automation: Its Impact on Business and Labor*, Planning Pamphlet No. 106 (National Planning Association, 1959).

59. The line that I am tracing is not included in his inventory. One effect of the internet on quotation culture has been the easy circulation of faux Aristotle quotes, tucked into a tweet (when they were still called that), pin, or post. On his blog Sententiae Antiquae, Joel Christensen uses the expressions quoted here in an entry titled "Meme Police: A Collection of Things Aristotle Did Not Say" (https://sententiaeantiquae.com/2018/09/23/meme-police-a-collection-of-things-aristotle-did-not-say/).

60. Gérard Genette, *Paratexts: Thresholds of Interpretation*, trans. Jane E. Lewin (Cambridge University Press, [1987] 1997), 160.

61. This begs the question of what a translation is, of course. Generally, I take a translation to be an interpretation of one language through another language where the objective is to make correspondences of varying amounts of creativity between the source language and the translation language.

62. The translations that contributed to this numerical average are: Aristotle, *Politics*, trans. H. Rackham (Harvard University Press, 1932); Aristotle, *Politics*, trans. Benjamin Jowett (Random House, 1943); Aristotle, *The Politics of Aristotle*, trans. Ernest Barker (Oxford University Press, 1946); and Aristotle, *The Politics*, trans. Thomas Allen Sinclair (Penguin, 1962).

63. William Francis Henry King, *Classical and Foreign Quotations: Law Terms and Maxims, Proverbs, Mottoes, Phrases, and Expressions in French, German, Greek, Italian, Latin, Spanish, and Portuguese with Translations, References, Explanatory Notes, and Indexes*, rev. ed. (Whitaker & Sons, [1887] 1889), vii.

64. King, *Classical and Foreign Quotations*, vii.

65. Gary Saul Morson, *The Words of Others: From Quotations to Culture* (Yale University Press, 2011), 94–95.

66. Aristotle, *Politics*, 1253a1.

67. Buckingham, *Automation*, 2.

68. Buckingham, 175; see also 177.

69. Buckingham, 188.

70. Buckingham, 189. During the spring of 1961, the year *Automation* was published, Buckingham served as director of a twelve-day series of hearings held by the House Subcommittee on Unemployment and the Impact of Automation. Hearings Before the Subcommittee on Unemployment and the Impact of Automation of the Committee on Education and Labor, House of Representatives, 8th Cong., 1st sess., General Investigation into Types of Causes of Unemployment, Hearings Held in Washington, DC, March 8, 10, 20, 21, 22, 27, 29, 29; April 12, 17, 18, and 25 (Government Printing Office, 1961).

71. L. F. Mihlon, "Plain Talk on Automation," *Factory* 120, no. 2 (1962): 224.

72. That fact was highlighted by *The New York Times* when it recognized him favorably in a small, anonymously written column after his death; see "John I. Snyder Jr," *New York Times*, April 26, 1965, https://timesmachine.nytimes.com/timesmachine/1965/04/26/101542508.html?pageNumber=30.

73. Beginning in the late 1960s, the foundation was run out of a brownstone townhouse in Manhattan called the Automation House, whose other spaces held art exhibits and organizations focused on mediation in community disputes and collective bargaining. For early hype about the space, see "Preview: Automation House, New York City," *Architectural & Engineering News* 10 (1968): 76–78. The foundation also cosponsored conferences and conference volumes—for example, a conference at the Waldorf-Astoria Hotel in New York City, "Solutions to Problems of Automation and Employment," on May 16, 1963. Its proceedings were published as Charles Markham, ed., *Jobs, Men, and Machines: Problems of Automation* (Frederick A. Praeger, 1964). Snyder cosigns its introduction (5).

74. Lyndon B. Johnson, Annual Message to the Congress on the State of the Union, American Presidency Project, https://www.presidency.ucsb.edu/node/242292.

75. Lyndon B. Johnson, "Economic Report on the Nation's Progress and Trends," *New York Times*, January 20, 1964, https://www.nytimes.com/1964/01/21/archives/text-of-president-johnsons-economic-report-on-the-nations-progress.html?searchResultPosition=43. Following the details of the policy work is Prout, *Chasing Automation*.

76. "Automation: Threat and Promise," *New York Times Magazine*, March 22, 1964, https://timesmachine.nytimes.com/timesmachine/1964/03/22/98447117.html?pageNumber=251.

77. Gardner Ackley, "Properly Harnessed, It Can Be a Blessing," *New York Times Magazine*, March 22, 1964, 16, 52, 54, 57.

78. John I. Snyder Jr., "We Must Begin a Search for Answers," *New York Times Magazine*, March 22, 1964, 16, 62, 66, 69–70; 16.

79. National Commission on Technology, Automation, and Economic Progress. Hearings Before the Select Subcommittee on Labor of the Committee on Education and Labor, House of Representatives, 88th Cong., 2nd sess., on H.R. 10310 and Related Bills, to Establish a National Commission on Automation and Technological Progress, Hearings Held in Washington, DC, April 14, 15, and 27, 1964 (Government Printing Office, 1964), 135–38, 138–41. The statement sent to Johnson by the Ad Hoc Committee on the Triple Revolution is the first supplementary item listed.

80. For example, David Sarnoff, "The New Computerized Age—3: No Life Untouched," in Hearings Before a Subcommittee on Government Operations, House of Representatives, 89th Cong., 2nd sess., July 26, 27, and 28, 1966 (Government Printing Office, 1966), 298–300; Charles R. Bowen, "Automation: The Paradoxes of Abundance," in *Automation, Education, and Human Values*, ed. William W. Brickman and Stanley Lehrer (School & Society, 1966), 75; and Jules Karlin, *Man's Behavior: An Introduction to Social Science* (Macmillan, 1967), 365 (Karlin includes Buckingham's *Automation* in his bibliography, but he does not link the Aristotle quote to it).

81. S. M. A. Hameed and Dallas Cullen, eds., *Work and Leisure in Canada* (Faculty of Business Administration and Commerce, University of Alberta, 1971), 98.

82. Arthur O. Lewis, "Utopian Approaches to Technology," *Bulletin of Science, Technology & Society* 7 (1987): 493–506, 493. Lewis cites Aristotle, *The Politics*, revised edition, trans. Thomas Allen Sinclair (Harmondsworth: Penguin, 1981).

83. Editorial View, "To Spark or to Smother—Which?," *World Vision Magazine* 10, no. 9 (1966): 32.

84. Aristotelis, *Ars rhetorica*, ed. W. D. Ross (Oxford University Press, 1959), 1394395. "Quotations," of course, are a modern notion; Aristotle writes of *gnōmai*, wisdom-packed insights of few words.

85. Aristotle, *The Politics of Aristotle*, trans. Ernest Barker (Oxford University Press, 1946), iii.

86. Robert K. Merton, *On the Shoulders of Giants: A Shandean Postscript, The Vicennial Edition* (Harcourt Brace Jovanovich, [1965] 1985), 41.

Chapter Six

1. Walter Prytulak, *Jobless, Moneyless, and Free: Prospects for a New Social Order* (Vantage, 1980), 100; Charles M. Savage, *Fifth Generation Management: Integrating Enterprises Through Human Networking* (Butterworth-Heineman, 1990), 132.

2. Maurice Balme, "Attitudes to Work and Leisure in Ancient Greece," *Greece & Rome* 31, no. 2 (1984): 140.

3. Erik Brynjolfsson and Andrew McAfee, *Race Against the Machine: How the Digital Revolution Is Accelerating Innovation, Driving Productivity, and Irreversibly Transforming Employment and the Economy* (Digital Frontier, 2012), 1. Their endnote—for which I thank them, since so few people cite their Aristotle source—indicates that this rendering of the line came from Aristotle, *Politics*, trans. William Ellis (Echo Library, 2006).

4. Brynjolfsson and McAfee, *Race Against the Machine*, 53. The endnote indicates the source as Havelock Ellis, *Little Essays of Love and Virtue* (1922). It appears in a chapter titled "The Individual and the Race," in which Ellis shows how replacement (e.g., machines for humans, "fit" humans for "unfit" humans) is the way of things. Havelock Ellis, *Little Essays of Love and Virtue* (George H. Doran, 1922), 177. One gets the sense that Brynjolfsson and McAfee did not seek out the text around the quotations they used. Incidentally, the volume *Automation, Education, and Human Values* (ed. Brickman and Lehrer) cited in chapter 4 features one epigraph, and it is this exact Ellis quote.

5. Antonio Regalado, "When Machines Do Your Job" (Q&A with Andrew McAfee), *MIT Technology Review*, July 11, 2012, 70–71. It appeared in a section called "The Future of Work" after a piece titled "Automate or Perish."

6. Regalado, "When Machines Do Your Job," 71. As far I can tell, "Digital Athens" first makes an appearance seventeen years earlier in the work of Dutch scholars wondering whether the future of information and communication technology would be more ancient Athenian or Orwellian. They forecast that Orwellian elements will get embedded in Athenian structures; see W. B. H. J. van de Donk, I. Th. M. Snellen, and P. W. Tops, eds., *Orwell in Athens: A Perspective on Informatization and Democracy* (IOS, 1995), 4.

7. Erik Brynjolfsson and Andrew McAfee, *The Second Machine Age: Work, Progress, and Prosperity in a Time of Brilliant Technology* (W. W. Norton, 2014), 250. This entire page is strikingly similar to Alice Mary Hilton, "Cyberculture in the Transition from a War to a Peacetime Economy," *Fellowship* (1964): 3–4.

8. Andrew McAfee and Erik Brynjolfsson, *Machine, Platform, Crowd: Harnessing Our Digital Future* (W. W. Norton, 2017).

9. McAfee and Brynjolfsson, *Machine, Platform, Crowd*, 24.

10. See my discussion of the Triple Revolution in chapter 3. For an analysis of King's use, see Tierney, *Dismantlings*, 93–111.

11. Leif Weatherby, "Delete Your Account: On the Theory of Platform Capitalism," *Los Angeles Review of Books*, April 24, 2018, https://lareviewofbooks.org/article/delete-your-account-on-the-theory-of-platform-capitalism/. Marx refers to Andrew Ure—*The Philosophy of Manufactures; or, An Exposition of the Scientific, Moral, and Commercial Economy of the Factory System* (Charles Knight, 1835)—as "the Pindar of the automatic factory" (*Capital* 1, 544) and as

"this Pindar of the manufacturers" (*Capital* 3, 510n75). Thanks to Leif for a fun chat about the Pindar burn.

12. Carl Benedikt Frey and Michael Osborn, "The Future of Employment: How Susceptible Are Jobs to Computerization?," Working Paper, Oxford Martin, 2013.

13. Carl Benedikt Frey, *The Technology Trap: Capital, Labor, and Power in the Age of Automation* (Princeton University Press, 2019), ix.

14. Frey, *Technology Trap*, 1.

15. Bhorat, "Aristotle on Automation," 16.

16. Frey, *Technology Trap*, xiv.

17. Aaron Bastani, *Fully Automated Luxury Communism: A Manifesto* (Verso, 2019), 50–65. He does not supply the page number for his quotation from *Grundrisse*, writing only that it comes from "the 'Fragment on Machines,'" but it can be found in Karl Marx, *Grundrisse: Foundations of the Critique of Political Economy*, trans. Martin Nicolaus (Penguin, [1973] 1993), 701.

18. Bastani, *Fully Automated Luxury Communism*, 54. Bastani sounds a bit like Arendt here.

19. Hesiod, *Works and Days*, 117–18 (*karpon d'ephere zeidōros aroura automatē pollon te kai aphthonon*). *Automatos* is the same adjective that Homer uses to describes Hephaestus's tripods and so appears in Aristotle's quotation in the automation sentence.

20. Athenaeus, *The Deiphnosophists*, vol. 1, trans. Charles Burton Gulick (Harvard University Press, 1927), 2.68. Telecleides's description will remind readers of what Alice Mary Hilton called "Schlaraffenland." He was likely amplifying similar scenes from earlier comedies of his contemporaries. For more on ancient Athenian comic playwrights who imagined objects and food moving on their own without human effort, see H. C. Baldry, "The Idler's Paradise in Attic Comedy," *Greece & Rome* 22, no. 65 (1953): 49–60, which concludes: "Whether the comic poets described the remote past or conjured up a fantastic future, the faults and foibles of their fellow-citizens were their main concern" (60). For a different view, see Devecka, "Did the Greeks Believe in Their Robots?"

21. Bastani, *Fully Automated Luxury Communism*, 67, italics in original. From my own legwork, I know that this translation came from Aristotle, *The Politics of Aristotle*, trans. Ernest Barker (Oxford University Press, 1946).

22. Aaron Benanav, *Automation and the Future of Work* (Verso, 2020), 82.

23. Benanav, *Automation and the Future of Work*, 83.

24. Kevin Rouse, *FutureProof: 9 Rules for Humans in the Age of Automation* (Random House, [2021] 2022), xxii. The source that Rouse cites is Sean Carroll, "Aristotle on Household Robots," *Discover*, September 28, 2010. Carroll is shouting out news of self-assembling robots, and he cites a lecture on Marx by Brad DeLong, wherein DeLong cites Marx citing Aristotle. Carroll ends his short piece with this line: "I suspect Aristotle would have been quite tickled at self-assembling robots" (https://www.discovermagazine.com/the-sciences/aristotle-on-household-robots).

Conclusion

1. Aristotle, *De arte poetica liber*, ed. Rudolph(us) Kassel (Oxford University Press, 1922), 1447b9–10.

2. For example, Cicero, *Rhetorica I*, ed. A. S. Wilkins (Oxford University Press, 1902); and Tullia D'Aragona, *Dialogue on the Infinity of Love*, trans. Rinaldina Russell and Bruce Merry (University of Chicago Press, 1997). Taking the form of a dialogue between Socrates and his

rhetoric teacher Aspasia is Bonnie Mak and Allen H. Renear, "What Is Information History?," *Isis* 114, no. 4 (2023): 747–68.

3. Sébastien Bubeck et al., "Sparks of Artificial General Intelligence: Early Experiments with GPT-4," *ArXiv* 1 (2023): 1.

4. This figure is figure 1.6 of Bubeck et al., with the caption "Hypothetical dialogues by Plato criticizing autoregressive language models written by GPT-4 and ChatGPT, and GPT-4's evaluation of those dialogues."

5. Bubeck et al., "Sparks of Artificial General Intelligence," 10.

6. A very modest sampling: Sarah Scullin, "Plato Would Have Wanted You to Unplug: Technology Addiction, Technophobia, and Kids These Days," *Eidolon*, October 2, 2017, https://eidolon.pub/plato-would-have-wanted-you-to-unplug-712a908a16e0; Ekaterina V. Haskins and Gaines S. Hubbell, "Plato's *Phaedrus* and the Ideology of Immersion," *Ancient Rhetorics and Digital Networks*, ed. Michele Kennerly and Damien Smith Pfister (University of Alabama Press, 2018), 154–75; Zeynep Tufekci, "What Would Plato Think About ChatGPT?," *New York Times*, December 18, 2022, SR7; and Isaac James Richards, "The Labyrinth: A Platonic Dialogue on What's Next, Featuring ChatGPT as Phaedrus," *Explorations in Media Ecology* 22, no. 2 (2023): 235–39. A noteworthy preference for the *Gorgias* occurs in the conclusion of Andrew Pilsch, *Transhumanism: Evolutionary Futurism and the Human Technologies of Utopia* (University of Minnesota Press, 2017), 197–203.

7. Bubeck et al., "Sparks of Artificial General Intelligence," 10.

8. "Elon Musk's Full Interview at Cannes Lions 2024: AI, Creativity, and the Future of X," YouTube video, 44:18, June 19, 2024, https://www.youtube.com/watch?v=84Q4dyK_urU (all quotes from 13:50–23). In early 2025 Musk said that he planned to roll out five thousand Optimus units by the end of 2025, "a Roman legion's worth." @ElonClipsX, ""This year we hopefully will be able to make about 5,000 Optimus robots,'" X, 6:33 a.m., May 14, 2025, https://x.com/ElonClipsX/status/1922601262366769440.

9. "Mark Zuckerberg on Life, History, and Being Human / The Circuit with Emily Chang (Bonus Clip)," YouTube video, 9:53, December 19, 2024, https://www.youtube.com/watch?v=R91_oQ4smys (from 8:38). Thanks to Damien Smith Pfister for alerting me to this interview.

10. For the math showing this as the unfulfilled "promise" of automation for decades, see Aaron Benavav, *Automation and the Future of Work* (Verso, 2020), chapter 1; and Antonio A. Casilli, *Waiting for Robots: The Hired Hands of Automation*, trans. Saskia Brown (University of Chicago Press, [2019] 2025), chapter 1.

11. This is not to say the subterranean does not hold appeal, too. For a general sketch of the billionaire prepper scene as it looked a few years ago, see Douglas Rushkoff, "The Super-Rich 'Preppers' Planning to Save Themselves from the Apocalypse," *Guardian*, September 4, 2022, https://www.theguardian.com/news/2022/sep/04/super-rich-prepper-bunkers-apocalypse-survival-richest-rushkoff.

12. Adam Becker, *More Everything Forever: AI Overlords, Space Empires, and Silicon Valley's Crusade to Control the Fate of Humanity* (Basic Books, 2025), 87.

13. Yanis Varoufakis, *Technofeudalism: What Killed Capitalism* (Melville House, [2023] 2024). In 2025, the term "technofeudalism" is starting to appear regularly in pieces and podcasts about tech billionaires.

14. Yanis Varoufakis, "George Varoufakis (1925–2021)," YanisVaroukakis.eu, September 30, 2021, https://www.yanisvaroufakis.eu/2021/09/30/george-varoufakis-1925-2021-english/.

15. Varoufakis, *Technofeudalism*, 216.

16. As detailed by classicist Johanna Hanink, *The Classical Debt: Greek Antiquity in an Era of Austerity* (Harvard University Press, 2017), 235–38. Varoufakis was finance minister as the global recession was hitting Greece hard. His rejection of the austerity measures pushed by other European countries and entities made him a legendary figure on the left. Alain Badiou recommends Greece's resistance during the crisis as a model for fighting neoliberal capitalism; see Alain Badiou, *Greece and the Reinvention of Politics*, trans. David Broder (Verso, [2016] 2018).

17. Varoufakis, *Technofeudalism*, 217.

18. For example, Ober, *Demopolis*, 88–93.

19. The US government spending megabill that made it out of the House in May 2025 stipulated that states could not regulate AI for a decade, but, under pressure from state governors, the Senate voted 99–1 to strike that portion; see David Morgan and David Shepardson, "US Senate Strikes AI Regulation Ban from Trump Megabill," Reuters, July 1, 2025, https://www.reuters.com/legal/government/us-senate-strikes-ai-regulation-ban-trump-megabill-2025-07-01/.

20. Aristotle, *Politics*, 3.5.1279b.

21. Eran Shalev, *Rome Reborn on Western Shores: Historical Imagination and the Creation of the American Republic* (University of Virginia Press, 2009).

22. Cartledge, *Democracy*, 306.

23. Aristotle, *Politics*, 4.7.1294b7–9.

24. John Gastil and Erik Olin Wright, ed. *Legislature by Lot: Transformative Designs for Deliberative Governance* (Verso, 2019); Alexander Guerrero, *Lottocracy: Democracy Without Elections* (Oxford University Press, 2024); Cristina Lafont and Nadia Urbinati, *The Lottocratic Mentality: Defending Democracy Against Lottocracy* (Oxford University Press, 2024); Adam Grant, "To Improve Democracy, Get Rid of Elections," *New York Times*, August 23, 2023, Section A, 22. I add, too, Yves Sintomer, *The Government of Chance: Sortition and Democracy from Athens to the Present*, trans. Sarah Louise Raillard and Patrick Camiller (Cambridge University Press, 2023).

25. Matthew R. Christ, "Liturgy Avoidance and *Antidosis* in Classical Athens," *Transactions of the American Philological Association* 120 (1990): 150.

26. Becker, *More Everything Forever*, 287–89.

27. Cartledge, *Democracy*, 205.

28. For instance, Mark Zuckerberg's annual salary from Meta is $1.

29. Aristotle, *Politics* (trans. Rackham), 5.2.1302b19–21; also 3.8.1284a.17–21.

30. Aristotle, *Politics*, 3.8.1284a21–22; see also 5.2.1302b.15–17.

31. Aristotle, *Politics* (trans. Rackham), 5.2.1302b15–17.

32. Danielle Allen, *Justice by Means of Democracy* (University of Chicago Press, 2023), 71.

33. Aristotle, *Politics* (trans. Rackham), 3.8.1284b8–13; see also 5.2.1302b35–40, 1303a1–3.

34. Aristotle, 3.8.128423–24.

35. For a reconstruction of the details from the limited evidence we have, see Cartledge, *Democracy*, 70–73.

36. Alex Zhang, "Ostracism and Democracy," *NYU Law Review Online* 96 (2021): 235–68; Emily Salamanca, "Pruning of the People: Ostracism and the Transformation of the Political Space in Ancient Athens," *Philosophies* 8, no. 81 (2023): 1–21.

37. See, for example, Frank Pasquale, *New Laws of Robotics: Defending Human Expertise in the Age of AI* (Belknap Press of Harvard University Press, 2020), 178; and Leif Weatherby, *Language Machines: Cultural AI and the End of Remainder Humanism* (University of Minnesota Press, 2025), conclusion (titled "Language as a Service, or the Return of Rhetoric").

38. Gabor, *Inventing the Future*, 31.

Bibliography

"About the Reith Lectures." BBC. Accessed June 23, 2024. https://www.bbc.co.uk/programmes/articles/4ZTNLKgrG2mSzfgC1ZYlNmV/about-the-reith-lectures#:~:text=The%20aim%20is%20to%20advance,significant%20issues%20of%20contemporary%20interest.

Ackley, Gardner. "Properly Harnessed, It Can Be a Blessing." *New York Times Magazine*, March 22, 1964, 16, 52, 54, 57.

Adler, Judith. "A Black Social Theorist? Reading *The Right to Be Lazy* by Paul Lafargue." *Society* 60 (2023): 750–60.

Akin, William E. *Technocracy and the American Dream*. University of California Press, 1977.

Allen, Danielle. *Justice by Means of Democracy*. University of Chicago Press, 2023.

Ampère, André-Marie. *Essai sur la philosophie des sciences: Ou, Exposition analytique d'une classification naturelle de toutes les connaissances humaines*. Bachelier, Libraire-Éditeur, Quai des Augustins, 1834.

Ampère, André-Marie. *Essai sur la philosophie des sciences: Ou, Exposition analytique d'une classification naturelle de toutes les connaissances humaines, seconde partie*. Bachelier, Libraire-Éditeur, Quai des Augustins, 1843.

Antipater of Thessalonica. "On a Water-Mill." In *The Greek Anthology*, book 9. Translated by W. R. Paton. Harvard University Press, 1917.

Arendt, Hannah. "From Hegel to Marx." In *The Promise of Politics*, edited by Jerome Kohn, 70–80. Schocken, 2005.

Arendt, Hannah. *Hannah Arendt Papers: Correspondence, 1938 to 1976; Organizations, 1943 to 1976; Conference on Cybernetics, New York, N.Y., 1964 to 1966*. Manuscript/mixed material. Library of Congress. Accessed November 12, 2025. https://www.loc.gov/item/mss110560 0339/.

Arendt, Hannah. *The Human Condition*. 2nd ed. Edited by Margaret Canovan. University of Chicago Press, [1958] 1998.

Arendt, Hannah. "Karl Marx and the Tradition of Western Political Thought." In *Thinking without a Banister: Essays in Understanding, 1953–1975*, edited by Jerome Kohn, 3–42. Schocken, 2018.

Arendt, Hannah. *The Modern Challenge to Tradition: Fragmente eines Buchs*. Edited by Barbara Hahn and James McFarland, with Ingo Kielich and Ingeborg Nordmann. Wallstein Verlag, 2018.

Arendt, Hannah. *On Revolution*. Penguin, [1963] 2006.

Arendt, Hannah. "On the Human Condition." In *The Evolving Society: The Proceedings of the First Annual Conference on the Cybercultural Revolution*, edited by Alice Mary Hilton, 213–19. Institute for Cybercultural Research, 1966.

Arendt, Hannah. "Socrates." In *The Promise of Politics*, edited by Jerome Kohn, 5–39. Schocken, 2005.

Arendt, Hannah. *Vita activa: oder, Vom tätigen Leben*. W. Kohlhammer, 1960.

Arendt, Hannah. "What Is Freedom?" In *Between Past and Future: Six Exercises in Political Thought*, 143–72. Viking, 1961.

Aristotelis. *Ars rhetorica*. Edited by W. D. Ross. Oxford University Press, 1959.

Aristotelis. *De arte poetica liber*. Edited by Rudolphus Kassel. Oxford University Press, 1965.

Aristotle. *Eudemian Ethics*. Translated by H. Rackham. Harvard University Press, 1935.

Aristotle. *Nicomachean Ethics*. Translated by H. Rackham. Harvard University Press, 1926.

Aristotle. *Parts of Animals*. Translated by A. L. Peck. Harvard University Press, 1961.

Aristotle. *Politics*. Translated by William Ellis. Echo Library, 2006.

Aristotle. *Politics*. Translated by Benjamin Jowett. Random House, 1943.

Aristotle. *Politics*. Translated by H. Rackham. Harvard University Press, 1944.

Aristotle. *Politics*, books 3 and 4. Translated by Richard Robinson. Clarendon, [1962] 1995.

Aristotle. *Politics*, books 7 and 8. Translated by Richard Kraut. Clarendon, 1997.

Aristotle. *The Politics*. Translated by Thomas Allen Sinclair. Penguin, [1962] 1980.

Aristotle. *The Politics*. Revised ed. Translated by Thomas Allen Sinclair. Penguin, 1981.

Aristotle. *The Politics of Aristotle*. Translated by Ernest Barker. Oxford University Press, 1946.

Armstrong, Tim. *The Logic of Slavery: Debt, Technology, and Pain in American Literature*. Cambridge University Press, 2012.

Arndt, David. *Arendt on the Political*. Cambridge University Press, 2019.

Arnold, Pauline, and Percival White. *The Automatic Age*. Holiday House, 1963.

"Astra Taylor on the Promise and Challenge of Democracy." Preposterous Universe (podcast), July 29, 2019. https://www.preposterousuniverse.com/podcast/2019/07/29/57-astra-taylor-on-the-promise-and-challenge-of-democracy/.

Atack, Carol. *Plato: A Civic Life*. Reaktion, 2024.

Atanasoski, Neda, and Kalindi Vora. *Surrogate Humanity: Race, Robots, and the Politics of Technological Futures*. Duke University Press, 2019.

Athenaeus. *The Deiphnosophists*. Vol. 1. Translated by Charles Burton Gulick. Harvard University Press, 1927.

"Automation and Technological Change." Hearings Before the Subcommittee on Economic Stabilization of the Joint Committee on the Economic Report Congress of the United States, Eighty-Fourth Cong., 1st sess., October 14, 15, 17, 18, 24, 25, 26, 27, and 28, 1955. Printed for the Use of the Joint Committee on the Economic Report. Government Printing Office, 1955.

"Automation: Threat and Promise." *New York Times Magazine*, March 22, 1964. Section SM, 16.

Badiou, Alain. *Greece and the Reinvention of Politics*. Translated by David Broder. Verso, [2016] 2018.

Bagrit, Leon. *The Age of Automation: The BBC Reith Lectures, 1964*. Mentor, 1965.

Baldry, H. C. "The Idler's Paradise in Attic Comedy." *Greece & Rome* 22, no. 65 (1953): 49–60.

Balme, Maurice. "Attitudes to Work and Leisure in Ancient Greece." *Greece & Rome* 31, no. 2 (1984): 140–52.

Bassett, Caroline. *Anti-Computing: Dissent and the Machine*. Manchester University Press, 2021.

Bassett, Caroline, and Ben Roberts. "Automation Now and Then: Automation Fevers, Anxieties and Utopias." *New Formations* 98 (2019): 9–28.

Bastani, Aaron. *Fully Automated Luxury Communism: A Manifesto*. Verso, 2019.

Bauman, Zygmunt. *Retrotopia*. Polity, 2017.

Becker, Adam. *More Everything Forever: AI Overlords, Space Empires, and Silicon Valley's Crusade to Control the Fate of Humanity*. Basic Books, 2025.

Bell, Daniel. *Work and Its Discontents: The Cult of Efficiency in America*. Beacon, 1956.

Benanav, Aaron. *Automation and the Future of Work*. Verso, 2020.

Benjamin, Ruha. *Race After Technology: Abolitionist Tools for the New Jim Code*. Polity, 2019.

Bhorat, Muhammed Ziyaad. "Aristotle on Automation: A Preindustrial Political Theory of Technology." PhD diss., University of California, Los Angeles, 2022.

Biese, F. *Die Philosophie des Aristoteles*. Vol. 2. G. Reimer, 1842.

Bloomberg, Warner, Jr. *The Age of Automation: Its Effects on Human Welfare*. League for Industrial Democracy, 1955.

Boggs, Grace Lee. "Panel Discussion." In *The Evolving Society: The Proceedings of the First Annual Conference on the Cybercultural Revolution*, edited by Alice Mary Hilton, 221–51. Institute for Cybercultural Research, 1966.

Boguslaw, Robert. *The New Utopians: A Study of System Design and Social Change*. Prentice-Hall, 1965.

Bond, Sarah. *Strike: Labor, Unions, and Resistance in the Roman Empire*. Yale University Press, 2024.

Bowen, Charles R. "Automation: The Paradoxes of Abundance." In *Automation, Education, and Human Values*, edited by William W. Brickman and Stanley Lehrer, 71–83. School & Society, 1966.

Boter, Gerard. *The Textual Tradition of Plato's "Republic."* Brill, 1989.

Breen, Benjamin. *Tripping on Utopia: Margaret Mead, the Cold War, and the Troubled Birth of Psychedelic Science*. Grand Central, 2024.

Broussard, Meredith. *Artificial Unintelligence: How Computers Misunderstand the World*. MIT Press, 2019.

Brynjolfsson, Erik, and Andrew McAfee. *Race Against the Machine: How the Digital Revolution Is Accelerating Innovation, Driving Productivity, and Irreversibly Transforming Employment and the Economy*. Digital Frontier, 2012.

Brynjolfsson, Erik, and Andrew McAfee. *The Second Machine Age: Work, Progress, and Prosperity in a Time of Brilliant Technology*. W. W. Norton, 2014.

Bubeck, Sébastien, Varun Chandrasekaran, Ronen Eldan et al. "Sparks of Artificial General Intelligence: Early Experiments with GPT-4." *ArXiv* 1:1–155.

Buchan, Jennifer. "Rhetoric, Gender, and Myth in the Age of the Technoapocalypse." Master's thesis, Pennsylvania State University, 2021.

Buck, Roy C. "Education, Technological Change, and the New Society." In *Automation, Education, and Human Values*, edited by William B. and Stanley Lehrer, 195–212. School & Society, 1966.

Buckingham, Walter. *Automation: Its Impact on Business and People*. Harpers & Brothers, 1961.

Buckingham, Walter. "The *Human Side* of Automation." *Business Horizons* 3, no. 1 (1960): 19–28.

Butler, Samuel. *Erewhon Erewhon & Erewhon Revisited*. Dover, [1872] 2015.

Campbell, Blair. "Paradigms Lost: Classical Athenian Politics in Modern Myth." *History of Political Thought* 10, no. 2 (1989): 189–213.

Canovan, Margaret. "Introduction." In *The Human Condition* by Hannah Arendt, edited by Margaret Canovan, vii–xx. 2nd ed. University of Chicago Press, [1958] 1998.

Canovan, Margaret. *The Political Thought of Hannah Arendt*. J. M. Dent, 1974.

Čapek, Karel. *RUR*. Translated by Paul Selver and Nigel Playfair. Dover, 2001.

Capurro, Rafael, and John Holgate. *Von Boten und Botschaften—Die Angeletik als Weg zur Phänomenologie der Kommunikation*. Wilhelm Fink Verlag, 2011.

Carlyle, Thomas. "Signs of the Times." *Edinburgh Review* 49 (June 1829): 439–59.

Carroll, Sean. "Aristotle on Household Robots." *Discover*, September 28, 2010. https://www.discovermagazine.com/aristotle-on-household-robots-26771.

Cartledge, Paul. *Democracy: A Life*. Oxford University Press, 2016.

Carver, Terrell, and Daniel Blank, ed., *Marx and Engels's "The German Ideology" Manuscripts: Presentation and Analysis of the "Feuerbach Chapter."* Palgrave Macmillan, 2014.

Casilli, Antonio A. *Waiting for Robots: The Hired Hands of Automation*. Translated by Saskia Brown. University of Chicago Press, [2019] 2025.

Chang, Emily. *Brotopia: Breaking Up the Boy's Club of Silicon Valley*. Penguin, 2019.

Charlesworth, James C. "A Bold Program for Recreation." *Annals of the American Academy of Political and Social Science* 313 (1957): 141–47.

Christ, Matthew R. "Liturgy Avoidance and *Antidosis* in Classical Athens." *Transactions of the American Philological Association* 120 (1990): 147–69.

Christiansen, Joel. "Meme Police: A Collection of Things Aristotle Did Not Say." Sententiae (blog), September 23, 2018. https://sententiaeantiquae.com/2018/09/23/meme-police-a-collection-of-things-aristotle-did-not-say/.

Chude-Sokei, Louis. "Race and Robotics." In *Cyborg Futures: Cross-Disciplinary Perspectives on Artificial Intelligence and Robotics*, edited by Teresa Heffernan, 159–71. Palgrave Macmillan, 2019.

Chude-Sokei, Louis. *The Sound of Culture: Diaspora and Black Technopoetics*. Wesleyan University Press, 2016.

Cicero. *Rhetorica I*. Edited by A. S. Wilkins. Oxford University Press, 1902.

Clarke, I. F. *The Pattern of Expectation, 1644–2001*. Basic Books, 1979.

Curtius, Ernst Robert. *European Literature and the Latin Middle Ages*. Translated by William R. Trask, with a new introduction by Colin Burrow. Princeton University Press, [1948] 2013.

D'Aragona, Tullia. *Dialogue on the Infinity of Love*. Translated by Rinaldina Russell and Bruce Merry. University of Chicago Press, 1997.

Davis, David Brion. *The Problem of Slavery in Western Culture*. Oxford University Press, [1966] 1988.

Davis, J. C. *Utopia and the Ideal Society: A Study of English Utopian Writing, 1516–1700*. University Press, 1981.

Davy, Thomas J., and Lloyd A. Rowe, "Précis of the Conference." In *Leisure in America: Blessing or Curse?*, edited by James C. Charlesworth, 70–90. American Academy of Political and Social Science, 1964.

Day, Ronald E. "The 'Conduit Metaphor' and the Nature and Politics of Information Studies." *Journal of the American Society for Information Science* 51, no. 9 (2000): 805–11.

DeLong, J. Bradford. *Slouching Toward Utopia: An Economic History of the Twentieth Century*. Basic Books, 2022.

Dechert, Charles R. "Cybernetics and the Human Person." *International Philosophical Quarterly* 5, no. 1 (1965): 5–36.

Devecka, Martin. "Did the Greeks Believe in Their Robots?" *Cambridge Classical Journal* 59 (2013): 52–69.

Dew, Thomas R. *An Essay on Slavery*. 2nd ed. Richmond: J. W. Randolph, [1832] 1849.

Diamond, Larry. "Liberation Technology." *Journal of Democracy* 21, no. 3 (2010): 69–83.

Diebold, John. "Automation: Its Impact on Business and Labor." Planning Pamphlet No. 106. National Planning Association, 1959.

Diebold, John. *Automation: The Advent of the Automatic Factory*. D. Van Nostrand, 1952.

van de Donk, W. B. H. J., I. Th. M. Snellen, and P. W. Tops, eds. *Orwell in Athens: A Perspective on Informatization and Democracy*. IOS, 1995.

Douglass, Paul F. "Foreword." *Annals of the American Academy of Political and Social Science* 313 (1957): ix–x.

Draycott, Jane. "Automata, Cyborgs, and Hybrids: Bodies and Machines in Antiquity." In *Body and Machine in Classical Antiquity*, edited by Maria Gerolemou and George Kazantzidis, 48–69. Cambridge University Press, 2023.

"Dr. Norbert Wiener Dead at 69; Known as Father of Automation." *New York Times*, March 19, 1964, 1.

duBois, Page. *Slaves and Other Objects*. University of Chicago Press, 2003.

Ducrocq, Albert. *Découverte de la cybernétique*. René Julliard, 1955.

Dziuba, Allison, and Jerry Won Lee. "Post-Aristotelianism and the Specters of Monolingualism." *Rhetoric Review* 40, no. 3 (2021): 257–69.

Editorial View. "To Spark or to Smother—Which?" *World Vision Magazine* 10, no. 9 (1966): 32.

Eglash, Ron. "Broken Metaphor: The Master-Slave Analogy in Technical Literature." *Technology and Culture* 48, no. 2 (2007): 360–69.

Ellis, Havelock. *Little Essays of Love and Virtue*. George H. Doran, 1922.

"Elon Musk's Full Interview at Cannes Lions 2024: AI, Creativity, and the Future of X." YouTube video, 44:19, June 19, 2024. https://www.youtube.com/watch?v=84Q4dyK_urU.

Emerson, Ralph Waldo. "Works and Days." In *Society and Solitude: Twelve Chapters*, 131–56. Sampson Low, Son, & Marston, 1870.

Engel, William E. "Marx's Scholia: Annotations Involving Classical and Renaissance Texts in *Capital*." *Connotations* 29 (2020): 189–219.

Euben, J. Peter. "Arendt's Hellenism." In *Cambridge Companion to Hannah Arendt*, edited by Dana R. Villa, 151–64. Cambridge University Press, 2000.

Euben, J. Peter. *Platonic Noise*. Princeton University Press, 2003.

"Father of Cybernetics Norbert Wiener's Letter to UAW President Walter Reuther." Libcom .org. Accessed November 12, 2025. http://libcom.org/history/father-cybernetics-norbert-wieners-letter-uaw-president-walter-reuther.

Fertik, Harriet. "Antiquity, Tradition, and Anti-Blackness in Hannah Arendt's Public Sphere." *TAPA* 154, no. 1 (2024): 271–94.

Finley, Moses I. *Democracy Ancient and Modern*. Rev. ed. Rutgers University Press, [1973] 2019.

Frey, Carl Benedikt. *The Technology Trap: Capital, Labor, and Power in the Age of Automation*. Princeton University Press, 2019.

Frey, Carl Benedikt, and Michael Osborn. "The Future of Employment: How Susceptible Are Jobs to Computerization?" Working paper, Oxford Martin, 2013.

Friedan, Betty. *The Feminine Mystique*. W. W. Norton, 1963.

Fuller, R. Buckminster. "Education Automation: Freeing the Scholar to Return to His Studies." In *Education Automation: Comprehensive Learning for Emergent Humanity*, edited by Jaime Snyder, 31–108. Lars Müller, 2010.

Gabor, Dennis. *Inventing the Future*. Knopf, 1964.

Galbraith, John Kenneth. *The Affluent Society*. Mentor, 1958.

Garnsey, Peter. *Ideas of Slavery from Aristotle to Augustine*. Cambridge University Press, 1996.

Garvey, Michael Angelo. *The Silent Revolution; or, The Future Effects of Steam and Electricity upon the Conditions of Mankind*. William & Friederich G. Cash, 1852.

Gastil, John, and Erik Olin Wright, eds. *Legislature by Lot: Transformative Designs for Deliberative Governance*. Verso, 2019.

Gedichte aus dem Griechischen, Übersetzt von Christian Graf zu Stolberg. Carl Ernst Bohn, 1782.

Genelli, R. P. "Facteur humain ou facteur social du travail." *Revue française du travail* 7, no. 1–3 (1952):15–37.

Genette, Gérard. *Paratexts: Thresholds of Interpretation*. Translated by Jane E. Lewin. Cambridge University Press, [1987] 1997.

Geoghegan, Bernard Dionysius. *Code: From Information Theory to French Theory*. Duke University Press, 2023.

Geoghegan, Bernard Dionysius. "Textocracy, or, The Cybernetic Logic of French Theory." *History of the Human Sciences* 33, no. 1 (2020): 52–79.

Gerolemou, Maria. *Technical Automation in Classical Antiquity*. Bloomsbury, 2023.

Geroulanos, Stefanos, and Leif Weatherby. "Cybernetics and the Human Sciences." *History of the Human Sciences* 33, no. 1 (2020): 3–11.

Gibson, William. *Neuromancer*. Ace, 1984.

Gines, Kathryn T. *Hannah Arendt and the Negro Question*. Indiana University Press, 2014.

Goldberg, Maxwell H. ". . . And See it Whole." In *Automation, Education, and Human Values*, edited by William B. Brickman and Stanley Lehrer, 342–59. School & Society, 1966.

Goldberg, Maxwell H. "Continuous Education as a Way of Life." *Adult Education* (1965): 3–10.

Goldberg, Maxwell H. "The Displacement of Human Labor: Historic Trends." In *The Evolving Society: The Proceedings of the First Annual Conference on the Cybercultural Revolution*, edited by Alice Mary Hilton, 153–58. Institute for Cybercultural Research, 1966 .

Goldberg, Maxwell H., and Patricia Kochanek, ed. *Technical Change and Human Dignity: A Study in Human Values. Text with Questions and Readings from the CCLE-IBM Humanities Project on Technological Change*. Center for Continuing Education at Penn State University, 1966.

Grant, Adam. "To Improve Democracy, Get Rid of Elections." *New York Times*, August 23, 2023, A22.

Greenberg, Stephen. "Ward Family Papers, 1870–1953." Compiled 1990. Humanities and Social Sciences Library, Manuscripts and Archives Division, New York Public Library.

Greenwood, Emily. "Reconstructing Classical Philology: Reading Aristotle *Politics* 1.4 After Toni Morrison." *American Journal of Philology* 143, no. 2 (2022): 335–57.

Guerrero, Alexander. *Lottocracy: Democracy Without Elections*. Oxford University Press, 2024.

Guilbaud, Georges-Théodule. *La cybernétique*. Presses universitaires de France, 1954.

Guilbaud, Georges-Théodule. *What Is Cybernetics?* Translated by Valerie MacKay. Grove, 1960.

Gunkle, David J. *Person, Thing, Robot: A Moral and Legal Ontology for the Twenty-First Century and Beyond*. MIT Press, 2023.

Hall, Edith, Richard Alson, and Justine McConnell, eds. *Ancient Slavery and Abolition: From Hobbes to Hollywood*. Oxford University Press, 2011.

Hall, Edward T. *The Silent Language*. Doubleday, 1959.

Hameed, S. M. A., and Dallas Cullen, eds. *Work and Leisure in Canada*. Faculty of Business Administration and Commerce, University of Alberta, 1971.

Hanink, Johanna. *The Classical Debt: Greek Antiquity in an Era of Austerity*. Harvard University Press, 2017.

Hanink, Johanna. "It's Time to Embrace Critical Classical Reception." *Eidolon*, May 1, 2017. https://eidolon.pub/its-time-to-embrace-critical-classical-reception-d3491a40eec3.

Hanink, Johanna, and Demetra Kasimis. "Introduction: In Terms of Athens." *Ramus* 50, nos. 1–2 (2021): 1–8.

Hariman, Robert. "Political Parody and Public Culture." *Quarterly Journal of Speech* 94, no. 3 (2008): 247–72.

Harrington, J. Drew. "Classical Antiquity and the Pro-Slavery Argument." *Slavery and Abolition* 10, no. 1 (1989): 60–72.

Harvey, David. *A Companion to Marx's "Capital": The Complete Edition*. Verso, 2018.

Haskins, Ekaterina V., and Gaines S. Hubbell. "Plato's *Phaedrus* and the Ideology of Immersion." In *Ancient Rhetorics and Digital Networks*, edited by Michele Kennerly and Damien Smith Pfister, 154–75. University of Alabama Press, 2018.

Havelock, Eric A. *Preface to Plato*. Harvard University Press, 1963.

Hawhee, Debra, and Christa J. Olson. "Pan-Historiography: The Challenges of Writing History Across Time and Space." In *Theorizing Histories of Rhetoric*, edited by Michelle Ballif, 90–105. Southern Illinois University Press, 2013.

Hayat, Samuel. "Les controverses autour du travail en 1848." *Raisons politiques* 47 (2012/13): 13–34.

Hayles, N. Katherine. *How We Became Posthuman: Virtual Bodies in Cybernetics, Literature, and Informatics*. University of Chicago Press, 1999.

Hayward, Herbert Layton. "Panel Discussion." In *The Evolving Society: The Proceedings of the First Annual Conference on the Cybercultural Revolution*, edited by Alice Mary Hilton, 59–68. Institute for Cybercultural Research, 1966.

Hearings Before the Subcommittee on Unemployment and the Impact of Automation of the Committee on Education and Labor, House of Representatives. 87th Cong., 1st sess., General Investigation into Types of Causes of Unemployment, Hearings Held in Washington, DC, March 8, 10, 20, 21, 22, 27, 29, 29; April 12, 17, 18, and 25. Government Printing Office, 1961.

Heims, Steve Joshua. *The Cybernetics Group*. MIT Press, 1991.

Hesiod. *Theogony, Works and Days, Testimonia*. Translated by Glenn W. Most. Harvard University Press, 2018.

Highet, Gilbert. *The Classical Tradition: Greek and Roman Influences on Western Literature*. Oxford University Press, 1949.

Hill, Samantha Rose. *Hannah Arendt*. Reaktion, 2021.

Hilton, Alice Mary. "The Bases of Cyberculture: Scientific, Technical, Philosophical, Socioeconomic, Political." In *The Evolving Society: The Proceedings of the First Annual Conference on the Cybercultural Revolution*, edited by Alice Mary Hilton, 7–21. Institute for Cybercultural Research, 1966.

Hilton, Alice Mary. "Basic Assumptions." In *The Evolving Society: The Proceedings of the First Annual Conference on the Cybercultural Revolution*, edited by Alice Mary Hilton, 2–6. Institute for Cybercultural Research, 1966.

Hilton, Alice Mary. Correspondence, 1963, Box 1, Folder 17. James and Grace Lee Boggs Papers, UP001342. Walter P. Reuther Library.

Hilton, Alice Mary. "Cyberculture in the Transition from a War to a Peacetime Economy." *Fellowship* (May 1964): 3–8.

Hilton, Alice Mary. "Cyberculture—The Age of Abundance and Leisure." *Michigan Quarterly Review* 3, no. 4 (1964): 217–29.

Hilton, Alice Mary. "Cybernetics and Cybernation." *Science Teacher* 40, no. 2 (1973): 34–40.

Hilton, Alice Mary. "Cybernetics and the Future." Interview with Studs Terkel, WFMT Radio Network (Chicago), July 12, 1965.

Hilton, Alice Mary. "Cybernetics: Its Impact on the Processes of Learning, Politics, and Production." In *Progress of Cybernetics*, vol. 3, edited by J. Rose, 1287–97. Gordon & Breach Science Publishers, 1970.

Hilton, Alice Mary. "Dr. Alice Mary Hilton in Conversation with Studs Terkel." Interview with Studs Terkel, WFMT Radio Network (Chicago), 1967.

Hilton, Alice Mary. "An Ethos for the Age of Cyberculture." In *AFIPS Conference Proceedings, Vol. 25: 1964 Spring Joint Computer Conference*, 139–53. Spartan, 1964.

Hilton, Alice Mary. "The Evolving Society." In *The Evolving Society: The Proceedings of the First Annual Conference on the Cybercultural Revolution*, edited by Alice Mary Hilton, 144–52. Institute for Cybercultural Research, 1966.

Hilton, Alice Mary. "Homo Faber, Homo Sapiens, Homo Poeta." *American Journal of Psychotherapy* 20, no. 4 (1966): 627–35.

Hilton, Alice Mary. "Individual Responsibility in a Cybercultural Society." *Quest* 5, no. 1 (1965): 37–47.

Hilton, Alice Mary. *Logic, Computing Machines, and Automation*. Spartan, 1963.

Hilton, Alice Mary. "Panel Discussion." In *The Evolving Society: The Proceedings of the First Annual Conference on the Cybercultural Revolution*, edited by Alice Mary Hilton, 221–51. Institute for Cybercultural Research, 1966.

Hilton, Alice Mary. Private papers. Shared with the author.

Hilton, Alice Mary, ed. *Against Pollution and Hunger: Notes Toward a New World*. John Wiley & Sons, 1974.

"History." Charles H. Kerr Publishing Company. Accessed November 12, 2025. https://charleshkerr.com/about-1.

Hogan, Sarah. *Other Englands: Utopia, Capital, and Empire in an Age of Transition*. Stanford University Press, 2018.

Holmes, George Frederick. "Observations on a Passage in the Politics of Aristotle Relative to Slavery." *Southern Literary Messenger* 16 (1850): 193–205.

Holmes, George Frederick. *A Science of Society*. Anderson Brothers, 1884.

Homeri. *Opera*. Vol 2. Oxford University Press, 1920.

Honig, Bonnie. "What Kind of Thing Is Land? Hannah Arendt's Object Relations, or: The Jewish Unconscious of Arendt's Most 'Greek' Text." *Political Theory* 44, no. 3 (2016): 307–36.

Houghton, James. "Panel Discussion." In *The Evolving Society: The Proceedings of the First Annual Conference on the Cybercultural Revolution*, edited by Alice Mary Hilton, 221–51. Institute for Cybercultural Research, 1966.

Huhtamo, Erkki. "From Kaleidoscomaniac to Cybernerd: Notes Toward an Archaeology of the Media." *Leonardo* 30, no. 3 (1997): 221–24.

Hutchins, Robert M. *The University of Utopia*. 2nd ed. University of Chicago Press, [1953] 1964.

Izaguirre III, José G. "Reckoning with Tlateloloco: Arturo Rosenblueth and a Cybernetic Rhetoric." *Rhetoric & Public Affairs* 25, no. 2 (2022): 57–90.

"John I Snyder Jr." *New York Times*, April 26, 1965. https://timesmachine.nytimes.com/timesmachine/1965/04/26/101542508.html?pageNumber=30.

Jameson, Fredric. "History and Salvation in Philip K. Dick." In *Archaeologies of the Future: The Desire Called Utopia and Other Science Fictions*, 361–83. Verso, 2007.

Jameson, Fredric. "Varieties of the Utopian." In *Archaeologies of the Future: The Desire Called Utopia and Other Science Fictions*, 1–9. Verso, 2007.

Johnson, Christopher. "'French' Cybernetics." *French Studies* 69, no. 1 (2014): 60–78.

Johnson, Lyndon B. "Annual Message to the Congress on the State of the Union." American Presidency Project. Accessed November 12, 2025. https://www.presidency.ucsb.edu/node/242292.

Johnson, Lyndon B. "Economic Report on the Nation's Progress and Trends." *New York Times*, January 20, 1964. https://www.nytimes.com/1964/01/21/archives/text-of-president-johnsons-economic-report-on-the-nations-progress.html?searchResultPosition=43.

Johnson, Lyndon B. "Remarks upon Signing Bill Creating the National Commission on Technology, Automation, and Economic Progress." American Presidency Project. Accessed November 12, 2025. https://www.presidency.ucsb.edu/node/241917.

Juvenal and Persius. Translated by G. G. Ramsey. William Heineman, 1918.

Kahn, Tom. *The Economics of Equality*. League for Industrial Democracy, 1964.

Kaiser, Bruno. *Ex Libris Karl Marx und Friedrich Engels: Schicksal und Verzeichnis Einer Bibliothek*. Berlin: Dietz Verlag, 1967.

Kamen, Deborah. *Greek Slavery*. De Gruyter, 2023.

Karlin, Jules. *Man's Behavior: An Introduction to Social Science*. Macmillan, 1967.

Kastely, James L. *The Rhetoric of Plato's "Republic": Democracy and the Philosophical Problem of Persuasion*. University of Chicago Press, 2015.

Katz, Claudio. "The Socialist Polis: Antiquity and Socialism in Marx's Thought." *Review of Politics* 56, no. 2 (1994): 237–60.

Kelly, Kevin. *The Inevitable: Understanding the 12 Technological Forces That Will Shape Our Future*. Penguin, 2017.

Kennerly, Michele. "Cybernetics in the Republic." *History of the Human Sciences* 36, no. 1 (2022): 80–102.

Kennerly, Michele. "The Place of Ancient Greece in W. E. B. Du Bois's 'The Workers' (1948)." Forthcoming.

Keynes, John Maynard. "Economic Possibilities for our Grandchildren." In *Essays in Persuasion*. Ebook. W. W. Norton, 2011.

Keyt, David. "Plato and the Ship of State." In *The Blackwell Guide to Plato's "Republic,"* edited by Gerasimos Santas, 189–213. Wiley, 2006.

King, William Francis Henry. *Classical and Foreign Quotations: Law Terms and Maxims, Proverbs, Mottoes, Phrases, and Expressions in French, German, Greek, Italian, Latin, Spanish, and Portuguese with Translations, References, Explanatory Notes, and Indexes*. Rev. ed. Whitaker & Sons, [1887] 1889.

Kline, Ronald R. *The Cybernetics Moment; or Why We Call Our Age the Information Age*. Johns Hopkins University Press, 2015.

Konstan, David. "The Greek Polis and Its Negations: Versions of Utopia in Aristophanes's *Birds*." In *The City as Comedy: Society and Representation in Athenian Drama*, edited by Gregory W. Durbov, 3–22. University of North Carolina Press, 1997.

Krajewski, Markus. *The Server: A Media History from the Present to the Baroque*. Translated by Ilinca Iurascu. Yale University Press, [2011] 2018.

Krell, Jacob. "What Is the 'Cybernetic' in the 'History of Cybernetics'? A French Case, 1968 to the Present." *History of the Human Sciences* 33, no. 1 (2020): 188–211.

Lafont, Cristina, and Nadia Urbinati. *The Lottocratic Mentality: Defending Democracy Against Lottocracy*. Oxford University Press, 2024.

Lafargue, Paul. *The Right to Be Lazy*. Translated by Charles H. Kerr. Charles H. Kerr, 1989.

Lafargue, Paul. *The Right to Be Lazy and Other Essays*. Translated by Alex Andriesse. New York Review, 2023.

Lafontaine, Céline. *L'empire cybernétique: des machines à penser à la pensée machine. Essai*. Éditions du Seuil, 2004.

Lane, Melissa. *Plato's Progeny: How Plato and Socrates Still Captivate the Modern Mind*. Duckworth, 2001.

Latil, Pierre de. *La pensée artificielle: Introduction à la cybernétique*. Gallimard, 1953.

Latil, Pierre de. *Thinking by Machine: A Study of Cybernetics*. Translated by Y. M. Golla. Houghton Mifflin, 1957.

Leff, Michael C. "The Topics of Argumentative Invention in Latin Rhetorical Theory from Cicero to Boethius." *Rhetorica* 1, no. 1 (1983): 23–44.

Leigh, Matthew. *From* Polypragmon *to* Curiosus*: Ancient Concepts of Curious and Meddlesome*. Oxford University Press, 2013.

Leonard, Miriam. "Arendt's Revolutionary Antiquity." *Classical Philology* 113 (2018): 53–66.

Leonard, Miriam. "Hannah Arendt and the Ancients: Preface." *Classical Philology* 113 (2018): 1–5.

Lepore, Jill. *If Then: How the Simulmatics Corporation Invented the Future*. Liveright, 2020.

Lepore, Jill. "The Failed Ideas That Drive Elon Musk." *New York Times*, April 4, 2025. https://www.nytimes.com/2025/04/04/opinion/elon-musk-doge-technocracy.html.

Le Roux, Ronan. *Une histoire de la cybernétique en France (1948–1975)*. Classiques Garnier, 2018.

Leroy, Justin. "Racial Capitalism and Black Philosophies of History." In *Histories of Racial Capitalism*, edited by Destin Jenkins and Justin Leroy, 169–84. Columbia University Press, 2021.

Lewis, Arthur O. "Utopian Approaches to Technology." *Bulletin of Science, Technology & Society* 7 (1987): 493–506.

Lewis, M. J. T. *Millstone and Hammer: The Origins of Water Power*. University of Hull Press, 1997.

Litwack, Michael. "Extensions After Man: Race, Counter/Insurgency and the Futures of Media Theory." *Media, Culture & Society* 43, no. 7 (2021): 1350–63.

Livingstone, Niall. *Athens: The City as University*. Routledge, 2017.

Loraux, Nicole. *The Invention of Athens: The Funeral Oration in the Classical City*. Translated by Alan Sheridan. Zone, [1991] 2006.

McAfee, Andrew, and Erik Brynjolfsson. *Machine, Platform, Crowd: Harnessing Our Digital Future*. W. W. Norton, 2017.

McCarthy, George E. *Marx and the Ancients: Classical Ethics, Social Justice, and Nineteenth-Century Political Economy*. Rowman & Littlefield, 1990.

McCarthy, George E., ed. *Marx and Aristotle: Nineteenth-Century German Social Theory and Classical Antiquity*. Rowman & Littlefield, 1992.

McLuhan, Marshall. *The Classical Trivium: The Place of Thomas Nashe in the Learning of His Time*. Edited by W. Terrence Gordan. Gingko, 2006.

McLuhan, Marshall. "Cybernation and Culture." In *The Social Impact of Cybernetics*, edited by Charles R. Dechert, 95–108. Simon & Schuster, 1966.

McLuhan, Marshall. *The Gutenberg Galaxy: The Making of Typographic Man*. University of Toronto Press, 1962.

McLuhan, Marshall. *Understanding Media: The Extensions of Man*. 2nd ed. Signet, 1964.

Ma, John. *Polis: A New History of the Ancient City-State from the Early Iron Age to the End of Antiquity*. Princeton University Press, 2024.

Mailloux, Steven. "Re-Marking Slave Bodies: Rhetoric as Production and Reception." *Philosophy and Rhetoric* 35, no. 2 (2002): 96–119.

Mak, Bonnie, and Allen H. Renear. "What Is Information History?" *Isis* 114, no. 4 (2023): 747–68.

Malamud, Margaret. *African Americans and the Classics: Antiquity, Abolition and Activism*. I. B. Tauris, 2019.

Malamud, Margaret. "The *Auctoritas* of Antiquity: Debating Slavery Through Classical Exempla in the Antebellum USA." In. *Ancient Slavery and Abolition: From Hobbes to Hollywood*, edited by Edith Hall, Richard Alson, and Justine McConnell, 279–318. Oxford University Press, 2011.

"Mark Zuckerberg on Life, History, and Being Human / The Circuit with Emily Chang (Bonus Clip)," YouTube video, 9:53, December 19, 2024. https://www.youtube.com/watch?v=R91_oQ4smys.

Markham, Charles, ed. *Jobs, Men, and Machines: Problems of Automation*. Frederick A. Praeger, 1964.

Marshall, David L. "The Polis and Its Analogues in the Thought of Hannah Arendt." *Modern Intellectual History* 7, no. 1 (2010): 123–49.

Marshall, David L. "Warburgian Maxims for Visual Rhetoric." *Rhetoric Society Quarterly* 48, no. 4 (2018): 352–79.

Marx, Karl. *Capital: A Critique of Political Economy*. Vol. 1. Translated by Ben Fowkes. Penguin, 1990.

Marx, Karl. *Capital: A Critique of Political Economy*. Vol. 2. Translated by David Fernbach. Penguin, 1992.

Marx, Karl. *Capital: A Critique of Political Economy*. Vol. 3. Translated by David Fernbach. Penguin, [1981] 1991.

Marx, Karl. *Grundrisse: Foundations of the Critique of Political Economy (Rough Draft)*. Translated by Martin Nicolaus. Penguin, 1993.

Masani, Pesi Rostum. *Norbert Wiener (1894–1964)*. Birkhäuser Verlag, 1990.

Mayor, Adrienne. *Gods and Robots: Myths, Machines, and Ancient Dreams of Technology*. Princeton University Press, 2018.

Medina, Eden. *Cybernetic Revolutionaries: Technology and Politics in Allende's Chile*. MIT Press, [2011] 2014.

Merton, Robert K. *On the Shoulders of Giants: A Shandean Postscript. The Vicennial Edition*. Harcourt Brace Jovanovich, [1965] 1985.

Messer-Kruse, Timothy. *The Yankee International: Marxism and the American Reform Tradition, 1848–1876*. University of North Carolina Press, 1998.

Michael, Donald N. *Cybernation: The Silent Conquest*. Center for the Study of Democratic Institutions, 1962.

Michael, Donald N. "Free Time—The New Imperative in Our Society." In *Automation, Education, and Human Values*, edited by William W. Brickman and Stanley Lehrer, 293–303. School & Society, 1966.

Michael, Donald N. "On Thinking About the Future." *Journal of Humanistic Psychology* 20, no. 1 (1989): 37–53.

Michael, Donald N. "Reviewed Work(s): *The Age of Automation* by Leon Bagrit." *Technology and Culture* 7, no. 2 (1966): 257–61.

Mihlon, L. F. "Plain Talk on Automation." *Factory* 120, no. 2 (1962): 224.

Miles, Edwin A. "The Old South and the Classical World." *North Carolina Historical Review* 48, no. 3 (1971): 258–75.

Mindell, David A., Jérôme Segal, and Slava Gerovitch. "From Communications Engineering to Communications Science: Cybernetics and Information Theory in the United States,

France, and the Soviet Union." In *Science and Ideology: A Comparative History*, edited by Mark Walker, 66–96. Routledge, 2003.

Moore, Kelly. *Disrupting Science: Social Movements, American Scientists, and the Politics of the Military, 1945–1975*. Princeton University Press, 2008.

More, Thomas, *Utopia*; Francis Bacon, *Atlantis*; Henry Neville, *Isle of Pines*. Oxford University Press, 2008.

Morgan, David, and David Shepardson. "US Senate Strikes AI Regulation Ban from Trump Megabill." Reuters, July 1, 2025. https://www.reuters.com/legal/government/us-senate-strikes-ai-regulation-ban-trump-megabill-2025-07-01/.

Morson, Gary Saul. *The Words of Others: From Quotations to Culture*. Yale University Press, 2011.

Monoson, S. Sara. "Navigating Race, Class, Polis, and Empire: The Place of Empirical Analysis in Aristotle's Account of Natural Slavery." In *Reading Ancient Slavery*, edited by Richard Alston, Edith Hall, and Laura Proffitt, 133–51. Bristol Classical Press, 2011.

Monoson, S. Sara. "Recollecting Aristotle: Pro-Slavery Thought in Antebellum America and the Argument of *Politics* Book I." In *Ancient Slavery and Abolition: From Hobbes to Hollywood*, edited by Edith Hall, Richard Alston, and Justine McConnell, 247–78. Oxford University Press, 2011.

Morozov, Evgeny. *To Save Everything, Click Here: The Folly of Technological Solutionism*. PublicAffairs, 2014.

Morrison, Donald R. "The Utopian Character of Plato's Ideal City." In *The Cambridge Companion to Plato's "Republic,"* edited by G. R. F. Ferrari, 232–55. Cambridge University Press, 2007.

Mumford, Lewis. *The Story of Utopias*. Azafran, [1922] 2017.

Mumford, Lewis. *Technics & Civilization*. University of Chicago Press, [1934] 2010.

Napoli, Davide. "The Shape of Early Greek Utopia." *Classical Quarterly* 71, no. 2 (2021): 467–81.

Natale, Simone. *Deceitful Media: Artificial Intelligence and Social Life After the Turing Test*. New York: Oxford University Press, 2021.

National Commission on Technology, Automation, and Economic Progress. Hearings Before the Select Subcommittee on Labor of the Committee on Education and Labor, House of Representatives, 88th Cong., 2nd sess., on H.R. 10310 and Related Bills, to Establish a National Commission on Automation and Technological Progress. Hearings Held in Washington, DC, April 14, 15, and 27, 1964. Government Printing Office, 1964.

Nederman, Cary J. "Men at Work: *Poesis*, Politics, and Labor in Aristotle and Some Aristotelians." *Analyse & Kritik* 30, no. 1 (2008): 17–31.

Nersessian, Anahid. *Utopia, Limited: Romanticism and Adjustment*. Harvard University Press, 2015.

"The New Negro Movement: Where Shall It Go Now?" *Dissent* (1964): 279–95.

Norbert Wiener Papers. Massachusetts Institute of Technology Libraries, Department of Distinctive Collections.

Ober, Josiah. *Demopolis: Democracy Before Liberalism in Theory and Practice*. Cambridge University Press, 2017.

Ober, Josiah. *Mass and Elite in Democratic Athens: Rhetoric, Ideology, and the Power of the People*. Princeton University Press, 1989.

Oliver, Robert T. "Education in the Year 2000 A.D." *Michigan Quarterly Review* 3, no. 4 (1964): 233–36.

"Osborne Ward's Ancient Working People." Classics and Class. Accessed November 12, 2025. https://www.classicsandclass.info/product/166/.

Palaephatus. *On Unbelievable Tales*. Translated by Jacob Stern. Bolchazy-Carducci, 1996.

Parmenter, Christopher S. "'But They Were a Race of Whites': Race and the Making of Ancient Slavery in the Anglophone World, 1785–1980." *TAPA* 154, no. 1 (2024): 295–330.

Pasquale, Frank. *New Laws of Robotics: Defending Human Expertise in the Age of AI*. Belknap Press of Harvard University Press, 2020.

Padilla Peralta, Dan-El. *Classicism and Other Phobias*. Princeton University Press, 2025.

Penny, Simon. "Machine Culture." In *SISEA Proceedings*, edited by Wim van der Plas, 184–91. SISEA, 1991.

Peters, John Durham. "'You Mean My Whole Fallacy Is Wrong': On Technological Determinism." *Representations* 140 (2017): 10–26.

Peters, John Durham, and Benjamin Peters. "Norbert Wiener as Pragmatist." *Empedocles* 7, no. 2 (2016): 157–72.

Pieper, Josef. *Muße und Kult*. Kösel-Verlag, 1948.

Pilsch, Andrew. *Transhumanism: Evolutionary Futurism and the Human Technologies of Utopia*. University of Minnesota Press, 2017.

Pitkin, Hanna Fenichel. *The Attack of the Blob: Hannah Arendt's Concept of the Social*. University of Chicago Press, 1998.

Plato. *Euthyphro; Apology; Crito; Phaedo*. Translated by C. Emlyn-Jones and W. Preddy. Harvard University Press, 2017.

Plato. *Gorgias; Menexenus; Protagoras*. Translated by Malcolm Schofield. Cambridge University Press, 2009.

Plato. *Laches; Protagoras; Meno; Euthydemus*. Translated by W. R. M. Lamb. Harvard University Press, 1924.

Plato. *Lysis; Symposium; Gorgias*. Translated by W. R. M. Lamb. Harvard University Press, 2001.

Plato. *Republic*. Books 1–5. Translated by Chris Emlyn-Jones and William Preddy. Harvard University Press, 2013.

Plato. *Republic*. Books 6–10. Translated by Chris Emlyn-Jones and William Preddy. Harvard University Press, 2013.

Plato. *Statesman*; *Philebus*; *Ion*. Translated by H. N. Fowler and W. R. M. Lamb. Harvard University Press, 1925.

Popper, Karl. *The Open Society and Its Enemies, Vol. 1: The Spell of Plato*. Routledge, [1945] 2011.

"Preview: Automation House, New York City." *Architectural & Engineering News* 10 (1968): 76–78.

"Prof. Ben Seligman of Massachusetts U." *New York Times*, October 25, 1970, 92.

Prout, Jerry. *Chasing Automation: The Politics of Technology and Jobs from the Roaring Twenties to the Great Society*. Cornell University Press, 2022.

Prytulak, Walter. *Jobless, Moneyless, and Free: Prospects for a New Social Order*. Vantage, 1980.

Regalado, Antonio. "When Machines Do Your Job" (Q&A with Andrew McAfee). *MIT Technology Review*, July 11, 2012, 70–71.

"Reith Lectures Will Be on Automation. Sir Leon Bagrit." *London Times*, May 22, 1964, 8.

Resnikoff, Jason. *Labor's End: How the Promise of Automation Degraded Work*. University of Illinois Press, 2021.

Resnikoff, Jason. "The Myth of Black Obsolescence." *International Labor and Working-Class History* 102 (2023): 124–45.

Rhee, Jennifer. *The Robotic Imaginary: The Human and the Price of Dehumanized Labor*. University of Minnesota Press, 2018.

Richards, Isaac James. "The Labyrinth: A Platonic Dialogue on What's Next, Featuring ChatGPT as Phaedrus." *Explorations in Media Ecology* 22, no. 2 (2023): 235–39.

Rickover, Hyman G. *American Education—A National Failure: The Problem of Our Schools and What We Can Learn from England.* E. P. Dutton, 1963.

Rickover, Hyman G. "A Humanistic Technology." In *The Social Impact of Cybernetics*, edited by Charles R. Dechert, 109–28. Simon & Schuster, 1966.

Rice, Warner G. "Humanities in the Sixties." In *Automation, Education, and Human Values*, edited by William W. Brickman and Stanley Lehrer, 87–98. School & Society, 1966.

Rid, Thomas. *Rise of the Machines: A Cybernetic History*. W. W. Norton, 2016.

Robertson, Aaron. *The Black Utopians: Searching for Paradise and the Promised Land in America.* Farrar, Straus & Giroux, 2024.

Rouse, Kevin. *FutureProof: 9 Rules for Humans in the Age of Automation.* Random House, [2021] 2022.

Rushkoff, Douglas. "The Super-Rich 'Preppers' Planning to Save Themselves from the Apocalypse." *Guardian*, September 4, 2022. https://www.theguardian.com/news/2022/sep/04/super-rich-prepper-bunkers-apocalypse-survival-richest-rushkoff.

Russell, Bertrand. "In Praise of Idleness." *Harper's*, October 1932. https://harpers.org/archive/1932/10/in-praise-of-idleness/.

Salamanca, Emily. "Pruning of the People: Ostracism and the Transformation of the Political Space in Ancient Athens." *Philosophies* 8, no. 81 (2023): 1–21.

Samuel, A. L. "Some Moral and Technical Consequences of Automation—A Refutation." *Science* 132, no. 3429 (1960): 741–42.

Sannwald, Rolf. *Marx und die Antike.* Verlagsanstalt Benziger, 1956.

Sarnoff, David. "The New Computerized Age—3: No Life Untouched." In Hearings Before a Subcommittee on Government Operations, House of Representatives, 89th Cong., 2nd sess., July 26, 27, and 28, 1966, 298–300, in Washington, DC. Government Printing Office, 1966.

Savage, Charles M. *Fifth Generation Management: Integrating Enterprises Through Human Networking.* Butterworth-Heineman, 1990.

Scullin, Sarah. "Plato Would Have Wanted You to Unplug: Technology Addiction, Technophobia, and Kids These Days." *Eidolon*, October 2, 2017. https://eidolon.pub/plato-would-have-wanted-you-to-unplug-712a908a16e0.

Segal, Howard P. "Practical Utopias: America as Techno-Fix Nation." *Utopian Studies* 28, no. 2 (2017): 231–46.

Segal, Howard P. *Technological Utopianism in American Culture.* University of Chicago Press, 1985.

Segal, Jérôme. *Le zéro et le un: histoire de la notion scientifique d'information au 20e siècle.* Éditions Syllepse, 2003.

Seligman, Ben B. *Most Notorious Victory: Man in an Age of Automation.* Free Press, 1966.

Seligman, Ben B. "The Social Costs of Automation." In *The Evolving Society: The Proceedings of the First Annual Conference on the Cybercultural Revolution*, edited by Alice Mary Hilton, 159–66. Institute for Cybercultural Research, 1966.

Selisker, Scott. *Human Programming: Brainwashing, Automatons, and American Unfreedom.* University of Minnesota Press, 2016.

Shalev, Eran. *Rome Reborn on Western Shores: Historical Imagination and the Creation of the American Republic.* University of Virginia Press, 2009.

Shore, Daniel. *Cyberformalism: Histories of Linguistic Forms in the Digital Archive.* Johns Hopkins University Press, 2018.

Silvey, Ted F. "Production Control." In *The Evolving Society: The Proceedings of the First Annual Conference on the Cybercultural Revolution*, edited by Alice Mary Hilton, 127–30. Institute for Cybercultural Research, 1966.

Simbirski, Brian. "Cybernetic Muse: Hannah Arendt on Automation, 1951–1958." *Journal of the History of Ideas* 77, no. 4 (2016): 589–613.

Sintomer, Yves. *The Government of Chance: Sortition and Democracy from Athens to the Present*. Translated by Sarah Louise Raillard and Patrick Camiller. Cambridge University Press, 2023.

Smith, Merritt Roe. "Technological Determinism in American Culture." In *Does Technology Drive History? The Dilemma of Technological Determinism*, edited by Merritt Roe Smith and Leo Marx, 1–35. MIT Press, 1994.

Snyder, John I., Jr. "We Must Begin a Search for Answers." *New York Times Magazine*, March 22, 1964, 16, 62, 66, 69–70.

Spies, August. *Auto-Biography; His Speech in Court, and General Notes*. Nina Van Zandt, [1887] 1939.

Stabile, Donald R. "Automation, Workers, and Union Decline: Ben Seligman's Contribution to the Institutional Economics of Labor." *Labor History* 49, no. 2 (2008): 275–95.

Stanley, John. "The Marxism of Marx's Doctoral Dissertation." *Journal of the History of Philosophy* 33, no. 1 (1995): 133–58.

Steigerwald, David. "Walter Reuther, the UAW, and the Dilemmas of Automation." *Labor History* 51, no. 3 (2010): 429–53.

Stowe, Harriet Beecher. *Uncle Tom's Cabin*. Edited by Jean Fagan Yellin. Oxford University Press, [1852] 1998.

Sutherland, Williard C. "A Philosophy of Leisure." *Annals of the American Academy of Political and Social Science* 313 (1957): 1–3.

Taplin, Jonathan. *The End of Reality: How Four Billionaires Are Selling a Fantasy Future of the Metaverse, Mars, and Crypto*. Public Affairs, 2023.

Taylor, Astra. *Democracy May Not Exist, but We'll Miss It When It's Gone*. Metropolitan, 2019.

Thucydides. *History of the Peloponnesian War*. Vol. 1. Translated by C. F. Smith. Harvard University Press, 1919.

Tierney, Matt. *Dismantlings: Words Against Machines in the American Long Seventies*. Cornell University Press, 2019.

Towns, Armond R. *On Black Media Philosophy*. University of California Press, 2022.

Trentowski, Bronisław. *Stosunek filozofii do cybernetyki, czyli sztuki rządzenia narodem*. Nakładem Ksiegarni J. K. Żupańskiego, 1843.

Triclot, Mathieu. *Le moment cybernétique: la constitution de la notion d'information*. Éditions Champ Vallon, 2008.

"The Triple Revolution: An Appraisal of the Major US Crises and Proposals for Action." *International Socialist Review* 25, no. 3 (1964): 85–89.

Tufekci, Zeynep. "What Would Plato Think About ChatGPT?" *New York Times*, December 18, 2022, SR7.

Ure, Andrew. *The Philosophy of Manufactures; or, An Exposition of the Scientific, Moral, and Commercial Economy of the Factory System*. Charles Knight, 1835.

Vanderford, Chad. "Proslavery Professors: Classic Natural Right and the Positive Good Argument in Antebellum Virginia." *Civil War History* 55, no. 1 (2009): 5–30.

Varoufakis, Yanis. "George Varoufakis (1925–2021)." YanisVaroukakis.eu. September 30, 2021. https://www.yanisvaroufakis.eu/2021/09/30/george-varoufakis-1925-2021-english/.

Varoufakis, Yanis. *Technofeudalism: What Killed Capitalism*. Melville House, [2023] 2024.

Walker, Charles R., and Robert H. Guest. *The Man on the Assembly Line*. Harvard University Press, 1952.

[Walker, Timothy]. "Art. V. Defence of Mechanical Philosophy." *North American Review* 9, nos. 2–3 (July 1831): 122–36.

Wallis, David. "After Cyberoverkill Comes Cyberburnout." *New York Times*, August 4, 1996, Section 1, 43.

Ward, Cyrenus Osborne. *The Ancient Lowly: A History of the Ancient Working People from the Earliest Known Period to the Adoption of Christianity by Constantine*. Vol. 1. 9th ed. Charles H. Keer, 1888.

Ward, Cyrenus Osborne. *The Ancient Lowly: A History of the Ancient Working People from the Earliest Known Period to the Adoption of Christianity by Constantine*. Vol. 2. *Origins of Socialism*. W. H. Lowdermick, 1900.

Ward, Stephen M., ed. *Pages from a Black Radical's Notebook: A James Boggs Reader*. Wayne State University Press, 2011.

Weatherby, Leif. "Delete Your Account: On the Theory of Platform Capitalism." *Los Angeles Review of Books*, April 24, 2018. https://lareviewofbooks.org/article/delete-your-account-on-the-theory-of-platform-capitalism/.

Weatherby, Leif. *Language Machines: Cultural AI and the End of Remainder Humanism*. University of Minnesota Press, 2025.

Weber, Max. *The Protestant Ethic and the "Spirit" of Capitalism*. Translated by Peter Baehr and Gordon C. Wells. Penguin, 2002.

Weinberg, Alvin M. "Can Technology Replace Social Engineering?" *Bulletin of the Atomic Scientists* 22, no. 10 (1966): 4–8.

Wiener, Norbert. *Cybernetics; or, Control and Communication in the Animal and the Machine*. 2nd ed. MIT Press, [1948] 1962.

Wiener, Norbert. *God and Golem, Inc.: A Comment on Certain Points Where Cybernetics Impinges on Religion*. MIT Press, 1964.

Wiener, Norbert. *The* Human *Use of Human Beings: Cybernetics and Society*. Houghton Mifflin, 1950.

Wiener, Norbert. *The Human Use of Human Beings: Cybernetics and Society*. Rev. ed. De Capo, 1954.

Wiener, Norbert. *I Am a Mathematician*. In *A Life in Cybernetics* (*Ex-Prodigy: My Childhood and Youth* and *I Am a Mathematician: The Later Life of a Prodigy*). MIT Press, [1956] 2017.

Wiener, Norbert. "A Scientist Rebels." *Atlantic Monthly* 179 (1947): 46.

Wiener, Norbert. "Some Moral and Technical Consequences of Automation." *Science* 131, no. 3410 (1960): 1355–58.

Wiener, Norbert, and Donald Campbell. "'Automatization': Norbert Wiener's Concept of Fully Mechanized Industry." *St. Louis Post-Dispatch*, December 5, 1954, 1.

Winner, Langdon. *Autonomous Technology: Technics-out-of-Control as a Theme in Political Thought*. MIT Press, [1977] 1978.

Winner, Langdon. *The Whale and the Reactor: A Search for Limits in an Age of High Technology*. 2nd ed. University of Chicago Press, [1986] 2020.

Winterer, Caroline. *The Culture of Classicism: Ancient Greece and Rome in American Intellectual Life*. Johns Hopkins University Press, 2002.

Wish, Harvey. "Aristotle, Plato, and the Mason Dixon Line." *Journal of the History of Ideas* 10 (1949): 254–66.

Woodruff, Paul. *First Democracy*. Oxford University Press, 2005.

Woods, Ellen Meiksins. *Peasant-Citizen and Slave: The Foundations of Athenian Democracy*. Verso, [1988] 2015.

Woody, Thomas. "Leisure in the Light of History." *Annals of the American Academy of Political and Social Science* 313 (1957): 4–10.

Wurgaft, Benjamin Aldes. *Thinking in Public: Strauss, Levinas, Arendt*. University of Pennsylvania Press, 2016.

Zamalin, Alex. *Black Utopia: The History of an Idea from Black Nationalism to Afrofuturism*. Columbia University Press, 2019.

Zhang, Alex. "Ostracism and Democracy." *NYU Law Review Online* 96 (2021): 235–68.

Index

The letter *f* following a page number denotes a figure.